Praise for *Flying Free*

"*Flying Free*...should be required reading for everyone...Dr. Aragon's struggles as a youth, and her fight to win those struggles, provides motivation to others facing similar situations."

—ANN QUIROZ GATES, professor, University of Texas at El Paso, and director, Computing Alliance of Hispanic-Serving Institutions

"I loved watching Cecilia's transformation as she discovered her love of flying and just went for it, challenging all the stories that her upbringing had taught her...Through cheering her on in this book, I also started cheering on myself."

—SARAH E. MCQUATE, science writer and biochemistry PhD

"Dr. Cecilia Aragon in her book *Flying Free* tells a story of courage and perseverance, one that needs to be heard. Her story is one laced with grit and determination."

—DR. TELLE WHITNEY, cofounder, Grace Hopper Celebration Conference

"This is a must-read book for anyone who has ever had any doubts about what they can achieve! Cecilia chronicles her path from a young Latina, who experienced racism verbally and physically, to a confident and very successful professor in computer science at a top university. Her passion for flying provided a path to face and overcome her fears to become the first Latina on the US Aerobatic Team and medalist at the World Aerobatic Championships. Her passion for flying gave her a strong voice for her personal and professional life!"

—VALERIE TAYLOR, CEO and president, Center for Minorities and People with Disabilities in Information Technology

Flying Free

Flying Free

My Victory over Fear to Become the First
Latina Pilot on the US Aerobatic Team

Cecilia Aragon

**BLACK
STONE**
PUBLISHING

Copyright © 2020 by Cecilia Aragon
Published in 2020 by Blackstone Publishing
Cover and book design by Alenka Vdovič Linaschke

Some names and identifying details have been changed
to protect the privacy of individuals.

Printed in the United States of America

First edition: 2020
ISBN 978-1-982642-46-4
Biography & Autobiography / General

1 3 5 7 9 10 8 6 4 2

CIP data for this book is available
from the Library of Congress

Blackstone Publishing
31 Mistletoe Rd.
Ashland, OR 97520

www.BlackstonePublishing.com

To my parents, Sergio and Katinka Rodriguez,
who always believed in me.

To Dave, Diana, and Ken,
whose love and support have always sustained me.

Courage is the price that Life
exacts for granting peace.
—Amelia Earhart

Introduction

In 1985, which is when this story begins, I, Cecilia Rodriguez Aragon, was twenty-five years old and scared of elevators. My graduate school administrator once found me crying in the ninth-floor women's restroom after I'd climbed eight flights of stairs, too frightened to jump onto the elevator. My fear immobilized me even in situations that didn't seem to bother anyone else, like when I climbed a ladder, shook hands with a stranger, or talked on the telephone. It seemed that whenever I had to perform, my brain circuits got jammed and I froze. I was terrified that people would find out the truth: that I was a Failure with a capital *F*. I believed my personality had been stamped into my genes from birth: INTF—Incompetent, Nerd, Terrified, Failure.

But by 1991, just six years later, I was hanging upside down a thousand feet in the air, performing loops and rolls at airshows in front of millions of people in California and across the country. That same year, I beat the national record for fastest time from first solo in an airplane to membership on the United States Unlimited Aerobatic Team. I became the first Latina to win a place on this team and earn the right to represent the US at the Olympics of aviation, the World Aerobatic Championships. I jumped out of airplanes and taught others how to fly. I learned how to fundraise and earned money to compete at the world level. I worked as a test pilot and contributed to the design of experimental airplanes, crafting curves of metal and fabric that shaped air to lift inanimate objects high above the earth.

Flying became my art, my science, and my passion. I used my training in math to optimize split-second performances in the air. In a span of just six years, I taught myself to overcome my self-doubt, shyness, and deep-seated fear of heights to become one of the best aerobatic pilots in the world.

But flying, it turned out, was just the beginning. Learning to face death at a few hundred feet above the runway was merely preparation for dismantling my self-doubt in the classroom and the workplace.

When I was a child, I was bullied by classmates, although it never occurred to me I might be a focus of discrimination. I also never understood why certain teachers looked at me the way they did, with a barely perceptible hostile expression hidden beneath a polite veneer. In books, quiet girls who did their homework were teacher's pets. I was a quiet girl who did her homework, so why didn't they like me?

The little girl I was thought it must be a flaw in my character. I was simply a bad person. And that feeling grew with me. As a teen, I didn't question why my math teacher mentored the second-best student instead of me, or why my English teacher graded me down for creating a disturbance in class, when it was the two kids behind me who talked all the time. These experiences left me with the feeling that there must be something intrinsically wrong with my personality, that my dreams were too big for my reality.

After the World Championships were over, I retired from the team and applied the strategies I'd used there to go after the dreams I'd deferred. In 2003 I went back to complete my PhD in computer science, the program I'd quit because I thought I wasn't smart enough. After that, I worked with astronomers to solve some of the greatest mysteries of the universe. I worked with Nobel Prize winners, taught astronauts to fly, and created musical simulations of the universe with rock stars. Then I applied for my dream job, a career I'd all but given up on because the odds against it were so great. I received six offers and landed what seemed to me to be the best job on the planet: professor in the College of Engineering at the

University of Washington. My students challenge and thrill me to this day. I've won major awards for my research, raised millions of dollars, and in 2009, President Obama shook my hand and congratulated me for my work in data-intensive science. Oh, and in the middle of all this, I did a stint at NASA designing software for Mars missions.

I've lived the kind of life I never would have dreamed of as a shy, awkward child in Indiana, a child no one expected much of, a child who was bullied because of her gender and race. And what's more, I found that the mathematical techniques I developed to overcome my fear of flying could be applied to other aspects of my life, leading me to accomplish many goals, both small and large.

This is my story of breaking free from expectations and prejudice, of rising above my own limits. I did it through a series of simple and rather ordinary steps by combining math and logic with passion in an unexpected way. But you don't have to be a math whiz to learn from my story. You just have to want to break free and learn to soar.

Chapter 1

"Want to go flying?" my coworker Carlos shouted over the clatter of cooling fans in the machine room.

It was July 1985, and I was a new software developer at Digital Equipment Corporation's latest research lab in Palo Alto. I'd only been on the job a week, but I already knew I'd found a friend in Carlos with his love of the Unix operating system and ability to deliver rapid-fire banter on all things programming. A geek after my own heart—that was my initial impression of him. But this flying idea crossed a line. I froze, and the circuits of my brain jammed with fear for a moment.

"You mean in a small plane?" I asked, stalling for time. Did I want to risk death? Um, no. I liked Carlos, and I was grateful he'd set up my workstation on my first day at the job, but I wasn't the kind of person who flew in small airplanes. Nope.

I sneaked a glance at Carlos, not sure how he was going to take it when I told him no. I didn't want to hurt the feelings of one of the few people I felt comfortable with in this new, intimidating world of high tech.

As he waited for me to reply, he closed the back panel of one of the computers with a snap. "I rent a Piper Archer from the Palo Alto Flying Club. It's a beautiful plane."

I hadn't ever thought of airplanes as beautiful. Loud and reeking of kerosene, yes. Maybe sleek and fast, if I wanted to be positive. But didn't every aviation scene in the movies end in engine failure, followed by the inevitable nosedive to the ground? My imagination raced ahead, placing us both in a smoke-filled cockpit with Carlos yelling over the intensifying shriek of the engines, "Grab the wheel! Help me pull out of this dive!"

I blinked and glanced once again at Carlos's eager expression. If I said no, he might never ask me again. It would become yet another in a series of missed opportunities, like "taking a leave" (the polite way of saying "dropping out") from UC Berkeley's computer science PhD program. I'd dreamed of becoming a professor, like my father, for years. But the few available tenure-track faculty positions were in high demand with as many as four hundred applicants for a single opening. I was afraid not only that I couldn't compete against four hundred smart people, but worse, that I wasn't even intelligent enough to finish the required dissertation. So I'd simply given up.

Instead, I'd landed a job in Silicon Valley on the strength of my partially completed graduate work and undergraduate degree in math. But after only a week, I was terrified here too. Entering DEC's brand-new building, I'd suddenly found myself inside something nascent and burgeoning—a movement perhaps?—surrounded by people with the heady conviction that technology was about to change the world. In the neighborhood surrounding the Stanford campus, the scent of falafel curled into the air, and words like "microprocessor," "external cache," and "high-performance CPU" emanated from restaurants packed with geeks.

Yet, despite all the exhilaration around me, despite the fact that DEC had hired me, I was scared I didn't belong. I was the only female programmer on the team, and everyone else seemed so confident, so driven. Surely, they'd soon realize that they'd made a mistake. I kept having flashbacks to how I was bullied as a child. But I needed to find a way to keep the job. My new husband, Ben, and I had been struggling to rent rooms in pricey Berkeley while I was still a student. We'd gotten married in 1984 but had been keeping our finances separate, carefully dividing shares of the rent, utilities, and food. With only a student income, I was the weak link in the financial chain, barely making enough to pay my share. Until now, we'd had to share our living quarters with a series of weird housemates.

This was my first real job, one that might even lead to a career, and I had to hang onto it. I *wanted* to hang onto it. I had to succeed at *something*. And DEC was an exciting place to work in 1985.

Most everyone else in the spanking-new DEC Workstation Systems Engineering Group was a superstar. My boss had invented the famous Bourne shell on the Unix operating system. Another coworker came to us from Microsoft, where he'd developed an operating system called Windows. He seemed to think it was going to revolutionize personal computing.

And then there was me, the kid once assigned to slow reading groups in elementary school back in West Lafayette, Indiana. The girl who'd been diagnosed with a speech impediment in second grade, whose teachers had shaken their heads about my immigrant parents, native speakers of two different languages: my mom, Tagalog, and my dad, Spanish. The kid who'd been ostracized. It was clear I didn't belong. I felt like a bit player on a Broadway stage.

But right there, in that moment, with Carlos waiting on my answer, I decided it was time to face my fears just this once. Maybe it was a stupid risk, but I wanted to *enjoy* this adult life. After way too many years of being broke and afraid, I knew something was wrong with how I'd been living my life. It had become so very narrow. Every year my world contracted as I closed down another path, placed another fetter on myself. *It's not safe. I don't belong. I'm not that kind of person.* Somewhere along the way, I'd lost that connection to something I'd known as a small child, to something vast and deep, to the essence of the person I was meant to be.

And if I wanted a more expansive life, if I wanted to succeed in this career, I was going to have to keep my fears from ruling me. I might as well start with trusting Carlos's offer.

"Sure!" I said with fake enthusiasm, not fully believing what I'd just done.

Carlos grinned with delight. "I'll make the reservation," he said, as though it were as simple as going out to lunch.

* * *

I managed to avoid thinking about the upcoming flight all week. Avoidance was always one of my superpowers. But the following Saturday, I arrived at the Oakland North Field Executive Terminal early. The automatic glass doors slid open, and cold air blasted me in the face. I tried to act like I belonged in the snazzy lounge, its occupants all either in pilots' uniforms or business suits. I was the only woman other than the neatly coiffed and immaculately made-up blond attendant behind the counter.

I sat down in one of the plush chairs and pretended to be engrossed in a magazine labeled *Flying* in bold capital letters across the front. Every now and then I glanced up through the wall of glass at the tarmac, where dozens of small propeller airplanes lined the fence, and sweat chilled me in my thin T-shirt. I was trembling a little. Purely because of the cold, of course.

The doors swooshed open. Warm, briny air from the marsh surrounding the airport swirled in, and then Carlos appeared. "Ready to go?" he asked with a grin.

"Sure," I lied and followed him out to the death trap … er … Piper Archer. This so-called beautiful plane was shockingly tiny, with wings spanning maybe thirty feet, and less than that from nose to tail.

"I got the nicest airplane in the fleet," he boasted. "It's a 1985 model and has all the latest instruments."

The plane had only one door, and four narrow seats packed inside the minuscule cabin. Worse, the open door angled out over the top of one of the wings. I surely couldn't stand right on the wing, could I?

"Climb up and go inside," Carlos directed, busy with something under the belly of the airplane. I froze like a kid stuck on the ladder to the high diving board.

He reemerged from beneath the plane holding a clear plastic tube with a screwdriver on the end. He couldn't possibly be repairing the plane right before we took off, could he? Just to prove I could, I tentatively lifted my foot up onto the wing.

"No, don't step on the flap!" he warned. "Only the black area. That's designed to walk on."

Let's hope I hadn't damaged anything with my misstep. I climbed up on the black strip and stopped dead again. To get to the passenger seat, I'd have to step directly on the pilot's seat and then over a panel studded with multicolored levers. I glanced back at Carlos, still busy with some task probably crucial for the safe operation of the airplane. I didn't dare distract him. Fiery cinematic nosedives flashed before my eyes.

I surreptitiously wiped my shoes on my jeans, stepped onto the leather seat, and crawled past a dizzying array of dials, knobs, and bizarre-looking instruments. There was so much glass it looked like … a cockpit. A second steering wheel, just like the pilot's, protruded into the passenger side, and foot pedals extended over the floor mats. I didn't see how I could avoid bumping into one of the controls and causing certain death.

I vowed to sit absolutely still throughout the flight.

Carlos swung into the pilot's seat carrying a stack of multicolored maps, handed me a headset, and showed me how to adjust the microphone. "When I push this button, I'll be communicating with the tower, so please don't talk. I'll let you know when it's okay."

I nodded. I wouldn't say a word, no matter what. Nothing like, *Um, excuse me, I think I'm about to throw up all over these expensive leather seats.* Nope. Not a word.

Carlos opened a window vent, shouted "*Clear!*" and the propeller began to rotate. The blades blurred into a translucent disk, and the engine growled around my headset. The airplane shook and rumbled, lifting slightly off its wheels as though eager to fly. All at once, this strange and ungainly machine not much bigger than my Honda came alive, a giant bird flexing its wings. A rush of excitement surged through me. We were actually going to fly.

That is, if we didn't crash and burn first.

A nonstop current of voices surged through my headset, but I couldn't understand a word. We taxied out. Carlos gave me a thumbs-up, and I nodded weakly. He advanced the throttle, the engine roared, and we accelerated along the runway. I clutched the sides of the leather seat. Beyond the metal cowling, a view of the wide world opened out in front of me. The runway streamed away beneath us as we picked up speed. Gasoline fumes and burnt rubber dispersed as the roar and vibration increased. Then the plane lifted its nose, and we were airborne.

There was nothing to do but hold on.

The earth dropped away from us. Through the windshield, concrete and trees and endless blue sky pivoted as we wheeled away from land toward San Francisco Bay. Little sparkles of sunlight flickered on the waves beneath us, golden and sapphire.

We were *flying*.

And my heart lifted. I smiled so hard the muscles of my face ached.

Carlos pointed the plane toward the Golden Gate Bridge, a shimmering arc across the sea and sky. He dipped the nose gently, and we flew low over the California coastline, low enough that I could almost feel mist spray my face from waves breaking on the shore. The cliffs thrust up from the water, carved into the earth, vivid and sharp and near. Down we flew over mansions with their elaborate pools and gardens. I wondered if these affluent homeowners had any idea how naked they were to any ordinary citizen who happened to have a pilot's license. It was like having x-ray vision, a tremendous, secret delight.

Suddenly, Carlos tossed one of his complicated maps into my lap. "Quickly, find which radial of the Oakland VOR crosses the tip of Marin County."

Panic bubbled up in me. I had no idea what he was talking about, but I felt that I had to figure out what he needed or surely the plane would plunge into the ocean below us. I had to do something. I had to answer him, but instead I froze. As we sat in that tiny cabin suspended far above the earth, my hands sweated as I clutched the map.

* * *

Sweaty palms had been a humiliating trait of my body ever since childhood. The worst was when I faced heights, like riding the Ferris wheel with my dad at the Lafayette Fair, one evening when I was in sixth grade. At the moment we reached the top, the wheel lurched, and I clung to the bar while our pod rocked back and forth. Rust-colored sweat streaked my palms, and I rubbed them on the orange polyester pants my mom had bought on sale at Sears.

"What a beautiful view," my dad said, his smile gleaming in the reflected glow from lamps that looked like pinpoints beneath us.

I pressed my shoulder into the warmth of his sweater. My gaze trailed along the horizon, where the sky radiated a dusky apricot, sealing itself over cornfields in the distance. The air smelled different up here, purer, wilder, free of dust. Below my dangling feet, our town clung to the earth, the houses as tiny as Monopoly pieces in my mind, the people invisible. I raised a hand and imagined I could simply reach out and move those tiny pieces wherever I wanted.

Yet, if I leaned over the side and slipped, or if one of the bolts or rivets gave way, I'd plummet to certain death. I could imagine it: the rush of air, my terrified scream, the ground widening and expanding around me, closer and closer—then nothing.

I clutched my dad's arm with both hands.

"Whoa," he said, slipping his arm around me. "What's wrong?"

"We're awfully high up," I whispered.

"Shhh, it's fine." He pointed at a metal spoke. "See how wide those struts are? They're calculated to hold many times our weight. Remember I told you about the scientific method?" My dad was a physics professor and a mathematician, and if he said the ride was safe, it must be. In his arms, I relaxed—a little.

When the ride was over, my dad held my hand as we stepped onto solid ground. He kissed my forehead to say goodbye. "I have to work, but I'll pick you up in two hours. Unless you changed your mind and want to go home now?"

I shook my head, arms stiff at my sides. I wanted to stay at the fair, but I was considered too old to be babysat by a parent. I watched the stripes of his navy sweater get smaller and smaller until he vanished in the crowd while tinny music blared from loudspeakers all around me.

Alone, I shuffled my feet in the gravel, trying to decide what to do next. I knew the tilt-a-whirl would make me throw up and the roller coaster terrified me, but I had just enough money to buy cotton candy. I felt like a grown-up as I placed my order and a man spun frothy pink wisps into a huge solid ball. As I wandered down the path, the cloud of spun sugar hid my view of the crowd. The feathery strands melted to sweetness in my mouth. I relaxed a bit. This was fun after all.

"Hey, look, it's Rod-REE-kezz!" A familiar voice mispronounced my name, and I dropped the paper cone, backing against a wall plastered with posters.

Then I saw them across the midway—three of the classmates who most enjoyed making my daily life in sixth grade miserable, their faces blurred in the uneven lighting, their expressions identical and hostile. They wore matching short blond haircuts, and their pale hair gleamed under the lights. The tallest boy, Don Schwartz, stepped forward, flanked by his friends, grinning in anticipation. He scooped up the ruined cone and inspected the dirt-studded pink mass.

"I thought you spics were too poor to waste food." He thrust the mound of cotton candy at my face. "Eat it." His friends laughed.

I dodged his swipe and shrank back against the wall, frozen, glancing left and right for an escape path. Dozens of adults and kids streamed past, shouting and laughing over the music, but no one was paying attention.

Don stepped closer.

All I had to do was duck under his arm. I was a fast runner, faster than most of the kids in my class. But my feet were nailed to the ground, my body immobile except for the pulse drumming against my throat.

Time stretched out, and the smell of sugar and dust swirled into my nose.

"Why, how nice of you boys to share candy with your friend," an elderly woman behind them said, a yellow rose bobbing on her hat. "My grandson is waiting at the merry-go-round. Can you help me find it?"

I grabbed my chance and scurried into a thick crowd of adults. I ran under a ring of lights, hugging the walls and panting. I spent the rest of the evening lurking behind booths and checking the shadows for my tormentors.

* * *

That night was the last time I rode a Ferris wheel. I never saw the earth from above in that same way, not until this first flight in a small plane with Carlos. And just like that day over a decade before, time seemed to stretch while everything waited on my unfreezing. Carlos's question hung in the air as I stared at the map.

But this time I didn't have to run away. The chart on my lap held geometry and numbers—my strong suit. My muscles might have frozen, but my mind could still calculate.

"Three forty-seven," I said, following a line on the chart from the promontory of land to a funny little symbol on the Oakland Airport, noting the number where it crossed a blue circle.

Carlos grinned and fiddled with a set of dials on the dashboard, and we banked ever so slightly to the right. I breathed a sigh of relief.

I said little during the rest of the flight but never forgot the waves splayed out like lace against the cliffs, the sky cupping the ocean like a welcome, calling to me. Carlos let me take the controls, rotate the wheel left and right, and that sweet little Archer leaned into the wind at the touch of my hand. I felt profoundly blessed, touched by something beyond this world. We made a long arc over the East Bay and landed back at Oakland Airport. I was shaking as Carlos taxied the plane back to the Executive Terminal. He unlatched the cockpit door and took my hand to help me out. I inhaled deeply as my feet touched down on the solid concrete.

"Cheated death again," he announced with a grin.

I've heard people describe how alcohol or heroin seems to fill the hole in their heart, how it wipes all the pain away. That's the effect flying had on me. For so long, I'd been aching, lonely, missing something essential. Flitting from one failure to another. But that day, the hole in my heart was filled.

I *had* to go flying again, I realized. But when I pictured myself returning to the runway, I didn't see myself in the passenger seat. I saw myself at the controls. But what did this mean? It meant I would need to learn to fly. It meant that I would become a pilot.

There was only one problem, of course: fear.

I was terrified of operating machinery. Even driving a car scared me. And when I got scared, I got clumsy and awkward and made mistakes.

Aviation, they say, is "unforgiving of carelessness, incapacity, or neglect." Flying was dangerous for someone like me, whose fear often translated into panic and shutdown. I didn't perform well under pressure. Like the time at the fair when all my muscles locked up until chance freed me to run.

I couldn't help wondering if learning to fly would end up my final failure.

Chapter 2

As a child, my single greatest wish was to be able to fly. Not in a plane, but to levitate into the air the way fantastical creatures in books did, to play hide and seek among the branches of trees and rise above the ground, to be free of my ordinary life crowded with scary things and intimidating people. At every childhood birthday, for as long as I could remember, when I blew out the candles on my cake, I'd close my eyes and wish I could escape the life which shackled me to teachers who didn't care and classmates who bullied me.

It had gotten particularly bad with my classmates in sixth grade, when we moved across town to an apartment in a different school district.

"I wish I didn't have to go to school," I said at the breakfast table one morning, nursing bruises under my long sleeves and dreading another day of trying to avoid my classmate Don Schwartz and his friends. They'd gone from taunts at the beginning of the school year to physical attacks whenever they could get me alone. As the new kid, I didn't have any defenders.

My dad stopped pouring his cereal. "Not go to school?" His face fell. "Your Uncle Vicho used to skip school to go to the racetrack. He'd stay out all night. The next morning, he'd say he didn't feel well. My mother would allow him to stay home. Is that what you want?"

I shrank back across the table. "No, of course not." It hurt to disappoint him, worse than the bruises on my arm. My dad was the only person who reliably believed in me, who told me I was brilliant in math. Now he looked so sad. I wanted him to be proud of me, to puff out his chest and say, "My buttons are popping," like he did when I figured out some clever math trick, or brought home straight A's.

I often felt I had more educational advantages than he did, and I was letting him down. My dad was born in a small farming town in the south of Chile. As a boy, he'd been passionate about math and physics and spent all his allowance on textbooks mail-ordered from overseas. He dreamt of becoming a physicist, but his parents couldn't afford to send him to the US, which was the nearest country to offer the necessary studies at the level he desired. Instead, he was told to become a teacher, or maybe a farmer like his grandfather. It wasn't until he was in his midtwenties that an anonymous benefactor, thinking that my dad was the most brilliant mathematics student he'd seen, sent a check to cover his first year's expenses at the University of California, Berkeley. That gift, along with my dad's hard work, enabled him to achieve his dream career.

Setting the cereal box on the table, he said, "You could have a better career than me if you stay in school. Uncle Vicho never finished, and today he's a bum and a gambler." His shoulders slumped.

"It's not that I don't want to learn," I tried once again. "It's just that the boys in my class …"

My mom set down her coffee cup. "Cecilia, if the boys tease you, they probably like you."

I rubbed my mouth. Hitting me hard enough to leave bruises and calling me "dirty spic" meant they liked me? That couldn't be right, but I didn't have the nerve to question her.

My dad glanced at his watch. "I have to go. My student's having a problem with her visa, and I'm meeting her at the immigration office to help." He put his dishes in the sink.

My mom checked the clock. "You're going to be late for school," she said as she stood up from the table.

Resigned, I gathered my books and followed her to the car. I hid the science fiction book I was reading under my health textbook so none of my classmates could see the title. Liking to read was already suspicious, especially for a girl who did well in math. And to openly read science fiction and fantasy would brand me firmly as a nerd and an outcast.

In the books I read, kids had superpowers. They could fly. They could bring justice to the world. I couldn't fly, but my superpower was being good at math. I could see geometric patterns laid out before me. Mathematical induction seemed like a magic way of proving theorems like the domino effect. Step One: The first domino falls. Step Two: If any domino falls, the next one must also fall. Therefore, all dominoes will fall.

Math was beautiful, and it was fun, but it couldn't stop Don Schwartz from hitting me. Numbers and proofs didn't allow me to fly away from my problems on earth. I told myself flying was impossible. Fantasy was escapism. I needed to grow up and leave my impossible dreams behind.

* * *

During that first flight with Carlos, I realized my world had been transformed, and the first domino had fallen.

Step two would require quite a leap. I'd have to go from accepting a ride to learning how to be a pilot myself. I had to get up the courage to take lessons. Plus it was expensive, and Ben disapproved, telling me private flying was too dangerous. But since I was still living like a student while bringing home a programmer's income, the benefit of keeping separate finances in my marriage became clear. I had some extra cash, and I didn't need Ben's approval to spend it.

It helped that Carlos was constantly talking at work about the wonders of flight. "What a perfect day for flying!" he'd say when he caught me gazing out the window of my office. "The earth looks so beautiful from a couple of thousand feet in the air, doesn't it?" Having discovered a potential convert, he redoubled his efforts, constantly touting the benefits of flying instead of driving through the congested Bay Area.

Even after I decided to take my first lesson, I still had to figure out the logistics of where and what kind of airplane to fly. Flight instruction was expensive, but if I was careful, I could afford it. Unfortunately, I let

Carlos convince me to call and just ask for an instructor. When I finally picked up the phone, my voice was shaking. "I'd like to learn to fly." It didn't occur to me that selecting a flight instructor was one of the most critical decisions in pilot training, and by not doing research, I'd probably just picked the surefire way to get the newest and least qualified flight instructor in the club.

Nevertheless, on August 10, 1985, I pulled into the airport parking lot. A brackish, steady breeze blew across the bay from the northwest. Perched on a salt marsh, an ever-changing buffer between the saltwater of San Francisco Bay and the terrain known as Silicon Valley, the Palo Alto Airport merges with a complex coastal ecosystem. Like many small airports, it serves as a great nature preserve with its required acres of flat, undeveloped land. Tall, smooth cordgrass and glassworts thread their roots into the mud and surround the runway and taxiways. Sea lavenders, sedges, and rushes speckle the thick grass. I took a deep breath. From this day forward the smell of those wetlands would always be associated with excitement, with facing down fear and taking charge of my life.

I pushed open the glass door of the Palo Alto Flying Club, wiped my palms on my jeans and approached the woman behind the counter (women behind the desk, men on the flight line is an all-too-common situation at flight schools, as I was quickly learning). "I'm here for my first lesson with Brad Matthews."

The receptionist smiled widely. "That's great!" she said with more enthusiasm than anyone holding open the gates of death should possess. "Brad's just finishing up with a student. Can I get you some coffee?"

Coffee. Right. Like I needed to be more nervous. I pasted on a smile to match hers. "No, thank you, but could I use your bathroom?" My kidneys were running overtime in preparation for the death flight. What was I doing, trusting someone I barely knew with my life?

Hopefully Brad's previous student would take a long time. Maybe so long that there wouldn't be time for my flight today. I could see myself politely telling Brad that no, it was fine, I didn't mind. We could reschedule. Maybe sometime next week. Maybe sometime next *year*.

"Hi, Cecilia!" It was Brad, with every single blond hair in place, wearing a tie and crisp white shirt with … Wait, were those epaulets on the shoulders? He grabbed a clipboard from behind the desk, and we headed out to the flight line.

I followed Brad to a row of airplanes lined up on the asphalt in the August sun. My heart beat faster at the sight, and a rush spiraled through my body. Little puddles formed in the creases of my clenched hands. Would today be my last day on earth?

Brad patted the hood of a blue and white plane. "Here she is: November Seven Four Three Five Hotel, a 1978 model Cessna 152." In the United States, aircraft are identified by their "N-numbers," a unique string of numbers and letters, and often nicknamed by the last three digits. Only a little over twenty feet long, with two stubby exhaust pipes protruding from its sloping belly thick with grease, Three Five Hotel perched on three miniscule tires, smaller in diameter than those of a motorcycle. The wings stretched only inches above my head when I stood straight at my full height of five feet two inches.

Brad knocked on the metal surface, and it sounded hollow. It didn't seem nearly serious or miraculous enough to defy death. Something physical that could hold the dream of flight should be, I don't know, loftier, more elegant, simply *grander*. Not something with the heft of a cheap filing cabinet and all the glamour of a vintage metal garbage can, complete with streaks of dirt and oil. But I said nothing to Brad about any of this as we circled the Cessna. I was too busy being terrified.

To keep the plane from levitating away from its tie-down spot in a high wind, three long chains looped through metal rings welded to the airframe—two at the point where the struts attached to the wings and one at the tail. Brad assigned me the task of unchaining the airplane and freeing it for flight. The heavy chains left a metallic smell on my hands.

Brad tossed the clipboard onto the right-side seat. "We always start with a preflight inspection." Rapidly, he ran through a series of motions, wiggling parts of the airplane, taking fuel samples and wiping a dipstick with a rag, acting as though all this was completely obvious. Brad rushed through the inspection, brushing away my questions. I would later learn that he only got paid when the airplane engine was running, although payment wasn't his main concern. Brad came from a fairly well-to-do Palo

Alto family, and was working as a flight instructor solely to "build time for the airlines." I was one of his first students. He had recently gotten his instructor's rating with 250 hours in airplanes, but needed 1,500 hours before he could get the minimum certificate required to land a corporate jet job, the next step on the ladder toward becoming an airline pilot.

"Next time, you can do this on your own," he said at the end of his preflight inspection.

Say *what*? I had no idea what I would be looking for. Somehow, I managed to climb into the left side of the plane, the pilot's seat. There, I sat stiffly, shaking a little.

Inside the cockpit, the scent of heated plexiglass, vinyl upholstery, and gasoline and oil fumes mingled. This was a scent I would come to associate with terror, elation, and eventually, something more.

The panel, studded with dozens of complicated dials, gauges, and radios, supported a windshield crazed from seven years in the Palo Alto sun. Even with the seat cranked up to its highest position and slid all the way forward on its rails, I still couldn't peer over the dashboard, and my feet could barely reach the rudder pedals. It made me feel awkward, and I wondered if having limited vision and an imperfect connection to the controls would impact my ability to fly the plane. Unfortunately, Brad didn't seem to notice my feet dangling away from the pedals.

He climbed into the right seat, shouted "*Clear!*" and started the engine. The propeller turned over, growled, and the airplane shook itself and clanked. Carlos's Piper Archer had felt like a sleek, tiny version of a corporate jet. This 1978 Cessna clattered like a flying Volkswagen.

Simple, inexpensive, and fuel-efficient, the Cessna got the job done without frills. The 152 model was one of the safest aircraft ever built, with the lowest accident rate of any general aviation plane, despite having served as a workhorse training thousands of nervous student pilots how to fly. Still, the doors rattled, the windows didn't quite fit in their slots, and the cockpit sounded like a dozen jackhammers beating on garbage can lids. The Lycoming 235 engine up front was separated from the front seats by only a thin firewall, and when the four-cylinder reciprocating engine roared to life, it did so with gusto and volume.

Brad taxied us to the runway and did the takeoff from the right seat, telling me he'd let me handle the controls once we were at altitude. I was sitting
in the pilot's seat, but I still felt like a passenger—and a confused one at that.

Brad taught without headsets or intercom, which meant we could
barely hear each other, even when we shouted. His teaching method
involved bellowing over the earsplitting engine noise. "Now we're going
to do the four fundamentals! Watch while I demonstrate."

We hadn't talked about any of the maneuvers on the ground, and once
in the air, I was too swamped by fear to pay much attention. I assumed I
was simply a slow learner.

Brad turned the radio all the way up so we could hear the instructions
from the control tower blaring through the overhead speakers.

I shouted to Brad that I was having trouble understanding the garbled
instructions, and he yelled back, "Hey, you know why Cessna put fifty-
cent speakers in their aircraft?"

I shook my head.

He grinned. "Because they ran out of the twenty-five-cent ones!"

I had to laugh. Cessnas were far from luxury machines. This experience was already teaching me that aviation was very different from the
stereotype that all private pilots were wealthy and flew opulent aircraft.

The first lesson was mostly a blur. I remember being petrified, and I
remember that Brad did almost all the flying, telling me how much fun it
was. In all fairness to Brad, he genuinely tried to share his love of aviation
with me. Somewhere partway through the lesson, he even handed me the
controls and told me to make a few turns, then some climbs and descents.

And it *was* fun. We flew over the Dumbarton Bridge, across the Leslie
Salt flats, and over Fremont and on to the brown hills of the East Bay. I
gingerly turned the tiny plane to the left, then to the right. As our wings
bit into the atmosphere, I felt that deep thrill once again. *I was flying.* I
was controlling the airplane. Yes, it was scary, I couldn't understand most
of what Brad was saying, my ears ached from the throbbing racket of the
engine, but there I was, an ordinary human being flying like a bird. The
dun hills unrolled below us, and the scent of California scrub brush sidled
through the vents and soaked into my lungs, displacing the briny coastal air.

And I didn't die on that first flight. What I learned instead was that even if you take just a small step to face your fear—if you sign up for something you know is scary and make yourself do it—the range of what you can do becomes wider. Over the months and the years, when you look back over how far you've come, you'll realize how much you've grown and how much bigger the world has become.

It's just like mathematical induction. Step One: face your fear today. Step Two: If you did it today, you can do it again tomorrow. And the rest of the dominoes will fall in turn.

And that was exactly how I made it from my first flying lesson to my second. And from my second to my third and from my third to my—well, you get the idea.

Chapter 3

When I was sixteen, I met Ben Davidson, the man who would later become my husband. Eager to leave Indiana behind, I'd applied to college a year early and had been admitted to the California Institute of Technology. I met Ben my first week in Pasadena. He talked with me about the beauty of math, his pride in being an engineering major, and his excitement about the world around him. He was outspoken and iconoclastic, even among the brilliant nerds and outcasts at Caltech. He told me long rambling stories that made me laugh deep down in my belly.

One day he said, shocking my Catholic-girl heart, "I would make love to you if you wanted."

"Of course not," I retorted, but I'll admit I was intrigued. Ben was the first person who expressed attraction for me as a whole human being. He didn't focus only on my race, my immigrant parents, or my flat chest. Unlike the boys I encountered in high school, Ben saw me for who I was.

He stood long and lanky under his floppy hat, hair the color of wheat falling to his waist, a self-proclaimed hippie. It embarrassed me that he wore a belt buckle emblazoned with *love*, but I was charmed he'd created an imaginary language in high school and convinced several of his classmates to join his "Federation of Small Nations." They even held conventions to debate politics and grammar in his made-up language.

On one of our dates, he told me, "I see God in you." Then he completely spoiled the moment by adding, "But I see God in everyone."

On my first visit to Caltech, I'd talked to more guys my own age than I had in all my years in high school. I'd always assumed boys avoided me because I didn't really have breasts, my fashion sense was terrible, and I was shy. Or maybe some of it was because of prejudice. I remember a boy in high school telling me once, "You know I don't have anything against it, but my mother wouldn't approve of me dating you. She sees the name Rodriguez all the time in the police reports, and thinks all Hispanics do is pick crops and get in trouble."

So dates in high school were not for me. I told myself I didn't care. I still associated boys with the slurs, punches, and bruises I'd been trying for years to erase from my mind. But I could never erase from my memory the look of disgust on Don Schwartz's face as he hit me or the smell of bruised grass and clover.

It was the first warm day of 1970 in West Lafayette, Indiana. The May sun shone on the brilliantly green hillside behind Raleigh Elementary School, and fuzzy white and purple clover, yellow sourgrass, and tiny pale bluebells dotted the grass. Bees droned somewhere far away. I wandered out behind the school during recess, taking in great breaths of rich, sweet air.

Usually recess was my least favorite time, because none of the other kids wanted to play with me. But today my classmates were playing a game on the other side of the school, so I felt safe and free. I took another deep breath. It made me want to laugh.

Then suddenly Don Schwartz and his friends, Terry and Mike, rounded a corner, snickering.

Instantly my heart beat faster and my feeling of safety evaporated. I looked around for a place to hide. I had never understood why my mother said that it wasn't safe to be alone. I never felt in danger when I was alone. It was when other people were around that I wasn't safe.

Terry spotted me and nudged Don. I didn't like the flat look in their eyes, so I tensed, spun around, and ran.

I was ten years old and skinny. It seemed that I had weighed fifty-four pounds and worn size 6X forever. My favorite green and orange dress was

pulled tight with a bow at the back of my waist. I loved the soft feel of
the fabric against my bare legs, even though the knot in back dug into my
vertebrae when we did sit-ups in gym. My mother had taken me to the
shoe store the day before, so I wore brand-new shoes still sporting slick
beige soles since they hadn't been roughed up by walking on concrete.

I was a fast runner and normally wouldn't have had a problem outrun-
ning those three. But that day somebody had pulled a metal bar off the
playground equipment, maybe from a jungle gym, and had laid it out
there behind the school in the long grass.

Glancing over my shoulder to check the position of the boys, I tripped
over the bar (those slick new shoes didn't help) and fell hard, sprawling
full-length into the warm grass. I hit the ground with a heavy thump.

Long green grass streaks and splotches of mud coated my legs. The
scent of the grass was suddenly overpowering. Still dizzy from the fall, I
pushed myself up.

A shadow fell over me, and my skin felt abruptly cold. The three boys
were standing over me. Don's broad shoulders blocked out the sun, and
his face lay in shadow. "Rod-REE-kezz, you freak," he sneered.

Refusing to look at him, I said nothing. I started to get to my feet, but
he shoved me hard, and I stumbled, laid out once again on my back. Mike
sat on my stomach. I yelped and struggled.

"You dirty spic. What the fuck you doing?" Don picked up the metal
bar and leaned over me, still pinned down in the warm grass. He glanced
over his shoulder at the brick wall. No teachers in sight. "Huh," he said,
and his lip curled. His eyes became narrow slits. My heart pounded, and
I desperately tried to get out from under Mike, who weighed twice what I
did. Don's grip on the metal bar tightened. He lifted it, and a clod of dirt
fell off the pointed end into the grass. I struggled harder. Then he flipped
the bar and slid it in between my legs.

I redoubled my efforts to get away, but Don lifted the bar and brought
it down hard against my flesh. I screamed. Pain—intense, shocking
pain—flared and radiated from between my legs and took over my entire
body. Something hit me again. I flailed and struggled to no avail. The pain
crested until I couldn't bear it anymore.

The next thing I remember, I was lying alone in the warm, sweet-smelling clover, dizzy and in agony. The boys were gone.

I felt a sharp, strange ache somewhere in between my legs. It hurt so much, and I noticed with shame that I must have peed myself because my panties were wet.

I struggled to my feet. I could stand, though I was still dizzy. My ears rang, and the pain made it hard to see. My dress was dirty, and my legs were smeared with mud. I tried to brush some of the dirt off my dress, arms, and legs. Slowly, I limped back to the classroom, where all the students were seated at their desks working. The bell had rung a long time ago. I got scolded by the teacher for being late. I slipped into my chair, avoiding the eyes of Don, Terry, and Mike.

It was a long and painful afternoon. I had never been happier to see my mother in our blue Dodge in the parking lot after school. She didn't notice how dirty I was, so I was spared having to explain. But when I got home, went to the bathroom, and sat on the toilet, I found I couldn't urinate. I panicked and cried, calling for my mother.

"What happened?" She stood in the bathroom doorway, wiping her hands on her blue-and-green flowered apron, her dark brown eyes concerned.

"I …" I hesitated. I wasn't quite sure what to tell her. "Some boys in my class were mean to me," I began.

A line appeared in the middle of her forehead. "Are they teasing you again? Maybe they …" She was going to tell me they liked me again.

I remembered vividly the flat look of disgust on Don's face. "No, they hate me."

"Oh, Cecilia. Don't be so dramatic. Nobody hates you."

I turned my face away, and tears dripped down my face. She wasn't going to understand.

"So what happened? Tell me, Cecilia."

What could I say? "I slipped on the monkey bars," I said between sobs. "My shoes were slippery."

"Oh, no." She gathered me in her arms and bent to examine me. "Let me see. Oh, you're bruised and bleeding there. I'll put you in a hot bath, and that'll loosen the dried blood. You'll be okay." She hugged me. "Don't cry. You'll be all right."

I sat in the warm water, still crying, and my mother perched on the lip of the tub in the blue-tiled bathroom, gently rubbing my arm and singing to me.

"Mommy? Is it okay if I pee right in the water?"

"Yes, just this once."

Eventually I relaxed in the soothing warmth, and released my urine. The water turned a muddy orange, and I felt ashamed that I was so dirty.

I laid my face against my mother's arm and cried some more. She drained the dirty water, ran another clean tubful of warm water, and washed me tenderly.

"You're all right now," she said, drying me with a soft towel.

But I wasn't. That was the day I realized there was no safety, that even though my parents loved me, they couldn't protect me. I realized that people were not to be trusted and that I was on my own. And that the only thing I could do was pick myself up and move on. I became the girl who never broke the rules, who never opened her mouth in class, who learned to stay invisible.

When Don Schwartz sneered at me and said, "You stink, you dirty spic," I didn't say anything.

When my eighth-grade teacher scolded, "Why are you working so hard at math? You should be getting a boyfriend!" I stared at my shoes.

When my tenth-grade geometry teacher silently passed me over in favor of the second-best student in class, I didn't complain.

I never said anything. Never talked back, never stepped out of line. Because I was ashamed.

I knew that whenever bad things happened to me, it was my fault. There was something wrong with me, and there wasn't anything I could do about it.

* * *

I was nineteen and Ben was twenty-one when he wrote me a seventeen-page letter. In it, he waxed enthusiastic about many of the women he had known and loved and declared that of all the wonderful women in his world, there was only one with whom he'd want to spend the rest of his life. My chest tightened, thinking he'd found someone else and this was a Dear John letter. On the last page he wrote, "That woman is you."

Even though I slept in his room every night, I was terrified of sex due to my strict Catholic upbringing and perhaps because of the assaults I experienced in childhood, although I didn't share those memories with Ben. But whenever the topic of sex came up, he said, "I'll wait until you're ready, however long it takes."

On a golden afternoon in Berkeley, the sun filtering through the persimmon tree that shaded our bedroom, we lay together on our foam mattress. He'd planted lavender and jasmine in our garden, and the warm, mingled scents swept in through the open window. The sun played over Ben's skin, dappling the hair on his forearms. He enveloped me in his arms, and the clean scent of him drifted to my nostrils. I was trembling.

"I'll be gentle," he said. And he was, slow and sweet and intensely passionate, so that when he finally slipped inside me, it didn't even hurt.

We wrote our own wedding vows, and took the dramatic step of taking a new name together to celebrate our new life—Aragon, the province in Spain that reflected both of our European and Hispanic ethnicities—despite objections from all four of our parents. I promised I would love him "in life and beyond" on a sunny afternoon in June 1984 under a canopy of shagbark hickory and slippery elm trees in my parents' backyard in Indiana.

"Love doesn't just sit there, like a stone." I handed Ben a bouquet of calla lilies and recited Ursula Le Guin's words as I looked into his eyes. "It has to be made, like bread; remade all the time, made new." We kissed, and the breeze smelled rich with lilies and roses. His arms curled around me as the music soared.

In the video filmed right at the peak of the ceremony, a small plane appears in the distance, coming closer over the trees, until the noise of its engine drowns out the minister's words. Viewing that video years later, I couldn't help thinking it was a portent, a warning that flying might one day interfere with what I had once thought was an ideal relationship.

* * *

It was now September 1985, and I was pushing myself to take lessons at the Palo Alto Airport three times a week before work. When I wasn't flying, I was talking about flying. When I wasn't talking about flying, I was dreaming about how I could be flying. And, as I became more and more obsessed with flying, I started spending less time with Ben. In September, I made a major decision, against Ben's wishes, that even my pilot friends thought was crazy.

"You're going to do *what*?" Carlos squinted at me over the top of my workstation. He and I had become frequent flying buddies, pooling our funds to fly to a nearby airport for a "hundred-dollar hamburger" for lunch (burger, five dollars; airplane rental, ninety-five dollars). For both of us, it was fun to find someone with whom to share the passion of flying. Carlos had been delighted when I began to love flying as much as he did. But sometimes even he thought my enthusiasm was over the top.

"I'm going to buy a used Cessna," I said.

"You haven't even soloed. Are you sure it's wise to buy an airplane when you can't even fly it?"

"People buy cars before they have a driver's license," I pointed out.

He looked dubious. "Not often."

Refusing to be discouraged, I launched into my argument. "It'll actually save me money to buy an airplane."

He raised his eyebrows. I pulled out the spiral notebook where I'd made my computations. "Look. It costs thirty-five dollars per Hobbs hour to rent a Cessna 152, plus eighteen dollars per hour for the instructor. I make five landings in one point oh Hobbs hours, so that's more than ten dollars per landing." Another great thing about hanging out with Carlos was he knew stuff like a Hobbs hour was an hour when the engine is running. I never had to stop and explain any geeky aviation details to him.

"You only make five landings per hour during your lessons?"

"Brad won't do touch-and-goes," I explained. My instructor didn't like his students to touch down on the runway and immediately apply full throttle for takeoff because he claimed it was unsafe, even though all the other instructors were fine with it. Instead, he had me land, brake to a full stop, and taxi off the runway. Palo Alto was such a busy airport that we had to wait in line each time behind six to eight other airplanes preparing to take off. Airplanes are rented by the Hobbs hour, regardless of whether the engine is idling on the ground or flying at full cruise at three thousand feet.

"That's going to slow you down," Carlos said, his forehead wrinkling. "Are you sure he's a good instructor?"

Carlos had located the exact center of my worry. It was true that Brad's insistence on full-stop landings meant that I was only getting half as many landings as other students. But I didn't want to think about the possibility that Brad was a bad instructor. If he were, I'd have to do something about it, and that was the type of conflict I wasn't willing to take on yet.

"He says I'm not flying well enough for touch-and-goes," I explained, staring at the ground. Brad was the instructor, so he was in charge. Plus, I was too timid to say anything, and I assumed any problems I was having were my fault. Although I was frustrated, it didn't occur to me that his constant dismissal of my abilities might slow my learning.

I tapped the next page. "Suppose I bought a used Cessna 152. It burns five gallons of gas per hour. That's nine dollars per hour to fly, plus eighteen for Brad, so it comes to only five dollars per landing! See, it saves me money."

"I guess," he said with a shrug.

"I want to learn to fly," I told Carlos. "As a matter of fact, I *need* to fly, like I need food and water."

Carlos rolled his eyes at my melodramatic claim. But as a pilot himself, he understood, and it was a relief that someone did, after Ben's disapproval.

The night before, I'd been running through the numbers and finally had the courage to tell Ben my plan to buy a plane.

Each lesson was costing me about $50, I'd explained, adding up to nearly $600 a month for flying lessons, significantly more than my $400 share of the monthly rent. I'd budgeted that—assuming I could get a loan—I could afford $5,000 for a used airplane, less than some new cars cost in 1985. Watching my paycheck disappear into rental fees, I'd begun to haunt the aviation bookstore at the airport, devouring information about aviation and reading articles about budgeting flying costs. New airplanes were far beyond my price range, but hardly anybody I knew bought an aircraft new. Used planes, unlike used cars, were legally required to be maintained under strict FAA regulations and therefore tended to be in good shape.

If I continued to live like a student, my software engineering salary of $24,000 a year could cover my share of the rent, utilities, and food, and I'd still have enough left over for my new obsession.

After listening to me explain all this, Ben ran a hand through his hair in frustration. "Buying a plane is crazy. You've never bought anything this big before."

I frowned. "I can cover it with my salary. It won't affect you."

He shook his head, but reluctantly agreed after checking over the numbers.

I told myself I could handle Ben's displeasure. Even as a child, I'd vowed to never let a man make decisions for me. My real concern was that my fear of flying, combined with my frugal tendencies, might give me an excuse to avoid taking lessons. And then that would be it for flying. Another lost opportunity.

So, to guard against self-sabotage, I needed to take money-saving steps. I turned to the superpower that had never failed me yet: I approached the problem mathematically. Math's promise of a rational world amid unpredictability brought me peace. In order to overcome my fear of flying, I reasoned, I had to turn the equation around. Instead of "Thrift + Fear = Grounded," I had to devise a calculation that would make my instincts work *against* my fear of flying and *toward* my goal of flying more often.

I needed to create incentives in favor of flying. Flying *was* expensive, but it turned out that if I bought a used plane and flew it two hundred hours a year, my total costs for everything from parking and insurance to fuel would run around nineteen dollars an hour. Far less than the thirty-five dollars per hour I paid to rent. And, the more I flew, the cheaper the hourly cost. If I owned an airplane, I couldn't afford *not* to fly. It was a great psychological ploy. My own stinginess would force me to fly. An ideal antidote for fear.

The loan was the most challenging part of my plan. Banks were not necessarily convinced by my mathematics. I applied for several loans and was turned down. Finally, I walked into the bank where I'd had an account for five years, lugging a stack of credit card bills, all paid on time. "I have a perfect credit rating," I said. "I've saved up one thousand dollars, and I'm only asking for four thousand, eighty percent of my aircraft purchase."

The banker behind the desk scratched an ear. "You've never borrowed that amount of money before. What if we make it twenty-five hundred dollars, or fifty percent of five thousand, the total purchase price?"

I pressed my elbows into my sides. That wouldn't work, obviously. I saw my dream evaporating, but the banker must have realized he needed my business. Or maybe he had a quota. In any event, he signed the loan approval, and I was on my way to becoming an aircraft owner! I had to hide my grin and keep myself from skipping all the way out of the bank.

At that point, Carlos became an enthusiastic participant in the aircraft search. I think he was vicariously living out his own dream of becoming an aircraft owner without the burden of a loan payment. I didn't mind because now I had a supporter for my wild schemes. Ben, of course, stayed distinctly lukewarm on the airplane-buying idea. He didn't oppose it overtly, since I'd shown I could cover the payments with my own salary, but he made it clear that he thought flying was an impractical hobby. Ben loved me and wanted to me to be happy, but he sincerely hoped this flying obsession would pass.

But it didn't pass, and I made time to fly even though I faced a daily commute from Berkeley to Silicon Valley and back, two hours a day, five days a week. I reminded Ben we'd once made an agreement to live halfway between our jobs, but he refused to move out of Berkeley, where he worked. Frustrated, I threatened to move out and get an apartment in Palo Alto, near my job (and the airport, though I didn't mention that). We spent less and less time with each other, and whenever we did get together, we argued. He told me I was no fun anymore, and in response I did my best to avoid him. No more gardening together, going out to movies or on long walks. Instead, I spent weekends at the airport and went flying many nights after work.

"You used to be a fascinating conversationalist on anything under the sun, and now all you talk about is flying," Ben said one evening at dinner.

I had to admit he was right. I couldn't stop thinking about being up in the air.

Why had flying come to mean so much to me? Even though it terrified me, I *had* to take that lesson every day. I wanted it with such intensity that I'd do anything for it. I was already choosing my friends based on how interested—or willing—they were to talk about flying. I displayed what I'd been told were classic signs of drug addiction: hanging out with a different crowd, abandoning social activities, lying to my parents.

I hadn't told my parents I was taking flying lessons. No way would I ever tell them I was buying an airplane, because I knew they would be sensible and tell me not to. My mother would cry and tell me I should think about my family before taking up such a life-threatening hobby. My father would say I was making a mistake and that I should put more focus on my career. They would both tell me a plane was a selfish waste of money.

Selfish—it was one of the first words I learned as a very young girl. In a memory or perhaps a dream, I come downstairs to find my parents and younger sister eating orange popsicles in the dining room, the double kind with two sticks. A box with one remaining popsicle sits on the table.

"Can I have it?" I ask.

My sister, an orange ring around her mouth, protests. "I want another one!"

My mother tears open the bag and carefully splits the last popsicle in two, giving half to my sister and half to me. "There! I've divided it equally between you to be fair," she says.

Before I can complain, she scolds, "Don't be so selfish, Cecilia."

It was selfish to disturb Mom during her nap, selfish to ask to play with a friend, selfish to ask for more food at the dinner table. I could never get away from being selfish. It felt like my defining characteristic and my consummate shame. No matter how hard I tried to be a good girl, I felt like I was inherently bad—bad on the inside.

When I was older, my mother informed me, "When you get married, don't think it'll be fifty-fifty. A good relationship needs to be sixty-forty, and it's the woman who has to give the sixty."

I didn't *want* to give 60 percent. It seemed to me that women were getting a bad deal. Was it selfish to want 50 percent? My mom told me a good woman is generous, a giver, someone who sacrifices for her husband and children. She's not supposed to admit that sometimes she doesn't even want to be a mother, that she has days when she plops the kids in front of the TV to spend some blissful alone time. She's never supposed to turn away from that tradition of service and sacrifice.

My Filipina mother was born in Manila in 1935 and raised Catholic. Her beloved oldest brother was killed while serving as a volunteer in the American army fighting the Japanese during World War II. He was one of over a million Filipinos who died during the war. (It wasn't until 2017 that my uncle's sacrifice was recognized with the Congressional Gold Medal. His family never received the veterans' benefits promised by then-president Franklin Roosevelt in 1941.) One of my mom's earliest memories involved a bomb falling within a few feet of her house right after the Pearl Harbor attack.

My mom grew up with open sores on her legs, raised by a series of poverty-stricken relatives after her own mother died while she was still a baby. She was so hungry during the war that she ate cooking fuel. She told me stories of sitting in her family's roofless bamboo outhouse wiping herself with cut-up newspaper while Japanese planes flew overhead.

Despite the deprivations, she excelled in school, and eventually won a scholarship to the University of California, Berkeley. She emigrated from the Philippines at age nineteen and earned both a bachelor's and a master's degree.

Her journey across the world intersected with my dad's in Berkeley, where they both lived in the International House, met, and fell in love, though their relationship developed its own significant turbulence. They'd gotten together despite all odds, were driven apart by cultural forces, and at last, were drawn together again by their love to be married in Seattle only ten months before I was born.

Despite all she'd done to get her education, my mother gave up her career to support my father's dreams. She left her position as a social worker in San Francisco and followed my father to a tiny town in the Midwest, encountering snow, broiler ovens, and deep racial prejudice for the first time in her twenties. The contrast between my mother's life and my own seemed to get starkest when I examined the choices of her adult life after she married my father. My mother, far removed from the Filipino culture that had raised her, gave up her career to be a stay-at-home mom in an isolated Midwestern town. It was hard not to look at my dreams of flying solo, and even living alone, as individualistic to a fault. Or, as my mom once said, selfish.

My mother gave birth to two little girls in an area where she and her culture were about as alien to the local environment as you could get. In the Philippines, new mothers were surrounded by older female relatives. They helped with breastfeeding, dispensed advice, and shared in the task of childrearing. My mother lived practically intertwined with her six brothers and sisters in World War II Manila, sleeping four to a room on tatami mats. She was so accustomed to a communal society that she described her childhood to me in first-person plural.

"When we were children, we always celebrated my birthday by going to the cemetery. We played hide-and-seek behind the gravestones, calling out in subdued voices because if we shouted, our aunt would reprimand us for not showing respect for the dead."

How different it was in the Midwestern United States. When my mother gave birth to me in a hospital, none of her relatives were there. She was alone, with no one to give her advice. The nurse said her breasts were too small to breastfeed me, and that she should use formula instead.

On the second day of my life, the nurse brought her the wrong baby to feed.

My mother gazed down at the infant with straight black hair and Chinese features. "I'm sorry." She smiled apologetically. "This isn't my daughter."

The nurse checked the baby's wrist tag and laughed. "Oh, this is the Chan baby. They look so alike."

No, my mother wanted to say. *They don't look alike at all.* But she said nothing.

It was important to be good, to be quiet—whether it meant surviving the bombing of Manila or the overwhelmingly white population of the Midwest. When someone threatened you, it was important to stay hidden, to stay small. Fear helped keep you safe.

If I weren't selfish, maybe there was some other explanation for how divergent our lives were. There had to be as now I was on the cusp of buying a propeller plane, the object of one of my mother's greatest childhood fears. "Whenever I hear one flying overhead, I remember hearing that same kind of engine as a child and looking up and seeing the Japanese planes on their way to bomb Manila," she told me once. "I can't stop myself from reliving that memory and remembering that my brother died in the war."

I felt guilty to be enjoying something she was so afraid of. I felt I was going against all of my mother's hard-won wisdom by buying a plane, having the audacity to think I could be a pilot. Was it selfish for me to say that I didn't want a life like hers? That I didn't want to be defined by fear and sacrifice?

When I'd talked to Ben about buying a plane, his face had twisted in worry. I could see that he wasn't so much angry as frightened. He loved me and thought I was going off the deep end. What was this flying addiction doing to me, to our relationship, to my family life? Ben only wanted the best for me, and instead I was sneaking out to go flying. It was like I was having an illicit affair with aviation.

He was right; it was a risk. Once I signed on the dotted line, I'd be responsible for this machine. The loan payments and other expenses would come due every month. There would be no backing out.

Exactly.

These were the very stakes I needed to ensure that I'd actually follow through all the way to getting my pilot's license, and that I wouldn't let my fear of being selfish or causing others to worry allow me to back out. I was going to keep doing it. I was going to give myself this.

To become the person I wanted to be, I had to keep on flying, no matter what anyone said, even Ben. I tacked up a poem by Amelia Earhart over my desk. It began, "Courage is the price that Life exacts for granting peace." I knew I had to pay that price.

* * *

"You have to get a subscription to *Trade-a-Plane*," Carlos said later that week at the flying club, showing me a copy of the thick want-ad newspaper with distinctive yellow pages dedicated to the used aviation market. *Trade-a-Plane* contained about 180 pages of three-line classified ads in six-point font and was packed with incomprehensible initialisms like SMOH and TTAE.

Scanning the pages, I soon realized I couldn't even afford a used Cessna 152 and would have to step down to an older model, the Cessna 150. I made a list of Northern and Central California area codes and wrote down all the cheapest 150s within range of Palo Alto. I called a number in the 408 area code, and the man on the other end said the plane was tied down at Salinas Airport, only a little over an hour's drive away.

The next Sunday, October 13, 1985, Carlos and I drove down to Salinas. It was another gorgeous California fall afternoon, the sun glowing over golden hillsides dotted with live oaks. As we drove, I watched Latino farmworkers gathered in the artichoke fields.

Was it actually possible that I was about to become an aircraft owner? It had always been hard to figure out who I was, what my identity was.

I suppose this went as far back as my childhood. Was I Chilean, like my father, or Filipina, like my mother? "Spics are Mexicans," my father said. "You're not Mexican." Was I white, like my father claimed, or black, like my second-grade teacher told me to mark on multiple-choice forms?

I'd listened to Cher's song "Half Breed" on the radio until my father banged on the door. "Turn that trash down! Why don't you play classical music?"

I was half Chilean and half Filipina—what was that? There wasn't even a word for my racial background. Could you call me "Chilipino"? It sounded like a meal you'd order from one of the "ethnic" restaurants in West Lafayette.

I didn't speak Spanish or Tagalog. I'd never visited my mother's country, and on my occasional trips to Chile, my cousins made fun of me and called me a gringa. I spoke English with an American accent, even, sometimes, with a Hoosier twang, and I grew up in a rural environment, far from the big cities my parents grew up in.

What was I? I was influenced by my Hoosier environment, despite fleeing it as early as I could, leaving for college at age sixteen. In those sixteen years, I learned to appreciate silence and nature and open space. I felt squeezed by the dense housing in cities. I soaked in the values of independence and self-reliance from the farmers and small-town residents I grew up around. I learned how to pick myself up and keep moving forward. It seemed cowardly to blame my environment for my own shortcomings. I made my own decisions. I knew deep down that the victim mentality was dangerous.

So, really, what was my identity? Chilean, Filipina, Asian, Hispanic, Latina, Hoosier, American? White, black, brown, biracial, first-generation, intellectual, nerd, geek, student, programmer? None of the above?

In twenty-five years, I still hadn't found where I belonged.

But now, maybe I had.

I was a pilot and—maybe—soon to be an aircraft owner.

* * *

When I wasn't lost in thought, Carlos and I spent the drive talking about flying. It was such a contrast to my unhappy discussions with Ben. Only the night before, we'd had a major argument, and I'd told him I was moving out. That morning, I'd started searching for apartments in Palo Alto. Although we hadn't talked about divorce, I felt I was now independent. Ben and I kept separate finances, and now we were going to live apart. We'd be officially separated. It felt like I was starting an outrageous new life. And the trip to Salinas to consider buying a new airplane symbolized the beginning of that life.

We drove past the gleaming jet center and onto the low-rent side of the field, where battered green T-hangars stood in rows. And my Cessna was there, tied down at the weedy end of a narrow taxiway. Its red-and-white paint job was faded, the plexiglass windows yellowed, and the bottom of the tail tie-down ring shaved off. But already I loved it.

The owner, an affable man of about sixty with thin gray hair, introduced himself as Joe Holton. He wore a faded red T-shirt with STOCKTON WARBIRDS emblazoned over his paunch. We walked around the plane several times as he extolled its many virtues. All the while, I couldn't help thinking he had no need to convince me.

"Want to go up for a flight?" he offered, adding with a sidelong glance, "Seeing as you're still a student pilot, how about if I fly?"

I nodded, and it didn't take long before we were two thousand feet over the fields of Salinas, leaving Carlos behind on the taxiway.

"She's a sweet little airplane!" Joe yelled above the smooth roar of the Continental engine. I already knew I wanted this plane. It vibrated under my touch on the yoke, and I thrilled at the thought that this miraculous machine might soon be mine.

"The 150 is better than the 152!" Joe shouted. "Let me show you!" We flew around the traffic pattern, and he demonstrated a landing. "See that? Forty degrees of flaps. The 152 only has thirty. They said it was a safety improvement, but look at this; you can land this baby in almost no runway. Just be careful you don't try to take off with all the flaps down!" He braked the plane to a stop in less than five hundred feet.

I was sold. I was also able to follow Joe's fast-moving technical language. Brad made me feel like a bit of an imposter, never quite good enough, but now I felt that I was at last becoming a full member of the world of aviation.

Back on the ground, Carlos and I checked the aircraft logbooks, dating back to the plane's first flight from Kansas in 1973.

"I wish I didn't have to sell her, but I have to buy a boat," Joe said as I was closing up the last logbook.

Carlos's eyes and mine met in disbelief. Why would anyone trade in the joys of flight for something as wet and mundane as a boat?

After a prepurchase inspection, a mechanic pronounced November Eight Two One Niner Seven (One Niner Seven for short) in good shape. Joe and I haggled a little and settled on a purchase price of $5,000.

"He seems like a nice guy," I told Carlos as we left. "Pretty good-natured, too."

Carlos grinned. "You know the two happiest days in an aircraft owner's life?"

I raised my eyebrows.

"The day he buys his plane—and the day he sells it."

The next week, I signed the loan papers at my bank and got a cashier's check for $5,000 made out to Joseph Holton. On Saturday, Carlos flew Brad and me to Salinas in the Piper Archer. I signed the paperwork, and Brad and I took off, heading home to Palo Alto. One Niner Seven was mine.

Chapter 4

"That's *it?*" Carlos asked, raising his eyebrows at the nearly empty U-Haul.

I'd loaded up the truck with all my possessions and driven it to the loading dock of my new apartment in Palo Alto. It wasn't much. All the furniture in Berkeley belonged to Ben. I'd reserved the freight elevator for four hours that day, but I was only going to need about thirty minutes tops.

I shoved a box against the padded elevator wall and shrugged. "I was couch-surfing for a month in 1979, so I learned to never buy more stuff than I could carry."

He hefted one of the boxes and rested it on the edge of a potted plant. "You can carry this? It's sure heavy."

"Books," I said. "I collect lots of books. But since I can pack them in small boxes, it's okay." I didn't tell Carlos I still had all my grad school textbooks in those boxes. Sometimes I'd thought about selling them, since the odds of ever returning to the PhD program seemed slim, but the finality of that made me ache. It meant openly admitting my failure. So instead, I lugged them around with me wherever I went.

"And now you own an airplane."

I grinned. "That's okay too, because it can carry *me*."

It was a Saturday, and we'd taken a break from flying so he could help me move into my new place. Due to our shared fanaticism about flying,

Carlos and I had been hanging out together often after work and on the weekends to talk aviation and fly my new plane. My budget could stretch to accommodate a lot more flying now that I didn't have to pay for aircraft rentals. And the Cessna 150 was significantly cheaper to operate. Sure, it was a little slow for an airplane, topping out at about a hundred miles per hour. But that was fine for now.

It had been a rough couple of weeks with Ben in Berkeley. He hadn't said a word as I packed up all my clothes in one large box and my stacks of books and notebooks in many small ones. I was secretly hoping he'd come right out and ask me to stay. But he never did. I think now that he was in too much pain to talk. But at the time, I told myself he didn't care enough to tell me not to go. I hesitated before the final trip out to the U-Haul. "Do you want me to leave my keys?"

He tightened his lips and shook his head.

Maybe that was a signal he wanted to keep a link between us. "Sure you don't want to find a place halfway between both of our jobs?" I asked one more time.

He scowled. "Who wants to live in Hayward?"

I sighed. It was the same old impasse. I carried the last box out to the U-Haul and started the engine. I wasn't sure if I was angry or sad, excited or depressed, or maybe all of the above.

My willingness to pack up and move had deep roots. My father thought nothing of packing up the entire family and dragging us halfway across the world to new academic positions, physics conferences, sabbaticals, or lecture series. We moved sixteen times in sixteen years. It was assumed that a physicist with a thriving career would move whenever needed, and his wife and children were supposed to follow along without complaint. But on top of the career-related relocations, my father possessed an internal restlessness. When we'd finally be settled in a town, he'd find fault with each house and uproot us every year or two. From kindergarten in 1965 through my senior year in high school in 1976, I never attended the same school more than two years in a row. I came away with a constant feeling of rootlessness, an inability to belong.

Maybe that was part of why I'd been willing to leave my husband even though I still loved him. While I knew it hurt him. I, too, was restless, driven by the imperative to become the best I could be. Yet that imperative was in direct conflict with my mother's desire for me to be good, to be small. Not because she wanted less of me, but because she loved me and knew the danger women faced when they tried to take up more space, or in my case, to be brilliant in a male-dominated career like math or science. I desperately wanted a larger life, so in the end I left, but not without feeling guilty.

Ben, unlike me, was rooted in white, Anglo-Saxon Protestant traditionalism. His parents traced their ancestry back through several generations of Americans, through Scottish and German roots. His mother was an Ohio farm girl, his father a Korean War veteran and a general in the Air Force. His father spent long hours at work as an engineer and rocket scientist, returning late at night to his wife and children. His mother quit her job when she married and stayed home as a military wife from then on. Despite his father's military background, Ben had moved far less frequently than I.

I was attracted to Ben's nonconformism, but when we got married, his traditional side emerged. He stopped sharing his feelings with me. He arrived home after a long day on the job wanting only to discuss the interesting engineering problems he had solved that day. He stopped asking about my work and my interests. It was as though I was supposed to be quiet, be good, be someone more like his mother.

I wondered if Ben's interest in me had been a final act of rebellion against his parents. I wasn't used to living with someone white, someone who preferred silence over conflict, who didn't speak about feelings. My own family was boisterous and exuberant at home, shouting over each other at the dinner table. Everyone served themselves, reaching right past others' plates. My mother sang, "I Left My Heart in San Francisco" as she pulled dishes out of the oven and plopped them directly onto the kitchen table.

At Ben's parents' house, on the other hand, food was scooped into formal serving dishes. You *never* used an oven dish on the dining table. You had to politely ask, "Please pass the pot roast," and no one ever interrupted. Singing? It was almost a capital offense. Ben became disturbed if I hummed at the table.

Despite my having moved more than thirty times by then, this particular move, at age twenty-five, was the first into my very own place. It was
the most beautiful apartment I'd ever lived in. On the fifteenth floor of
a brand-new tower in Palo Alto, every window framed a panoramic view
of the city and San Francisco Bay. After Carlos finished helping me move
in, I stood on the balcony and breathed in the clear air. This perch, this
high-up place of my own, felt like something I'd been searching for without ever knowing it.

At last I wasn't dependent on anyone else, financially or emotionally.

"A woman must have money and a room of her own," Virginia Woolf
had famously said. I finally had both. Nevertheless, it was scary and went
against everything I'd been taught. I was supposed to get married and be
dependent on a man. As usual, my feelings were a mass of contradictions, and
despite my longing for freedom, I felt guilty about the separation from Ben.

Mine was the only signature on the lease, and no one else had a key to
my apartment. Going solo was thrilling and scary at the same time.

The prospect of my first solo flight was also on my mind during these
early days in my new apartment.

"Is Brad going to solo you soon?" Carlos asked me the next week at work.

Carlos's comment brought me down to earth like a hard landing, and I
resorted to my usual defense mechanisms. Brad hadn't said anything about
letting me fly on my own. "I'm probably not ready yet," I rationalized.

"You've got seventeen hours of flight time. That's more than enough."

I'd been looking forward to my first solo with a mixture of dread and
anticipation ever since I'd started flying. All the books and magazines I
read spoke of it as a milestone.

Carlos talked reverently of his first solo experience. "I took off for the
first time alone, and as I reached pattern altitude and saw the world spreading out below me"—he made a sweeping gesture with his arm, eyes fixed
on the far distance—"I knew that one day I'd fly everywhere I could see."

Sometimes I wasn't sure I'd ever get good enough to solo. Brad's reluc-
tance to solo me at the usual time was just confirmation of my lack of
ability. I'd always seen myself as clumsy at operating mechanical devices.
I didn't learn to ride a bike until I was eleven because I was so scared of

tipping over that I couldn't lift my feet onto the pedals. My driver's education teacher snorted over my attempts at parallel parking. Until I got the
job at DEC, I'd resisted driving, taking the bus all over the Bay Area, even
though I witnessed gambling, theft, knife fights, and even the attempted
murder of a bus driver by a passenger one day.

The irony was that I was more scared of operating a motor vehicle on
my own than I was of getting knifed on the bus. I trusted myself less than
a knife-wielding stranger. I didn't believe I was competent enough to drive
a car, so how could I possibly manage the complicated task of operating
an airplane? A car navigated in two dimensions; an airplane in three—and
the complexity of air navigation was unimaginable. I'd need to use both
hands and both feet to fly the airplane. To solo, I'd need to be able to land.
Up in the air, I was doing well as long as I got it right within fifty or a
hundred feet. Landing demanded accuracy within two to five feet.

It wasn't a problem flying with my instructor beside me. He'd be there
to catch any errors, to make sure the plane landed safely. He was my
safety net and my security blanket. But someday I'd have to fly without
an instructor.

By the time I had twenty hours logged in the airplane, even I could see
that I was landing the plane smoothly and correctly every time. Brad never
had to touch the controls. During each of our lessons after that magical
twenty-hour mark, I half-expected him to suggest that it was time for me
to solo. But he never did.

At first, I was grateful Brad wasn't pushing me, that he was allowing me time to hone my skills to be absolutely sure I'd be safe. But as
my twenty-five-hour mark approached, I was getting frustrated seeing my
bills mount up as we waited in line for takeoff. Brad whistled as he stared
out the window, joked with the air traffic controllers on the radio, and
after every lesson eagerly wrote down another hour in his logbook.

When I completed twenty-five hours, I finally broached the subject
with him. His eyes flicked away from me. "I'm just waiting until you can
land perfectly," he said.

It was then that I realized Brad had never soloed a student. It's a
big step for an instructor. Maybe *he* was nervous. Or could it be he was

especially nervous about *me*? He'd been making a lot of jokes recently, even passing around a cartoon that showed two airplanes labeled His and Hers. His was pristine and clean, while Hers was dinged up and dented. I'd laughed obligingly, like the time I had to force a laugh when the male programmers told the math joke about "pretty little Polly Nomial," who essentially gets raped by "Curly Pi." In the eighties, women who didn't laugh at such jokes were called humorless prudes, and the phrase "gender harassment" didn't exist.

And sexist jokes weren't the only ones Brad found funny. After my lesson one day, he and a couple of other instructors in the flight lounge were chuckling about the foibles of another student. "I'd be careful with Rajiv," one said. "Every time I've flown with guys from his neck of the woods, I found they just can't seem to pick up the skills very well. I don't know what it is. Maybe because they're only used to riding camels or something."

Watching the three blond men laughing together reminded me of Don Schwartz and his friends. I shook myself in irritation. That was crazy. They were nothing alike.

When I passed thirty hours in my logbook, and still no solo, I knew I had to take action. If I didn't speak up, I might never move forward. I steeled myself, my mouth dry. "Brad," I said, "I think I'm ready to solo." Inside, I felt lousy. It wasn't the magical solo experience so many pilots spoke of.

Brad looked away. "Um, let's see how you do today, and we'll see."

That day, we spent over two hours in the air going through all the maneuvers one more time, doing landing after landing. Brad could find no fault with anything I did.

"I'm ready, Brad," I said confidently.

Finally, after spending about five minutes on the taxiway with the engine idling, while he repeated that the plane would fly differently without his two hundred pounds in the right seat, he finally got out.

After he closed the door, I glanced all around the cockpit. There was no one to rely on but me. My breath quickened more from excitement than fear. Then I took off in a plane alone for the first time—in the plane I alone owned.

As I climbed into the air, the plane felt light and vibrant. The sun glittered on the waves of the bay, and shimmered in the haze to the north, toward San Francisco. At last, I was taking the first step into a wider world. Sure, I could use the plane to travel to distant places, but what mattered more was that I was flying, dancing in the air, despite what everyone had told me, despite what I had told myself. I gently caressed the control yoke and the rudders, making a small secret turn to the left and then one to the right, too small to be detected by the tower, and I grinned.

But trusting my own abilities was only the first step. I didn't want to be like the thousands of pilots who stopped at first solo, never to complete their license. I wanted to get my private pilot license, which was a daunting task. There was a long road from first solo to private pilot flight test, and it didn't look like Brad was going to get me there. So despite agonizing over hurting his feelings, I had to switch instructors. When I finally informed Brad of my decision, I heard my mother's voice in my head. "Cecilia, a woman needs to be nice. Aren't you being selfish?"

If I stayed "good," I would never get my license. Statistics show that women drop out of pilot training at a significantly higher rate than men. When I heard that, I decided, once again, that I had no use for being good.

I found another instructor—an experienced, salty pilot named Janet Michaels. She'd accumulated over five thousand hours and managed another flying club on the field. I was eager to fly with a woman pilot. Unfortunately, because of her job as club manager, she could only fly on weekends.

Everyone at the airport knew Janet. She bragged about having the keys to "over fifty airplanes on the field." She informed me she used to teach aerobatics. Intrigued, I asked her for more stories. She shrugged. "I quit because I got tired of washing vomit out of my hair."

I kept after her until she agreed to take me on as her student.

One Saturday in January 1986, I flew with Janet for the first time in One Niner Seven. Looking back, I think she only agreed because she was hoping that I would lease the Cessna 150 to her flight school. She was full of praise for my tattered airplane, but not so much for my flying.

"Flying is more than the rote memorization of numbers," Janet said as we taxied in after our flight. "You have to understand how the pressures in the control yoke and the rudders change as your airspeed changes.

Basically, you need a direct feedback loop between the controls and your brain. You don't have that," she said bluntly.

I knew she was right. I flew *mechanically*. I knew how to apply delicate touches to the controls so the instruments read exactly right, and I had memorized all the rules and guidelines and airspeeds. The indicator needle never deviated. I flew all the recommended speeds for takeoff, cruise, slow flight, and landing. In short, I had a lot of book learning about the airplane, but I still hadn't connected it to my body: I had no "feel" for the aerodynamics of flight. And without that feel, even a few seconds of distraction while flying could prove dangerous.

After the lesson with Janet, I was shaking and sweating as I shut down the engine. As she walked away, leaving me to tie down the airplane, tears leaked out of my eyes. Maybe I just didn't have the talent it took to be a pilot. Maybe I should give up after all.

But still, I went back the next week and the week after that. I might not be talented, but I was persistent. I absorbed more from Janet in a couple of flights than I'd learned in many hours with Brad. I admired her so much that I developed a secret fascination with aerobatics. Of course, that kind of flying was so far beyond my abilities that I knew I could never even try it. But I admired from afar the pilots who flew loops and spins and rolls, who soared straight up into the air and then dove back down to the earth at startling speeds. I tried to book as many lessons as possible with Janet, but she was so busy that I couldn't fly with her often enough to complete my license.

To finish the training, I'd need to find another instructor. Hank Kendall was a former commuter airline pilot who realized that flight instruction paid better than flying commuter jets. "You can't live on eight hundred dollars a month, especially when they want you to be available to fly seven days a week," he told me as we waited for the fuel truck after preflighting one morning.

Hank took being an instructor seriously. He charged twenty-five dollars an hour, significantly higher than Brad's eighteen per hour, and charged based on "block time." This meant that he looked at his watch the moment he sat down with me in one of the little classrooms at the flight school, and again at the end of the "block," or lesson, when he closed my logbook. The difference between the two was the amount of time he charged. It didn't matter if we were chatting or using the bathroom; he charged for all his time.

At first, I balked. At that time it was conventional for instructors to charge only for time in the plane. But after I had flown with him just once, I could see the difference. Hank explained everything thoroughly on the ground before we went up in the air. "The cockpit is a lousy classroom," he said.

He was right. His explanations on the ground translated into easier comprehension in the air. I began to understand how aerodynamics and flying really worked, although I was still lacking the "feel" of the airplane.

Hank owned an intercom and a pair of high-quality headsets he insisted we use on every flight. Not only did my headaches and the ringing in my ears subside, but I could actually hear Hank's directions. It was also easier to understand the tower. Plus, I found that without the constant battering of engine noise on my ears, I felt calmer on the flights.

All told, I'd fly only eleven flights with Hank, far fewer than the thirty-four I flew with Brad, but Hank was the one who really prepared me to become a private pilot.

From Hank, I learned the value of quality teaching. He taught people how to fly, rather than leaving them to figure it out themselves. Up until then, I'd believed that books were often better teachers than humans and that teachers frequently got in the way of learning. But Hank's thorough ground explanations led to rapid progress in the air, and maybe more importantly, Hank expected me to excel, unlike Brad, who always assumed I'd struggle.

* * *

During my sophomore year in high school, I learned firsthand that a teacher's expectations matter, regardless of subject area or student age. Our family had accompanied my father on sabbatical to Germany, where I didn't know the language. One of my teachers assumed I'd never master the material and simply told me to sit in the back and be quiet. But my French teacher insisted I do all the work, found me a tutor, and graded all my exams. All tenth graders in this German school took the same classes, so I was placed in *fourth-year* French even though I didn't know a word of the language. It was laughable when my teacher handed back German-to-French translations covered with red ink. How could she possibly expect a girl who barely spoke German and had never studied French to learn anything in her class?

Yet, goaded by her relentless encouragement, I did begin to learn. At the start of the second semester, she actually congratulated me when she handed back my test. I'd gotten the equivalent of a D-minus. My first passing grade in that class.

By the end of the school year, I'd not only caught up with the rest of the class, I was one of the top three students in French. My dad told me his buttons were popping. I'd picked up four years of high school French in a single year—in a class taught entirely in German.

As for the other teacher's class, I don't even remember what we covered that year. The teacher never bothered to grade my work, and I failed. It was a perfect laboratory experiment: all variables were held the same, except for one. I was the same person in both classes, and the only difference was what the teachers expected of me.

It was like a math formula. Low expectations produced low results. In the mathematical theory of complex systems, one teacher created a closed system, and the other an open system. My French teacher encouraged me to create complex structures in order to grow. She poured energy into her teaching, and I couldn't help but respond. Could I apply those same principles of complex systems to overcome my fears and get my pilot's license?

* * *

One major hurdle still remained, however. The private pilot certificate required twenty hours of solo flight time. But every time I drove to the Palo Alto airport, past the tiny building that housed the start-up Adobe Systems, and saw a Cessna coming in for a landing, my hands clenched on the steering wheel, and part of me hoped that my instructor would be sick or the airplane would be down for maintenance so that I wouldn't have to fly that day.

Yet each time I landed, I was so exhilarated that I'd eagerly schedule another lesson. I couldn't cancel it without disappointing my instructor or getting charged for the flight. These were powerful incentives to help me get over my fear. Research has shown that this kind of technique can be very effective. Facing my fear might be painful, but it was the only way I would become the person I wanted to be. I had to deliberately set up structures—what I called "scaffolds"—that would force me to keep flying.

Approaching it rationally, I knew my fears were mostly groundless. I studied the aviation accident statistics. Most of them were caused by pilot error, and 30 percent were alcohol related. So, if I always followed the law of "eight hours from bottle to throttle," my chances of surviving instantly leaped.

I calculated the ratio between joy and risk. It might have been safer for me to stay at home. But a colleague's neighbor in the Oakland Hills had been killed lying in bed one night when a tree blew over and fell on his house. So a safe life could kill me just as surely as flying.

I had a deep longing to grow. This longing resonated with a fundamental thermodynamic principle I'd studied as an undergraduate at Caltech, for which a physical chemist named Ilya Prigogine had won the Nobel Prize. Essentially, open systems which exchange energy with their environment, of which living organisms are a prime example, will create ever more complex structures, known as "dissipative structures," in order to grow. It's a defining element of the nature of the universe, like poet Dylan Thomas's "force that through the green fuse drives the flower."

Just as a plant builds cellular structures that can grow through rock, or as mathematics creates structures to shape thought, I was building mental structures to help me escape my cage of fear. Scheduling flights with an instructor was an important part of that process.

To hold myself accountable, I promised Hank I'd fly solo the day after each lesson. He wrote out the maneuvers for me to practice. One that particularly petrified me was known as a "stall." This didn't mean that the engine quits, but that the wing ceases to produce lift and the airplane stops flying. Learning how to handle a plane in a stall is crucial to flying at slow speeds in preparation for landing. I was also required to demonstrate stalls and recovery from stalls for the private pilot flight test. Book learning wouldn't get me out of this one.

Stalls were absolutely terrifying. I had only recently learned to trust that the long and elegant wings of my airplane would smoothly glide on their cushion of air and keep me aloft. Now I was going to deliberately induce them to stop doing that?

"I want you to practice steep turns, slow flight, and most importantly, stalls," Hank told me one day at the end of a lesson. "Next time I see you, I want you to report to me what you've done."

The next day, just as I had promised, I went up for a solo flight. In the practice area, I did some careful clearing turns. The California hills were green at this time of year after the wet winter, and the pale sun shone over their soft undulations. Everything smelled fresh and new with approaching spring. Acacia trees blossomed bright yellow, daffodils lined the fields, and forests shone in light-green swathes.

Okay, steep turns. I could do that. Carefully scanning the instrument that measured pitch attitude and bank angle, I banked so the little dial read 45 degrees, pulled back on the yoke just enough to keep my altitude, and completed a full 360. Now to the right. Slow flight. I could do that too by going through the procedure mechanically, reducing power, and then increasing it. Okay, done. More clearing turns. It's important to know if there's another aircraft in the practice area. I'm just being safe by making three or four clearing turns.

Now, time to do a stall.

Better do a few more clearing turns first. That's really important.

Now it's definitely time for a stall.

I gritted my teeth, reduced the throttle, and gradually raised the nose, my palms slick with sweat on the black plastic handgrips. It suddenly got way too quiet in the cockpit as the airflow past the fuselage diminished. I pulled the yoke nearly all the way back to the stop, and my biceps trembled from the exertion. The plane rattled. I smelled gasoline in the cockpit. The stall warning horn blared like an omen of imminent peril. The stall was about to happen ... about to happen.

Finally, I felt a sickening lurch in my stomach that meant the plane had stopped flying. The nose dropped, and I immediately shoved the yoke forward, pointing the plane at the ground.

The controls stopped shuddering, and I added throttle and gained airspeed. Air whooshed past the wings, and the wind and engine noise built back up into a roar. I dove at the ground thousands of feet below, trying not to think about smashing into the earth beneath me.

Then I pulled up into a climb to regain the lost altitude.

My heart pounded furiously. I'd done it. I'd completed my first solo stall.

I breathed deeply, shivering a little.

Time to head back to the airport and recover. Yes, at last.

Oh, but wait. If I went back now, I'd have to admit to Hank that I'd only done *one* stall. He'd said *stalls*—plural.

I argued with myself for a couple of minutes and did a few more clearing turns, just to be safe.

Finally I steeled myself, went through the process one more time, and did another very gentle stall.

Done!

I flew back to the airport in triumph. The next day, I was able to look Hank straight in the eyes and say that, yes, I had done steep turns, slow flight, and stalls. Plural.

Chapter 5

After eight months and eighty hours of flight time (much longer than the national average, I might add), I passed the private pilot flight test in my very own airplane. The flight examiner said, "You must have had a good instructor." I did. (Thanks, Hank.)

Now I looked for every excuse to take a friend for a ride. "Oh, you need to go to Monterey for work? Why rent a car? I'll fly you there!" "I hear there's a nice restaurant at the Santa Rosa airport. Why don't we have lunch? Yes, I don't mind spending fifty dollars for a hamburger." "You haven't seen San Francisco Bay from the air? It's spectacular, not to be missed."

After a while, people started glancing away, or even rushing off when they saw me coming. When Carlos's work schedule increased and mine took me away from Palo Alto, we gradually saw each other less and less and eventually lost touch. But I'd never lose the love for flying, which he was the first to instill in me. Even after our close friendship faded, I knew he had left me with a lifelong gift.

I got an aviation map of California, mounted it on the door of my bathroom, and circled in red Sharpie all the airports where I had landed. Even so, it was still a big effort to psych myself into flying. Every time I preflighted my airplane, I worried that this might be the time I crashed, the flight where something major went wrong. And then there were the scary incidents up in the air. Once, I discovered a mechanical problem called carburetor ice when my engine suddenly quit at seventy-five hundred feet over Booneville, California. Luckily, turning on carburetor heat solved the problem. Flying out of Borrego Valley Airport one hot summer at sunset, I found myself unable to climb, even at full throttle, as we approached the mountains east of Los Angeles. The plane kept sinking toward the rocky ground, getting closer and closer no matter what I did, until at last I banked away from the slope and back toward the valley. I'd just encountered downdrafts. There were so many terrible and dangerous things that could happen; I had to be skilled enough to handle all of them.

Maybe I should quit, sell my airplane, and take up a safer hobby. That would be the sensible thing to do, for sure. I still hadn't admitted to my parents I was flying. When we talked on the phone, I focused on interesting technical problems at work with my dad, and with my mom, I discussed her hobbies of photography and quilting. I avoided talk of Ben's and my separation.

I missed Ben, particularly when I drove past a wall of morning glories on my way to work. He and I had planted morning glories from seeds at the edge of our garden in Berkeley, and every morning he would count how many had bloomed and write the number in a notebook. That notebook had gotten accidentally packed in one of my boxes, and I'd left it on the desk in my apartment, planning to give it back to him. Instead, I saw his handwriting every morning.

In the meantime, I decided having a new goal or two would help me push past the fear and unhappiness. I'd work toward obtaining more flight certifications: first the instrument rating, and then my commercial pilot license, which would allow me to get paid for flying. If I could take on a second job as a flight instructor, it would help pay for my expensive new hobby.

But maybe I was overreaching my abilities. I still flew by rote, placing too much reliance on the instruments. I had yet to achieve that "seat of the pants" knowledge that good pilots had. I couldn't tell when a stall was about to occur except by checking the airspeed indicator. And my landings were workmanlike but not spectacular. As an instructor, I'd need to allow students to make mistakes, to let them get into risky situations, to push the margin of safety out a little further than I normally liked. Could I handle shaving the safety margin?

One of the best ways to keep growing and learning is to teach. Becoming a flight instructor would make me a better pilot, I thought. I might even finally become an intuitive pilot who trusted her own instincts. In order to become the best possible instructor, and to stay safe, I'd need a top-notch, highly experienced pilot to teach me. This time I wasn't going to sign up with the first person who answered the phone. Instead, I did research and found the most thorough instructor around: a man by the name of Al Donahue. Best of all, if I trained with Al at the West Valley Flying Club, Janet Michaels said I could become an instructor there. Instructor jobs were hard to come by. Everybody wanted them as they were the best way to "build time for the airlines." Even though I had no desire to become an airline pilot, I'd be competing with all the other brand-new flight instructors, and so I was reassured to learn that I'd have a job waiting for me after certification.

And so, I earned my instructor certificate in May 1987, less than two years after I'd started flying. But my problems weren't over yet. By the time I graduated, there were no instructor jobs available at West Valley after all. I was disappointed but determined not to give up.

Finally, in July 1987, I got the call I'd been waiting for. The University of California Flying Club offered me an instructor position at the Oakland Airport. The airport is steeped in aviation history. Dedicated by Charles Lindbergh in 1927, early photos show it was once a grassy field on the edge of San Francisco Bay. Pilots pointed their taildraggers into the wind and bounced across the terrain before lifting off. Amelia Earhart took off from Oakland in 1937 on her attempted round-the-world flight. Looking back, I think the club only hired me because they were desperate for flight instructors. It certainly wasn't because of my experience—I had a scant four hundred hours of flight time.

The UC Flying Club had been plagued by bad luck. At meetings, I'd been regaled with stories about embezzlement, near financial disaster, canceled insurance, and multiple plane wrecks. The club's main claim to fame, other than having existed for nearly fifty years, was the fact that someone had written a book (later made into a movie) about surviving a crash in a club airplane.

Normally, new flight instructors spent hours manning the desk at their flight school, greeting potential students. But it turned out the club already had about a dozen students eagerly waiting for some instructor— *any* instructor—to teach them. The previous club instructor had left under suspicious circumstances. Some said he had found a flying job; another member muttered darkly that it had something to do with flying cargo below the radar across the border.

I heard from other pilots that new instructors get the students scraped from the bottom of the barrel—the throwaways, the students who've failed, the ones other instructors dropped because they're so difficult, the students *no one* wants to fly with.

I was, in fact, about to encounter such a student on my very first day as an instructor.

* * *

Jack Springer met me at the hangars called the "Old T's" at the Oakland North Field. He had a sandy-colored mustache, freckles, and a grand total of fifteen hours of flight time. I could tell he was already quite certain that a young woman half his size claiming to be a flight instructor was more likely to be an impediment than a help. *I* certainly wouldn't be able to teach *him* anything, because Jack already knew how to fly. He'd nearly soloed, after all, and even though his last flight had been six months ago, he told me all about his plan for our upcoming flight as soon as we met.

This was not a good situation for a brand-new instructor, particularly a timid and insecure one like me. No one had taught me what to do with an overconfident man a decade older than me and fifty pounds heavier, someone who clearly saw right through me and knew me for the imposter I was.

Jack glared at me over a Formica table as I struggled to come up with a plan for our unconventional lesson. "I want to practice landings," he said. "I was almost ready to solo, and I expect to just polish them up a bit so I can do my solo flight."

I hesitated. I wanted to make a good impression, but I was worried. "You haven't flown for six months. We'll make this a review flight. You demonstrate the pre-solo maneuvers to me, starting with air work, and then we'll come back into the pattern for some landings."

He scowled. "I already know how to do air work. It's landings I need to do." He propped his knuckles on the table, and his frown took on a menacing cast.

I swallowed. It would be crazy and even dangerous to attempt landings without seeing how he performed at a safe altitude, especially after half a year of inactivity. Still, I tried to be placating. "It's been a while since you've flown, so it'll be a good idea for you to review the air work first and get warmed up before you work on landings."

"As long as we do landings," he insisted.

I nodded timidly, and we headed out to the flight line.

The Old T's were the ratty end of the airport, literally a bunch of old, corroded metal T-hangars, battered, with peeling paint, definitely the low-rent side of the field, far away in every respect from the Executive Terminal, where I'd gone for my first ride.

The UC Flying Club's fleet, which consisted of two rather old and faded Cessna 152s and a Beechcraft Sierra, was tied down out in the elements. I unlocked the red Cessna and had Jack demonstrate his preflight inspection. He'd forgotten practically everything. When we climbed into the plane and started up the engine, my heart sank further as he demonstrated his lack of proficiency on taxi, takeoff, and climb out. Once in the practice area, his steep turns wandered all over the place, gaining and losing altitude like a roller coaster. His muscular arms gripped the yoke like he planned to wrestle the plane into submission.

Terror rose in my chest. This was a guy who planned to land after this flight, who thought he was almost ready to solo? He could barely control the airplane.

I decided I'd have him fly us into the pattern, but then I would demonstrate the landing. I reminded him to lighten up on the controls, check for traffic, and stop fixating on one instrument at a time.

When I broached my plan to him as we returned from the practice area, he scowled. "Nuh-uh. *I'm* doing the landing," he announced, gripping the yoke harder for emphasis.

Nothing I said could budge him, so I sat up straighter in my seat and reminded him once more that in an emergency, I would take control.

He barely made it into the pattern, despite both my verbal directions and my nudges at the controls. The plane veered from side to side as he jerked the controls back and forth, added a blast of power, or pulled the throttle back nearly to idle. I sat there in the right seat, fighting to remain calm as I imagined the headlines: FLIGHT INSTRUCTOR AT ILL-FATED FLYING CLUB CRASHES ON FIRST FLIGHT.

On the final approach to landing, Jack yanked the nose up so we were pointed straight up at the blue sky, and then pushed it down until we were staring at the ground.

"Easy does it," I said, trying to sound unruffled. "Small corrections on the controls." Flight instructors only sweat on the right side of their faces, they say.

In response, he banked hard to one side. We were now heading for the Oakland Hills.

"How about a gentle bank to the left so we can keep the runway in sight?" I suggested. There was no response.

His eyes had gone wide, and a muscle twitched in his jaw under his mustache.

"I'll help you out a little with the controls," I said. "I'm banking left with aileron and adding some left rudder." (Ailerons are panels at the tip of the wing used to bank the plane.) We started to point more or less at the runway. "Back off on the throttle now, just a little."

Instead, he jammed full throttle in and shoved the yoke forward. Our airspeed increased, and we began to plummet toward the earth.

"Reduce the throttle and raise the nose!" I shouted, my calm veneer slipping. "Here, I'll take it. My airplane." He wouldn't let go of the controls. In desperation, I knocked his hand off the throttle and reduced it myself. "*My airplane! Let go of the controls!*"

"I can do it!" he insisted.

"Then set up for a stabilized approach at sixty-five knots!"

I coaxed him through the correct movements, but we were still swinging side to side on the final approach as he overcorrected, back and forth. I'd thought I was going to die many times in my budding pilot career, but this felt like the closest I'd ever come.

Why, I berated myself, had I ever decided to become a flight instructor? Surely my life was worth more than twenty dollars an hour.

I talked faster and faster, doing my best to adjust the controls that Jack held in his death grip. We were now over the runway, preparing to round out for the landing. "Now flare," I said. "*No! Not that much!*"

We ballooned into the air, the stall warning horn went off, and Jack decided now was the correct time to jam in right rudder. Obediently, the plane swung hard to the right.

Even someone with no "feel" for flying could see we were headed for a crash. I grabbed the controls, got us straightened out, and at the last minute, applied a burst of throttle to cushion the landing.

We landed hard on runway 27 Right, and slowly rolled to a stop. We were both breathing hard and sweating. I allowed Jack to taxi us off the runway, finally feeling all my muscles unwind. We had made it. Thank goodness for the design of the Cessna 152, the safest airplane ever built. It could withstand student manhandling, new instructor timidity, and collisions on the controls. No harm done to the plane, I thought in relief.

I glanced over at Jack. At least it must have been a good lesson for him to learn some humility.

He popped open the window and rested an arm on the sill. With a jaunty grin, he asked, "So, you think I can solo next time?"

* * *

While I'd avoided the crash with Jack Springer, my personal life seemed headed for a crash of a different kind. My venture into solo apartment renting wasn't going well. Despite my lofty dreams of independence, financial reality was hitting hard. It was astonishing how much of the salary I once thought so generous vanished into Palo Alto rent and utilities. Ben and I had been maintaining a cool but not unfriendly relationship, chatting on the phone occasionally, and getting together every now and then. One night, Ben invited me over for dinner. Just to talk, he said.

I sat down at the familiar dining table as he scooped a bubbling enchilada out of the baking dish and set it on my plate. He placed three slices of perfectly ripe avocado on top and a dollop of sour cream beside it. It smelled so wonderful my stomach rumbled, and we both laughed.

I'd arrived on edge, but after the first warm and satisfying bite of corn tortilla filled with melted cheese, I relaxed. During dinner he told me funny stories about his coworkers. Then he told me that half his beard had fallen out after I left, and we ended up crying in each other's arms.

When my lease ended on the apartment in Palo Alto, I told Ben I wanted to move back in with him. I felt like I was simultaneously admitting defeat about living on my own *and* acknowledging my deep love for Ben. Could I be independent as part of a couple, or were the two mutually exclusive?

His eyes lit up, but then he said, "As long as we don't move to Hayward."

"I like living in Berkeley," I agreed, "even though I hate the commute."

He seemed happy with that.

We'd go back to splitting expenses, I said, but I wanted a room of my own, like Virginia Woolf. Protesting at first, he eventually agreed I could claim the guest room.

At work, I found myself dealing with what seemed like a steady push toward a slower career track. As a software engineer, I was required to document my code by adding comments that explained what it was supposed to do. While most of my colleagues found this obligation onerous and only did the bare minimum, I'd taken a great deal of care to use graceful and clear prose to explain exactly what my functions did and how I'd structured each piece.

One of my managers read my documentation with approval. "This is very well written, Cecilia. Have you considered a career as a technical writer?" He said it as if he clearly had the best intentions for me.

It took me a moment to find my voice. Transitioning to technical writing would mean a cut in pay. Maybe he was trying to tell me something. "I'm not performing well as a programmer?"

He smiled reassuringly. "No, no, I didn't mean that. You're doing fine. I just thought that you might find it rewarding. Documentation is extremely important, and we always need good tech writers."

I didn't know what to say. "Thanks, but I'm happy as a software engineer."

After I got back to my office, I thought again about what it meant to be the only female programmer in our group. More women in Silicon Valley were tech writers than software developers. And, of course, their salaries were lower across the board, despite the fact that documentation *was* important.

After that day, I forced myself to do something that went against everything I'd ever believed in. I made sure that my documentation was accurate, but nothing more. I didn't want to get nudged into a career based on a gender stereotype, no matter how necessary the work or how good I was at it. *Don't ever get too good at a traditionally female task, or they'll make you do it for the rest of your life*, I told myself.

My life was now going through a lot of turbulence, even though I'd avoided—for the moment—an actual crash. I was struggling and insecure in my personal life, my flying, and my career. It felt like I was going off course, but I wasn't sure what to do about it.

Chapter 6

"*Left rudder!*" my new instructor Maureen Richards shouted from the back seat.

Panicked, I jabbed the rudder with my left foot. The plane abruptly swung hard to the left, faster than I expected, and I didn't know what to do. I was losing control on my very first landing in the Citabria, an airplane that was a notorious taildragger. We were heading straight for the ditch at the side of Oakland's Runway 33.

"Too much!" Maureen called out. "Remember, pressure on one rudder pedal is always followed by pressure on the other."

My pedals moved under my feet as Maureen used her set of dual controls to keep us aligned with the runway. The nose straightened out, and we slowly coasted to a stop. I sagged in the seat, breathing hard. We hadn't crashed, but only because Maureen had been there.

* * *

I'd thought a lot about that first lesson with Jack over the previous weeks. I'd wanted to blame him for the nearly disastrous end to the flight, but eventually I realized I was the one at fault. It's the flight instructor's job to be pilot-in-*command*. I'd abdicated my command, soothing myself with platitudes such as "The customer is always right," and insecurities like "Maybe I'm being overly cautious." If I wanted to be a flight instructor, or a pilot—or even a person living a full life on this planet—I needed to take control. I needed to find a way to develop confidence. I had to put incentives in place for becoming confident—I knew that much—but still I had no real idea of how to go about it.

Part of my difficulty was with the word *command* itself. It shamed me. Issuing orders meant putting my own opinions and desires ahead of someone else's. It was something that seemed, well, selfish, and I wasn't used to it. All my life, I'd never been in a position of authority over another human being. I'd been a daughter, student, or individual contributor—taking orders, never giving them. I'd obeyed my parents' instructions. I'd been a good student, getting straight A's and following teachers' and professors' guidelines. At work, I listened to my managers and worked late into the night to make my code robust, clean, and bug-free. Being obedient and following orders felt like it would keep me safe, just as I'd tried to make myself invisible to my tormentors in school. Being quiet was my defense mechanism, my surest method to avoid trouble.

Now for the first time, at age twenty-seven, I had to make the decisions. As pilot-in-command, it was my responsibility to ensure safety in the cockpit for my students and for myself. But what if my decisions were wrong? The consequences could be deadly, not just for me, but for an unsuspecting student. I had two choices: give up being an instructor or learn how to make the correct decisions in an airplane.

I'd chosen aviation because I knew it would lead to growth. I knew it would help me overcome my fear. And to live a full life—to become the person I was meant to be—I needed to stop being afraid of being in command, whether it was command of myself or others.

I'd been raised to believe that women weren't supposed to give commands. No, instead, my teachers in middle school had taught me that women were merely supposed to look attractive. They wanted me to *be* and not *do*—unless it meant getting good grades or following orders with precision.

When I complained to my mother, she responded with a Philippine origin myth. A long time ago, she said, women held power in society.

In each village, a female leader, a *babaylan*, with the help of a council of women, issued all the decisions for the village. The source of the babaylan's power lay in a magical pouch containing a hot coal, necessary for restarting the village fires should they ever go out.

But one day a group of men sneaked into the women's tent and stole the magical pouch. They threatened to withhold life-giving fire if the village did not acknowledge their authority. The women's council met, and the babaylan said, "It's all right if we let the men run the village. After all, they may have stolen the pouch with the coal of fire, but we women each still have our own pouches—our wombs. That's all we need. Let them run what they like; we have the true power."

I thought it was unfair that the women gave up their power and didn't even try to fight back. My mother rubbed her forehead slowly and said the women were happy in the end. That didn't feel like enough. Maybe they were just saying they were happy to stay safe. It was only much later that I realized the story's underlying message, and perhaps, what she was trying to teach me. It was all about the deliberate choice to abdicate external power in favor of the power of sexuality. After all, it's the traditional role for a woman in our society. As an attractive, sexual being, power of a kind will be bestowed upon you.

But I didn't want to give up the means to define my own power. By relying on sexuality, I'd be contained and defined by others. Sexual influence operates over an inherently limited range, so giving up external power in the world would lead me to a smaller, less influential, less adventuresome life.

In my early teens, I rebelled against my mother, as well as my teachers and classmates, by disconnecting myself from my body, by refusing to wear fashionable clothes or makeup, by deliberately denying my sexuality. I turned to the world of the mind, the intellectual domain where my father excelled, and the power of logic and math to always produce the correct answer.

At first, it didn't seem like I was giving up much. When I got my period at age eleven, my mother told me, "Now you're a woman. Now you're vulnerable." This was around the time that the girls in my class started wearing short skirts and squealing around boys—the same boys who called me a freak and a spic. I couldn't see the appeal in trying to make them aware of me in any way. So I deliberately chose to be neutral, uncharged, unobtrusive.

This neutrality came in handy later, in college and at work, where I found myself one of very few women in science and engineering. It wasn't unusual for me to be one of two women in a computer science class of thirty or the only woman on a team of ten programmers. Over time, it became a survival strategy to be neutral, to be sexless, to act like one of the guys.

I didn't realize how much I'd lost by disconnecting from my female body. To operate an airplane safely, to be truly in command of such a machine, logic isn't enough. Yes, intellect and problem-solving are crucial to becoming a good pilot, but more is needed, especially when a pilot reaches the outer edges of the flight envelope, where aerodynamics invert the usual ground-based human instincts. Flying is so different from navigating in two dimensions on the ground. You have to relearn everything.

And what I was gradually coming to realize was that I now had to connect my body to the airplane on a visceral level. To become a good pilot, I'd have to develop an instinctual ability to sense what was going wrong in the air before it became a problem.

As a six-year-old, I loved to move my body to music and persuaded my parents to sign me up for a ballet class at the local YWCA. One day, as the teacher led us through some stretches, I placed the soles of my feet together and drew my heels all the way into my crotch. The teacher spent time praising everyone in the group but me. Finally I spoke up.

"See?" I asked. "Isn't this good?"

She flicked her eyes briefly in my direction and sniffed. "No. You're doing it wrong." Gazing over at another girl, she said, "Excellent job, Amy."

The tips of my ears burned with embarrassment. What was wrong with how *I* did it? Was I untalented, inflexible, ungainly? I kept trying, but her repeated criticism eventually convinced me I'd never be a dancer.

Luckily, flying was teaching me that I could reclaim my relationship with my body. I could buttress my weak areas and grow strong from within. I could learn to control a plane despite my fear and stiffness and lack of coordination. But to build the next piece of the scaffold, to develop a true *feel* for flying, I had to tackle a much more difficult kind of flight. A type of flying "beyond the reach," everyone said, of pilots who flew awkwardly and mechanically.

Small airplanes lay upon a status continuum, their unspoken rank determined by their difficulty to land. And of all planes that required pilot skill, there was one type in particular that had the reputation of requiring the rawest pilot ability, the highest degree of "seat of the pants feel." This was the taildragger.

* * *

Not too far away from the UC Flying Club's line, another flight school called Lou Fields Aviation boasted a large, battered hangar housing a fleet of five or so aircraft. An older, fabric-covered airplane known as a tailwheel aircraft or "taildragger" was tied down just outside. It was a jaunty orange-and-white Citabria. Much cooler than the workhorse Cessna 152, the plane even featured a secret within its name: "Citabria" is "airbatic" spelled backward. Taildraggers earned their moniker from the third landing gear located at the tail instead of the nose (hence, "tailwheel" rather than "nosewheel"), lending them a classic, slick appearance. Because they were notoriously difficult to land, I'd always automatically ruled them out. But now I was ready to take one on. I had to.

Unstable on the ground, the plane wanted to swap ends so its tail was leading it down the runway, a so-called ground loop. Landing a taildragger was like balancing a pencil on the end of your nose; it required the coordination of a juggler or dancer—exactly my weak area.

I signed up for a tailwheel "checkout," a series of flights in which a pilot is taught and evaluated for proficiency. And so one blustery fall morning, Maureen and I walked out to the bright-orange Citabria, canted back with its nose in the air like it was eager to fly. Every airplane possesses its own unique aroma. From the moment you unlock it as it sits on the ramp, a mixture of fascinating odors blasts into your face. Usually it's the smell of vinyl or leather that's been baking in the sun, overlaid with a hint of aviation fuel and just a touch of oil. But I'm sure there must be other molecules, complex aromatics, that explain the scent that greets you the moment you open the door.

This Citabria was no exception. Its seats were wide and cushiony, made from foam that had been overused until it sagged. But they felt comfortable, almost homey. Only a handful of knobs and switches protruded from the dashboard, and Maureen explained each of them.

"Notice the trim control is located directly below the throttle," she said. The trim control adjusts the pressure on the control stick to keep the plane flying in a steady state. Forward trim can cause the plane to dive uncontrollably. She continued, "If you're ever trying to increase power, but nothing happens and the airplane dives, it's *not* true that the engine has quit and it's time to declare an emergency." She smirked. "Instead, you've probably grabbed the trim by mistake."

I chuckled nervously.

Maureen pointed at the instrument panel. "That red knob is the mixture. Watch out if you're ever instructing a Cessna pilot."

Like me? I thought, flushing a little.

"He'll think he has to pull carburetor heat on the downwind leg. He's likely to pull the mixture all the way out instead." She paused and dead-panned, "It turns out there's just enough time for the instructor in the back seat to unbuckle her seat belt, stand up, lean over the student's shoulder, and push the mixture back in before the engine completely quits."

During the lesson, I mostly kept quiet, absorbing Maureen's instruction. She gave me a lot to think about. I wondered why both the female instructors I'd flown with presented tough façades, warning me about students trying to kill you by shutting off the engine or needing to wash vomit out of your hair.

As we climbed into the plane, Maureen added, "You're the first woman I've taught. I like it. Normally, with a guy in the front seat, whenever we land at another airport, people always assume he's the pilot taking his girlfriend out for a ride."

I had to laugh.

Despite my initial clumsiness with the plane, she was patient as she explained my mistakes and showed me how to improve. Somewhere in the middle of laughing at her brash comments, I got over my nervousness and started to feel the movement of the airplane from side to side on the landing roll and to learn to use my feet to compensate. I was connecting with the plane. Practice and good instruction were all I needed. If training proceeds step-by-step, a good instructor can teach anyone anything. Talent isn't all-or-nothing. Skills can be developed. Power and confidence can grow.

After several weeks, she signed me off to fly the Citabria on my own. I headed out to the plane one crisp, sunny morning to put into practice all that I had learned. But sitting in the cockpit, I had a terrible premonition that I was going to crash. I wasn't skilled enough to fly this tailwheel airplane. I slumped over the stick. Maybe I was asking too much of myself. It was enough that I'd learned to fly at all. I shouldn't push myself any farther.

Maybe I was inherently just a Cessna pilot. Taildraggers required a level of talent I just didn't possess. And now, facing this trial, I realized that I couldn't go through with it. I sat up straight in the cockpit. Yes, that was it; I'd have to cancel.

As I unbuckled the seat belt and started to climb out of the cockpit, I paused. Wait a minute. By now I'd gotten used to doing terrifying things on a daily basis, and I got through them by working through a checklist to determine whether my fears were rational or not. I needed to do just that now. Had I performed adequately during the checkout? Yes. Had I studied the manual carefully? Yes. Did I have sufficient time in a tailwheel airplane to satisfy the insurance requirements? Yes, more than the minimum.

So my fear must be irrational. The only reason not to fly was my fear. This was the fear that had kept me from accomplishing so many things I wanted to do in life. This fear, if I let it, would ensure that my life would be narrow and boring and unexceptional.

I tightened my seat belt, started the engine, and took off into the beautiful day. It was a wonderful flight. And when I came back at the end, I made a perfect landing.

So my intuition had been incorrect. My childhood conditioning had shaped my instincts, which had told me to stay safe, to *be* rather than *do*, to relinquish command to someone else, because *maybe* I was unqualified.

My personality type must be "JACP," "just a Cessna pilot," a physical klutz, untalented at dancing, a follower rather than a leader. I'd internalized all the low expectations teachers and adults had of me as a child, and turned those beliefs into something permanent: an inherent personality type that defined what I could and couldn't do for the rest of my life: INTF. Incompetent, Nerd, Terrified, Failure.

But here's the wonderful thing: instincts can be retrained. The brain is like a muscle; neurological research has confirmed this. If your instincts, shaped by your early life, are leading you down a path of weakness, you can make a change. It's not going to be instantaneous. You don't face your fears once and it's all over. You need to keep working at it, day after day, the way you make bread: each day anew. And when you face your fears, and triumph over them, life opens up before you, becomes more exciting, larger and more vibrant. You become more powerful, and you learn to be comfortable with that power, comfortable enough to save lives— including your own.

The common belief, encouraged by the drama of Hollywood stories, is that change happens all at once. With a thunderclap—*boom!*—the protagonist morphs into a new person. But in reality, change happens bit by bit. It is slow, like a tree grows: not with a bang but with a gradual unfurling. When I look back on those days, I can't point to a single, definitive turning point, a day when I was weak and insecure in the morning and by the afternoon had become confident and powerful, a master. Instead, it happened the way buds slowly swell on a tree in springtime. One morning, you wake up and realize the cherry tree is covered in blossoms.

Chapter 7

"I'm thinking about taking an aerobatic course," I said to Ben one day.

"Why? Why turn a perfectly good airplane upside down?" He gave me a skeptical sideways glance.

"I've been reading about it a lot lately. It'll make me a safer pilot, knowing how to recover from spins or getting flipped inverted."

He scoffed. "You're crazy. How often does *that* happen?"

"Once would be too often."

"Do whatever you want," he said, "but I still think you're crazy."

It annoyed me that Ben was still dismissing my opinions. After I moved back in, I'd started asserting myself more often, and this was one of those moments. In the past, I'd often deferred to him on larger decisions (such as where we would live) even though I told myself I was an independent woman, but now I was questioning him more often, and this usually led to arguments. Still grappling with the feeling that I was selfish to insist on my own needs, I felt like we were moving one step forward, two steps back. I still loved him deeply, but sometimes I was certain our relationship was hovering on the edge of disaster, just like a plane can suddenly spin out of control and plunge toward the ground if you make one wrong movement.

* * *

A week later, I was flying with a student named Josh near Hayward, California. "Raise the nose for a departure stall," I told him as we circled over the hills. His rapid breathing rasped over the intercom, and he was clenching his jaw. I inched my right hand onto my thigh and shifted my feet over the rudder pedals, preparing to take the controls if necessary. I couldn't help feeling a little nervous myself. Although I'd been instructing private pilot flight students for over six months, I still found stalls scary—especially if I wasn't the one performing them. Every stall carried with it the risk that the student might put the plane into a spin, a maneuver that had killed so many pilots that the FAA had banned it from private pilot flight training. I was about to learn exactly what could make stalls with a student pilot particularly frightening.

Josh jerked the nose upward, and the Cessna swung to the left.

"Right rudder!" I called, but it was too late. The nose dropped dramatically toward the ground and began to oscillate. Everything blurred. We were entering a spin!

"*My airplane!*" I shouted, and luckily, Josh immediately released the controls. It was all happening so fast. Holding down panic, I pushed hard on the right rudder pedal and reduced the throttle to idle, executing the drill for spin recovery. I was doing everything I'd been trained to do, but I'd completely lost the sense of our physical location in space. Finally, the view outside the windshield stabilized, and the voice inside my head stopped screaming. I gradually fed in throttle and raised the nose to level flight.

Josh and I were both breathing hard. I'd managed to save us this time, but it bothered me that I didn't understand *why* the spin recovery procedure worked. Sure, I'd followed the steps I'd been taught, but shouldn't I, as an instructor and supposedly an expert, have a deeper comprehension of the underlying forces involved? Shouldn't I have been able to feel what was going to happen *before* we got into the spin?

When my dad taught me math, he always made sure I understood *why* the proofs and equations were correct. "You shouldn't just memorize, but understand," he said. "Now I want you to derive this proof yourself. Work it out, step by step." He'd slide another piece of paper to my side of the desk, and I'd set to work. His method took longer, but whenever I saw a similar problem again, I could solve it.

Now I was dealing with the same principle, only this time my life— and the life of a student—might depend on it. Without understanding why, there was no guarantee I could recover from a spin. And if I'd been unable to recover, we could have lost control of the airplane and plunged into the hills below. Although I'd been trained in basic emergency proce- dures, I needed to go beyond rote memorization. I knew what I had to do next, but I'd been dreading taking that step.

This incident solidified why I needed to take an aerobatic safety course and learn more about what an aircraft was capable of—including spins, loops, and rolling upside down. As I'd just seen, my life might depend on learning this skill. Yet, the thought of aerobatic training terrified me more than just about any other flying experience I'd had. Lots of people got private pilot licenses, but few took aerobatic training.

Spin training and recovery used to be taught to all pilots. But in 1949, the Federal Aviation Administration, concerned with the high number of spin-related training accidents, removed the requirement for spins in the private pilot curriculum. Instructors are still required to receive basic spin training, but, perhaps because *their* instructors have had limited spin expe- rience, that training is minimal. Clearly, my own education hadn't been sufficient for me to understand what was going on. I promised myself I would only take the basic ten-hour aerobatic course, just enough to learn how to stay safe and improve my skills, and then I would never subject myself to that terror again.

* * *

The metal airport gate squeaked as I slid my security badge into the slot. It was the morning of my first aerobatic lesson, and I was more nervous than I'd been for quite a while. The aroma of the bay rushed in through my open window. I took a deep breath before driving onto the field. This was it.

George Newell met me in a small alcove in Lou Fields's hangar that doubled as a classroom. George was an experienced instructor, a large, soft man with an apologetic air that masked a deep and abiding enthusiasm for aerobatic flight. He carefully described the basic maneuvers we'd be doing today—the loop and roll—with the aid of a whiteboard and a model airplane mounted on a wooden dowel. He explained entry speeds and safety concerns in his calm, quiet voice, and demonstrated the use of Lou's old military surplus parachutes.

After the classroom lesson, we walked out to the same orange Citabria I'd flown with Maureen, tied down at the far edge of the taxiway. A trio of marsh birds squawked over a catch in the long grass by the edge of the slough. The fog had burned off, and the sky gleamed an eggshell blue. The temperature was in the low seventies with a touch of breeze, no more than five knots out of the northwest.

I'd flown this plane for many hours. But today its familiar lines took on a more intimidating aura. George removed the large orange cushions from the back seat, exposing black metal slats from the skeleton of the plane, to make room for him to sit on the thick parachute without bumping into the headliner. The visible bare metal underscored the plane's transformation from comfort to something more ominous.

We both strapped on our parachutes, required by law for all aerobatic flights, and I climbed into the front seat. Of course, I had no need to remove any cushions. Even with the parachute, I needed them and extras to reach the rudder pedals and to see over the nose. Most women pilots have trouble reaching the controls in small American planes, since they tend to be designed for the average male at five feet ten inches. (By contrast, Russian planes all use adjustable rudder pedals, enabling a much wider variation in pilot height.)

I did my usual obsessive double-checking of each headset connection, adjusting each strap, and tightening the seat belts repeatedly. George was patient with me, settling his bulk into the back seat of the Citabria while occasionally making a gentle comment or joke.

My adrenaline was pumping and my heart beating at what felt like two hundred times a minute at the thought of flying a loop or rolling the plane upside down, but I took a deep breath and started the engine. We taxied out, and I took off, heading to the tiny practice area George had marked on the map, next to Mount Diablo, twenty miles away. In the busy airspace of the San Francisco Bay area, there were only a few spots where aerobatics was legally permitted. And unfortunately, since the Citabria only had 115 horsepower, it was going to take a long time to get there and cost a lot of money in rental fees.

Finally, we arrived in the practice area, and I did four or five clearing turns.

Then George took the controls to demonstrate a roll. "I'm diving at a hundred twenty-five miles per hour," he explained. "Then I pitch up, neutralize the stick, apply full left aileron and some left rudder."

The horizon pitched and tilted crazily in the windshield. The heavy webbing of Lou's old green parachute cut into the skin of my arms and neck. My internal organs felt like they were shifting around inside my gut. My breathing accelerated, and I couldn't help clutching the metal bar under the instrument panel in a futile attempt to stay oriented.

Aerobatics is like nothing else in this world. It's strange and disorienting the first time you turn upside down in the middle of the air, the first time you feel yourself weighing too much or too little. We take the Earth's pull for granted. A lifetime of living in its gravity field has made us completely unaware of the millions of tiny bodily reactions, motions, and little bits of knowledge that we've incorporated into our perceptions.

The Citabria sported large windows on both sides, and even an overhead skylight. This gives you tremendous visibility, more than 180 degrees from left to right, and a significant range both above and below. It felt like I could see everything, like every sense was engaged as we dove for speed. The terrain whipped by faster and faster; my eyes darted back and forth, looking for other airplanes, checking for landmarks on the ground. As our speed increased, the clamor of air rushing past the plane intensified. The airplane's vibration surged. Even the scent of the air streaming in through the vents changed. At four or five thousand feet, I smelled the dry California scrub, thistle and broom, live oak and spurge on the steep hills below. As we dove, the scent intensified.

George pulled back on the stick, and centrifugal force pressed me into the seat. That strange change in perceived gravity known as "g-force" made itself known as it pulled every muscle and cell of my body downward, squeezing me into the cushions and drawing blood away from my brain. I tensed my muscles as George had taught, straining the long muscles of my quadriceps, drawing in my abdominals, breathing thick and fast through my mouth and nose to keep my brain oxygenated.

In front of me lay nothing but empty blue sky as we pointed the nose up into the air. As George released the pull, my stomach lifted into my ribs and I became light in the seat, freed from the relentless pull of gravity, with the spaces between my cells widening. George applied full left aileron for the roll, and the stick moved all the way to the left-hand stop. We pointed straight at Mount Diablo, and George told me the nose would inscribe a rough oval in the air with the peak of the mountain at its center. Of course, I couldn't see it. A quick glance out the skylight, and all I noticed was vineyards above my head. Beneath my feet, blue sky.

As earth and sky whirled around me, every muscle seemed to tingle. I was dancing! Dancing in the sky. I wasn't quite sure what had happened to my body and soul, but I knew my world had been irrevocably altered once again. Never again would I be content to keep the ground underneath my feet. Now I needed to be more than a Cessna pilot. I *needed* aerobatics. I needed to learn this new world of spinning and looping and flipping through the sky, just as a few short years ago I needed that first flying lesson.

Straight and level flying was wonderful, but twirling upside down was miraculous. This was it. I'd found my new calling.

First, though, I'd have to deal with one small problem—the waves of nausea sweeping over me.

George's cheerful voice came over the intercom. "How about if I demonstrate a loop now?"

"Ohhh," I groaned. I keyed the mic. "Uh, I think we need to head back. I'm not feeling so good."

I managed to avoid throwing up on the bumpy flight back to the

Oakland Airport. We'd done exactly one maneuver in 1.2 hours. One expensive-as-hell maneuver.

It felt like paradise had been offered and snatched away at the same time. I'd experienced such joy on that flight, but the combination of my tendency toward airsickness and my lack of funds was going to keep me from being able to repeat it. Gloomy, I pushed the airplane back into its spot, answering George with monosyllables. Then, as I carried my parachute and cushions back to the hangar, I rallied. Hadn't I had to steel myself to take that first flight lesson? Hadn't I once believed I was incapable of earning a private pilot license? I'd overcome my fears before. I'd found a way to earn the money I needed to get my private, commercial, and instructor certificates. I'd done it before, so I could do it again.

It was just like mathematical induction. I had to logically analyze the next challenges I needed to solve. Over the next few days, I came up with two major ideas to improve the ratio of time spent learning aerobatics to time spent getting airsick. First, I booked double lessons with George so that we could take a break at an airport closer to the practice area, either Livermore or Tracy. This gave my stomach time to settle, and we could discuss the maneuvers calmly on the ground, then it was a short flight back out to the practice area, which meant less rental time. Second, I spent as much time as I could visualizing the maneuvers on the ground.

Visualization, or imagining yourself doing a physical activity, is a technique for skill development that's well known in the sports world. In one famous study, kids learned basketball free throws better by simply imagining themselves putting the ball through the hoop than by actually practicing.

Visualizing aerobatic maneuvers cost me nothing, and I rapidly became very good at imagining myself strapped into the airplane, breathing in that distinctive blend of aviation fuel and native California vegetation from the ground below, feeling that heaviness in every muscle in my body as g-forces squashed me into the seat, as the horizon flipped and rotated in the windshield.

All the money I earned teaching was now going right back into buying aerobatic flight lessons. I sold my Cessna 150 to pay for Citabria rentals. I gave up other forms of entertainment. Who needs to go to movies, when no story could possibly compare with living the incredible dream of flying every day? Before I took up flying, I was often plagued by depression and sadness, the feeling that my life was empty, and there was no particular reason to get up in the morning. But now, every single time the wheels of my plane rose from the earth in preparation for an aerobatic flight, euphoria spread through me like the warmth of the sun.

Flying had eased my sadness, and aerobatics had lifted me into a life that was full of joy.

* * *

I'd spent most of my earlier life believing the world was a dark place—one where bullies got away with harming others and corruption and dishonesty were never punished. I'd believed that true joy was only found in books or fantasies.

In sixth grade, most of my school days were bad, but gym class was one of the worst parts of the day. It often allowed Don and his friends more creative means of attacking me under the guise of "sports." Don's friend once threw a basketball at me so hard it dislocated a bone in my finger. Then there were the relay races in which the smaller kids like me were carried piggyback across the gym by our bigger classmates. During one of these races, Don took the opportunity to drop me straight on my tailbone. I lay on the dirty gym floor writhing in pain.

Don kicked me hard in the ribs. "Get up, you faker!"

The teacher blew his whistle, and I saw the toes of his tennis shoes as he approached.

"She's just faking," Don said.

Instead of chastising Don, the teacher said, "Get up, Rodriguez. You're fine."

I struggled to sit up, pain lancing through my tailbone and ribs.

During those early years, I can't remember a single time a teacher took my side over that of a white male. It got to the point where I simply gave up and stopped protesting. I retreated into a world of fantasy and magic, searching for sources of happiness in books.

I spent my early years in a world where dreams never came true, where I was told I should expect less and "be more realistic."

In those days, looking up at the trees around my house in Indiana, my dream of levitating, of dancing in the air, of flying free from gravity, seemed unreachable. Only characters in books got to fly. Magic didn't exist. The world was a grim place.

But now, somehow, miraculously, I'd broken the rules. The thrill I felt with each takeoff made me believe that everything I thought impossible was within reach after all.

For the first time, I began to imagine a future I *knew* I could make real.

Learning aerobatics was worth overcoming every hurdle. I would beat back my fear. I would find the money to train. I would learn how to overcome my airsickness. I would do whatever it took to achieve perfection in my art, to touch and grasp that inner joy. Earning my private pilot license had marked the beginning of changing my life; it had been the first step in overcoming my fear so I could lead a larger life. But aerobatics felt to me like the culmination of flying, the art for which all my previous training had been only a preamble. Now I could *create* something larger than me in the world. I was going to work at it until I succeeded.

* * *

Every couple of days—in the early mornings or on afternoons stolen from work—I flew with George and learned how to make the Citabria spin, roll, and loop the way I'd imagined. Day by day, my nausea receded, and my expertise with the airplane increased. After only a few short months, I was performing maneuvers I'd only seen before in airshows, like the Immelmann turn (a half-loop followed by a half-roll upright), split-S (half-roll to inverted followed by a half-loop down, like the bottom half of an *S*) and half Cuban eight (five-eighths of a loop followed by a half-roll).

One afternoon I was winding the heavy tie-down chain through the tailwheel of the Citabria after a particularly exhilarating and sweaty flight, when George said, "Hey, you know what, Cecilia? There's going to be an aerobatic contest at Taft Airport in a couple of weeks. I think you should go."

I laughed. "A contest? Me?" Yes, I'd gone beyond the ten-hour course and never wanted to stop. But *compete*?

George snapped his seat cushion back into place and nodded vigorously. "You're doing very well."

"Are you sure you've got the right person?"

"It's informal and designed for beginners, like a neighborhood soccer game. You'd be flying in the Basic category, so it's not like anyone there would be an aerobatic expert. Even if you don't win, you'd learn a lot just from participating in the contest."

I paused. Put that way, it almost sounded like fun.

George was one of the most supportive people I knew, kind and relentlessly encouraging. He always had his students' best interests at heart. I'd spent enough flight hours with him to feel comfortable sharing confidences, so I told him my big fear in a quiet voice: "People would laugh at me."

George's broad forehead smoothed out. "Aw, nobody would. I've come in last many times. If nothing else, you'll make good friends with the person who came in second to last."

I hooked the chain into position and met George's eyes. His soft, round face expressed nothing but enthusiasm. He wouldn't be so eager if he didn't believe it was a good thing for me to do. Attending a contest, challenging though it might be, just might be the next step for me to take to grow as a pilot.

I signed up.

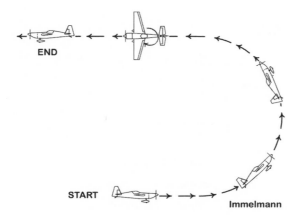

START → → →   **Immelmann**

END

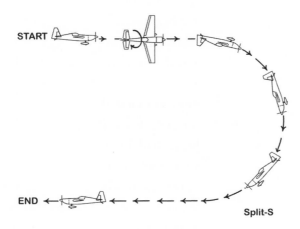

START → → →   **Split-S**

END ← ← ← ←

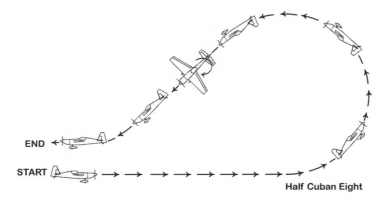

START → → → → → → →   **Half Cuban Eight**

END ←

Chapter 8

"Are you ready for this? Because I'm not," Adam Leblanc, another instructor at Lou Fields, said as we carried our parachutes out to the Citabria one bright Oakland morning in April 1988. He held out a hand. "Look, I'm actually trembling."

I was nervous too, but I was trying to keep it to myself. Adam and I were going to fly one of Lou's Citabrias to Taft Airport, where we would take turns flying at our first aerobatic contest. Over the past few months, we'd fallen into a kind of informal camaraderie after running into each other at the Oakland airport nearly every day. We were both new instructors fanatical about flying, and at the end of each day, we'd flop into folding chairs at Lou Fields's to hang on the words of the older pilots as they regaled us with stories of narrow escapes and flying adventures, in what was known as "hangar flying."

Adam was barely twenty years old and clean-shaven with light skin and curly brown hair. Everything was dramatic and emotional for him: he'd either flown with the *best* student ever or the *worst* that day. He told stories of near misses with relish, his eyes wide and voice breaking. He'd decided to forego college to become an airline pilot.

Neither of us had ever flown in an aerobatic contest, and we didn't know what to expect.

An hour by Citabria from Oakland, Taft is a dusty, potholed strip at the southwestern edge of the San Joaquin Valley, surrounded by oil fields and brown foothills stretching up into mountains to the west. A sleepy town with a shrinking population, Taft was once the site of the largest mouse infestation in US history. In 1926 an estimated one hundred million mice converged here. Devouring an entire lamb in its pen in a single day, the rodents scuttled through town until a horde of birds arrived and put the ecosystem back into balance.

On this day, there were no mice around that I could see. We arrived a little before eight in the morning, and the air was cool, although the sun clambering up the sky promised a scorching day.

When we landed, we were surprised to find the airport silent and empty. Unlike an airshow, there were no signs, crowds, or loudspeakers. If I hadn't known a contest was going on, I'd have thought it was a typical sleepy weekend at any small airport. A group of maybe thirty pilots milled around a dilapidated tie-down area, tending to their aerobatic planes. I recognized another Citabria, a Decathlon—which is a beefier version of the Citabria with more horsepower and a stronger airframe—and a couple of tiny biplanes that could fit inside a living room, most likely the famous Pitts Special, supposedly one of the best aerobatic airplanes ever built. I sighed at the tiny Pitts's beautiful lines. I had to admit it was far more elegant than the well-worn, familiar Citabria Adam and I would compete in.

Other than us, the field was deserted. A sagging barn at one end housed the FBO, or "fixed base operator," the fuel service on the field. Inside, a red-headed teenager lounged behind the Formica counter, facing a Naugahyde couch patched with duct tape along one side. I headed for the tiny bathroom. The toilet bowl was ringed with rust, and there was no soap.

When I came back out, the contest director, Roger Nichols, gathered everyone in front of a portable whiteboard set up on the tarmac for the official contest briefing. He explained the rules and safety procedures. Just to the east of the runway, there was an area where we would perform our maneuvers called the "aerobatic box," a cube of air about three thousand feet on a side. Roger read out the order of flight, and we all scattered; the pilots to prepare our airplanes and get ready to fly, the judges to drive out to the "line," where they would sit on folding chairs for a couple of hours, watching our maneuvers and scoring them on a scale of zero to ten.

Adam and I were flying in the lowest category, known as "Basic" and intended to introduce raw beginners to the joys of competition aerobatics. We would each fly three maneuvers: a single-turn spin, a loop, and an aileron roll in immediate succession. There were five categories in total. In order from least to most difficult, these were Basic, Sportsman, Intermediate, Advanced, and Unlimited. At most regional contests, all five categories flew.

I'd only practiced a sequence of spin-loop-roll a couple of times with George. Sequences are significantly more difficult than flying loops or rolls one at a time. Flying one maneuver directly after another meant that you didn't have time to set up your entry speed or even catch your breath between aerobatic figures. That made competition flying substantially more challenging than ordinary aerobatics.

Adam and I pushed the Citabria into position, and I waited anxiously for my turn to fly. I settled my headset onto my ears and wiped sweat off my forehead with the back of my hand. I took off, climbed to four thousand feet, and circled to the south of the airport.

When I finally got the signal to enter the box, I was more nervous than usual. The first maneuver was a spin. The top of the box was officially thirty-five hundred feet, but I entered at four thousand for safety. As I reduced the throttle to slow to stall speed in preparation for entering a spin, I checked the altimeter to make sure I wasn't losing altitude and then returned my eyes to the horizon. It was a beautiful day, the hazy blue sky arching overhead, the dry air seeping into my nose with hints of ranches and pastures, creosote and desert sage. The vibration of the airplane slowed, the engine coughed briefly, and my heart stuttered with the fear that it might quit. Fortunately, it resumed its purr.

Spins still terrified me, but I'd learned how to separate irrational fear, what kept me from taking action, from rational fear, what might save my life. My fear of spins had become relegated to the first category. Since I'd entered so many spins in the Citabria by now, I was convinced I could always recover. And the important thing about irrational fear was to not let it stop you. Stalls and spins were still scary, but I did them anyway.

I pulled the stick straight back into my stomach with all my strength, and the plane entered the spin. The roads and brown fields below me gyrated. The nose swung past vertical like it always did, and the rotation rate sped up. I sweated in my seat as the shrill, urgent voice inside my head screamed that I do something to recover from this spiral dive zooming toward the ground.

But, as I'd been trained, I waited. I held the controls in their positions against all common sense, keeping the plane in the spin when every part of me was yammering to recover, recover, *recover!* At last I saw the reference line flash into view at the left edge of the windshield, and with a sharp inhale, I pushed the stick forward and jammed on full right rudder simultaneously.

The Citabria recovered immediately from the spin like the sweet airplane it was. But (oops!) I'd misjudged the reference line and overshot, exiting about 30 degrees past where I should have been. George had told me if that happened I should just hold the line and sneak it out later as I pulled out of the dive, but without thinking, I instantly corrected with aileron. Wincing, I was sure the judges must have seen the "over and back" and would score me down. All I could hope for was that maybe they hadn't seen the full 30 degrees and would take off only three or four points out of ten instead of six. Maybe.

Even though I'd told both Adam and George, and even Ben, that I expected to come in last, I couldn't help secretly wishing I'd do better than expected. Ben, of course, thought the idea of competing in a flight contest was insane. But there was no time to think about that now.

To recover from the dive after the spin, I grabbed the stick with both hands and pulled. It was heavy, much heavier than when the plane was slow. I tensed my abdominal muscles and breathed fast through my mouth as the g-force came on like a huge hand slamming me into the seat. The edges of my field of vision turned gray—the first warning sign of impending loss of consciousness. I needed to finish the spin cleanly and get ready for the next maneuver, but more importantly, I needed to remain conscious.

I was almost back to horizontal and ready for the next maneuver, the loop, before I remembered, *Oops! I need to increase the throttle.* I shoved it forward and checked the airspeed indicator. I was supposed to be at 140 miles per hour, the safe entry speed for a loop. But my late power increase had left me at only 130.

It had been drilled into me not to start the loop at too low an airspeed—it could be dangerous. The Citabria could fail to make it past vertical and sustain damage to the control surfaces, maybe even come apart in the air. I really didn't want to test out one of Lou's old military parachutes today.

So I pushed forward on the stick to nose the airplane down a little. I dove at the ground, knowing the judges would see this as well, and would mark me down for it. One point for every 5 degrees off horizontal. I hoped I hadn't lost enough points to earn a humiliating zero on the loop. It wasn't looking good for avoiding last place.

My airspeed indicator reached 140 miles per hour, and I pulled the stick back. Again, the g-force, the heavy breathing, and the clenching of my abs and quads. This time my vision remained clear. I pulled up, up, up, nose pointed straight into the blue sky as I executed the first half of the loop. I shifted my gaze to the left wingtip, watching as the horizon rotated until I was nearly on my back. Then I eased off on the stick and floated, upside down, over the top of the loop.

Everything slowed down. The engine chugged away, but the airflow noise died down to a whisper. I floated in the seat, weightless, hovering at the top of a thousand-foot circle in the sky, held in place only by my seat belt. My headset slid up my ears, and connecting wires floated past my face. My spine lengthened, and all my muscles relaxed. I always loved this part of the loop—being suspended in the air for a few seconds of peace and quiet with everything moving more slowly—before the inevitable return to the bottom.

The nose was dropping faster, and the airspeed was building. Now I was pointed straight at the ground, losing altitude at a ferocious rate. I hauled back on the stick, harder, harder, harder, tightening my muscles again as the g's came on, filling my lungs with hot, dusty air that scratched the back of my throat.

And then I was horizontal again. But there was no time to relax, because I had to start the roll. A quick glance at the airspeed indicator showed I still had 140 miles per hour. All I needed was 120, so I was safe.

I pitched up and applied full left aileron with both hands on the stick to shove it to the stop with all my might. I slid sideways in the seat as the roll began. The belt had loosened, but there was no time to tighten it. As I rolled inverted, I dangled a couple of inches from the seat, and the stick slid from my grip, causing the airplane to hesitate upside down.

The engine coughed. It was a gravity-fed fuel system, and I'd just starved the motor of gas. It started to quit. I braced myself and pushed sideways with all my strength on the stick. Finally, the roll continued, the engine roared to life, the nose dropped, and the plane returned to normal upright flight.

It was over. I was level at fifteen hundred feet, right at the bottom of the box, completely drenched in sweat, with my muscles quivering, but I had just successfully flown my first aerobatic contest. We were supposed to give three wing wags at the end of the sequence, dipping one wing at least 45 degrees to indicate the finish. I managed one, maybe two slight dips of the wing, before I decided I really should tighten my seat belt.

And then I faced the most important part of the flight: the landing. George's voice echoed in my head. "You have to forget all about the sequence; don't analyze your maneuvers. Just focus on flying a normal pattern, looking for traffic, and making a safe landing."

I managed to land safely and taxied back to my tie-down spot. I was cheering inside, proud of myself, and a small part of me hoped that Adam or George would be waiting for me, grinning and giving me a thumbs-up.

But as I shut the airplane down, everybody was busy watching the next pilot fly, his 180-horsepower Pitts screaming through the air as its propeller spooled up. It drew an absolutely flawless loop in the sky, and then rolled so fast that I almost missed the wings' rotation. I sighed with longing.

Adam was waiting to climb into the airplane for his flight. "Great job," he told me, but I could see he was already nervous about his own turn in the box.

After the flights were over, I joined the group of pilots waiting at the whiteboard for their scores to be posted. I'd always been competitive, building a sense of self-worth on how well I did in contests, on standardized tests, or for scholarships. But this was different. I believed I had no talent for flying; I'd gotten to where I was through dint of hard work. It took me much longer to get my pilot's license than the national average. For someone who always scored in a high percentile on national tests, it was humbling to play in an arena where I performed below average. At the same time, it was somehow freeing. Knowing I wouldn't do well was kind of a relief. I no longer had to live up to my own insanely high expectations. I didn't have to kick myself if I didn't get a perfect score.

Still, old habits die hard. As I waited for the numbers to be posted, I couldn't help but daydream about scoring well. Of course there was that overrotation on the spin, the dive before the loop, and then the nose up before the roll. But maybe it wasn't as bad as it felt. Maybe the judges blinked or got some dust in their eyes at exactly the right moment.

When the scoring director's assistant finally emerged from the tiny office where they'd set up the computer, he taped the dot-matrix printout to the whiteboard. Everybody gathered around, but of course, I was too short to see over everyone's shoulders. Someone called out the names of the top three pilots, and there were cheers and laughter. Many of the people here knew each other well. The top pilots were all flying Pitts, and to my surprise, many of them had been flying for years. I thought the Basic category was just for beginners.

Finally, Adam and I got a chance to squint at the sheet of paper flapping in the breeze. I examined the scores. Out of eight pilots, Adam came in fifth and I came in sixth.

"At least we're not last!" Adam was exultant.

And at least I didn't get a zero on any of my maneuvers. The judges did detect every degree of overrotation on my spin, so I only got a four out of ten. So much for dust in their eyes. The other scores were respectable sevens and eights. My total score just missed 70 percent. *Not bad for a first-timer*, I told myself.

Adam and I grinned at each other and high-fived. Our first aerobatic contest was a success.

* * *

The contest got me thinking. I could have done better on the spin, but a competition roll was supposed to be flown without raising the nose beforehand, something that simply couldn't be done in the low-horse-power Citabria without an inverted fuel system. (This was the system that kept the engine running when the plane flipped upside down.) I could certainly improve my flying, but if I wanted to score well at contests, I'd need to find something other than the Citabria.

George told me the plane I needed to fly next was called a Super Decathlon, and that there was one available to rent down in San Jose. So, in May 1988, I scheduled a flight with the owner of Super Decathlon Three Eight Seven Juliett Lima. The outfit that rented it was a small flying club called Condor Flight, located in an obscure back corner of the San Jose Airport. I drove all the way down to San Jose and looped around the commercial flight operations to a small, slightly run-down corner of the field that reminded me of the Old T's, although perhaps even more decrepit.

Martin Johnson, a shaggy man about forty years old in a worn leather jacket, met me in front of a hangar piled high with pieces of broken wing spars, torn-apart engines, and two motorcycles with their cowlings off. He'd been washing the Decathlon, scrubbing grease off one side of its cowling.

He greeted me cheerfully. "I just changed her oil, so she should be ready to go. She hasn't flown in a while, so it's great to meet a pilot who wants to do aerobatics."

I checked the plane over dubiously. It was, without a doubt, the shabbiest-looking airplane I'd ever seen. Paint flaked off the fabric fuselage and wings, the doors rattled in their sockets, and grease leaked from every pipe and seam. I tested the controls carefully and peered in at the engine. Everything I could see looked okay. "How's the maintenance?" I asked.

"Oh, it's great! I know a mechanic on the field who's a real genius. He's not one of those high-priced corporate types, if you get what I mean, so his hangar is a little dirty, but what he's forgotten about maintenance isn't worth knowing. Kinda like Juliett Lima here." Martin patted the side of the airplane affectionately. "She may not be the spiffiest airplane on the field, but she's completely safe." He showed me the engine and airframe logbooks, and everything was, apparently, signed off properly.

We were getting ready to strap into the airplane when I asked him about his parachutes.

"Nope, don't own any 'chutes."

"Um, isn't it a legal requirement to do aerobatics?"

"No one flies aerobatics in this plane," he informed me.

Wouldn't that make me something of a test pilot?

"I'm just going to check you out on takeoffs and landings, since I'm not even an instructor. We're not going to fly aerobatics today."

I was a little distressed since I had driven all the way specifically for an aerobatic checkout and had told him over the phone that I wanted to fly aerobatics.

"Of course you can fly aerobatics in it on your own, if you have parachutes. I'm sure if you can fly aerobatics in a Citabria, you can fly them in a Decathlon." He grinned. "It's actually a lot easier in Juliett Lima because this old gal has more horsepower than your Citabria, a stronger airframe, an inverted fuel system, and a symmetrical airfoil."

I drove back from San Jose after the quickest checkout I've ever received. Was I making a mistake, flying this airplane? Unfortunately, it was the only Decathlon available for rent anywhere in the Bay Area. I'd looked up the prices to buy a Decathlon in *Trade-a-Plane*, and they were all well beyond my reach at $28,000 to $50,000. This plane seemed safe enough, even if in poor cosmetic shape. And I wanted to learn to fly more aerobatic maneuvers. I needed to learn the slow roll, and to master inverted flight. I wanted to fly hammerheads and Cuban eights—all maneuvers that were possible in the Citabria but could not be flown to competition standards without pushing Lou's little airplane too far.

It was Juliett Lima or nothing.

So I'd found myself a Decathlon, the plane that had been touted to me as one of the best aerobatic trainers ever made. But where was I going to find a good aerobatic instructor? George didn't want to teach in anything other than one of Lou's Citabrias.

Although it was true that the early barnstormers taught themselves aerobatic maneuvers, they didn't have a reassuring safety record. I called around, but there were no aerobatic instructors available anywhere in the

Bay Area. It was suggested that I fly to Southern California or Arizona, where there were established schools, but I couldn't afford that much time off work, especially added onto the costs of the training. I was told that what people at my stage usually did was buy their own airplane, but that was financially out of reach for me.

It looked like I'd hit a dead end ... or had I?

Chapter 9

"Why do you fly this piece-of-shit airplane?" Frank Greenberg asked as we finished a slow roll, and the Decathlon shuddered and its doors rattled.

"What do you mean?" I asked, my stomach twisting. He was insulting my beloved rental, Juliett Lima. Sure, she might be dowdy, but she was all I could afford. If Frank stopped having fun flying with me, he might break off our lessons, and then there would be no one to teach me advanced aerobatics.

I'd recently met Frank at one of the meetings of the local chapter of the International Aerobatic Club held every month at the Livermore Airport, twenty-five miles east of Oakland. I was always nervous meeting new people, especially when I was the single newcomer in a large group. But here I was enthusiastically welcomed by club members. During the snack break, pilots one by one approached me to talk. They knew about Lou Fields and were pleased to hear I was flying in a Citabria and Decathlon. Frank, a solidly built dark-haired man with pale skin and a trim beard, was particularly friendly. He owned a single-seat Pitts S-1S, was the president of his own software start-up in Silicon Valley, and had been involved with the local chapter for many years.

Frank invited me to attend one of the chapter's weekly practice sessions at New Jerusalem Airport out in the Central Valley. "We critique each other's flying every Saturday and Sunday afternoons. You're welcome to join us. Bring your Decathlon, and you can practice the Sportsman sequence."

"But I'm flying Basic," I objected. Sportsman was one level up and more difficult than Basic.

"No, you should fly Sportsman at the Paso Robles contest. It's a lot more fun than Basic."

"I don't know if I'm ready for Sportsman," I said aloud, but my inner self sat up and said, *Yes!*

He shrugged. "Come on out and fly, and we'll see."

New Jerusalem Airport consisted of a strip of pavement in the middle of some alfalfa and melon fields in the Central Valley. People sometimes thought that when I said there was "nothing" out at New J, it was figurative. Nope. There was literally not a single structure at the field, not a building or hangar, no bathroom or outhouse, not even a bench out in the blazing Central Valley sun. Frank remarked that the only improvement at New Jerusalem was a tie-down ring he'd hammered into the asphalt one year so that he could secure his Pitts during practice.

The most important feature of the airport, for the chapter's purposes, was the FAA waiver that allowed pilots to perform aerobatic maneuvers above the runway. Normally it was illegal to fly aerobatics at that location. A chapter member "activated the box" by calling the FAA four hours before practice time.

One hot Sunday afternoon, I landed at about 12:30 p.m. after circling the runway. It had been a long drive from foggy Berkeley that morning, and I'd left the house before Ben was up. Ben and I still hadn't resolved the conflict over how much control I should have over my own life. Whenever I asked him, Ben agreed I should be independent and make my own decisions. Yet whenever I told him about a new flight maneuver, or broached a plan to start competing more, he'd try to convince me to be "rational" and give up my dangerous hobby. Perhaps he didn't realize that if I couldn't fly, I'd lose something that mattered as much to me as my life. At the time, however, I didn't have the words to explain it.

I was working two nearly full-time jobs, instructing at Oakland Airport and taking on a series of contract programming gigs. I'd left DEC because I wanted the flexibility to set my own hours and quickly discovered that good programming skills were a valuable commodity in Silicon Valley in the late eighties. I never had trouble finding new contracts whenever one ran out.

My dad had once told me, "All that matters is the work. If you're good at math and physics, it doesn't matter what language you speak, what race, religion, or sex you are." Although that hadn't been my experience generally, it was certainly true during a labor shortage. Employers at that time didn't seem to care about my gender or ethnicity as long as I could deliver code reliably. It was a heady feeling to be in demand, to feel confident in my own abilities, and to be appreciated for doing something well. It almost made up for my shame at giving up on the PhD.

Ben was working similarly long hours, often not returning home until two or three in the morning. I was usually gone by the time he woke up and asleep when he returned. We got along fine in the brief interludes when our paths crossed, as long as we avoided talking about aerobatics, which he still disapproved of. But what was disapproval compared to the magic of twirling in the air? I'd already put up with far greater bumps on the path to aerobatic excellence. It was enough, for now, that Ben and I had become amicable roommates.

Bumping over the rutted New Jerusalem airstrip to a small paved pad at the north end, the heat hit me like a blast furnace, redolent with dust, melting asphalt, and sun-warmed alfalfa. I turned off at the end and shut down. Juliett Lima's engine ticked in the sudden silence. Heated air seeped through my open window; the forecast said it would hit ninety-five today. I unstrapped both the five-point aerobatic harness and the backup seat belt that was there in case the first one failed. The metal buckles were almost too hot to touch.

Frank had already arrived, and his tiny red Pitts was tied down at the ring he'd installed. Frank treated aerobatics like a religion. His entire life revolved around his pursuit of excellence in his Pitts. I tried hard not to fawn too much over his beautiful single-seat airplane. I couldn't help but fantasize about flying one myself, even though I knew it was impossible. Frank was currently practicing in Unlimited, the top category, performing unimaginably complex and physically demanding maneuvers, such as double outside snaps, tailslides, and lomcovaks (gyroscopic maneuvers whose name means "headache" or "strong drink" in Czech). He'd been practicing for two years but had yet to enter an Unlimited contest, judging himself not quite ready to compete without humiliating himself.

Another pilot named Stu Beyer arrived shortly thereafter. Stu had hand-built his own plane, a Christen Eagle, in his living room and garage over a period of three years. He knew every weld, fabric patch, and seam on the aircraft. It was a meticulous work of craftsmanship, complete with the most intricate paint scheme I'd ever seen on an airplane. He flew Advanced, the second highest category. Frank and Stu often landed with bloodshot eyes from the negative-g maneuvers like outside loops or inverted snap rolls I had yet to practice.

"Negative g's are like being stretched on a rack, only less fun," Frank told me that first afternoon, after my eyes had widened when I learned the sequence he planned to fly.

Stu wore shorts, and I was shocked to see heavy bruising on his thighs. I was glad Ben wasn't there to see it; I could picture his disapproval.

I'd come a long way since my first flight in the Citabria. But meeting Stu and Frank was humbling and made me realize how much more there was to aerobatics than I had assumed from hanging out with the group at Lou Fields. For one thing, the bewildering variety of complex figures in the upper categories made Sportsman look kind of wimpy. Watching the two of them fly thrilled me to the core.

I felt outclassed in my shabby rented Decathlon, just barely attempting Sportsman. I'd already practiced most of the requirements, like Immelmanns and half Cuban eights, in the Citabria with George, but I wasn't flying to competition standards. However, Frank and Stu were very supportive. Although I was normally shy around strangers, I was used to being the only woman on programming teams at job sites, and as long as the conversation remained limited to technical details about flying or computers, I could hold my own. It helped that Frank and Stu were especially pleased with how fast I learned to evaluate their maneuvers from the ground.

After we talked for a few minutes, we started our critique session. The first pilot to fly was Stu, and I listened closely as Frank evaluated his sequence, playing judge and giving feedback on the precision of the maneuvers into a mini-cassette recorder: "On the hammerhead, you're positive up, negative down, barreled the roll. Twenty-degree overrotation on the snap. Outside loop is pinched at the top."

A hammerhead maneuver draws a shape in the sky that looks a little like its name. You pull to a vertical climb, nose pointed straight at the sky, until the plane slows down, then pivot 180 degrees around your vertical axis until the nose is aimed directly at the ground. Frank's critique meant Stu didn't fly a perfect vertical line up; his nose was tipped slightly forward, or "positive." On the downline, his nose was tucked a little, known as "negative." "Barreled the roll" implied that the airplane didn't rotate precisely around its roll axis, but wobbled. On his snap roll, he didn't stop in time, going 20 degrees past where he should have been. "Pinched" meant the loop was pointy at the top.

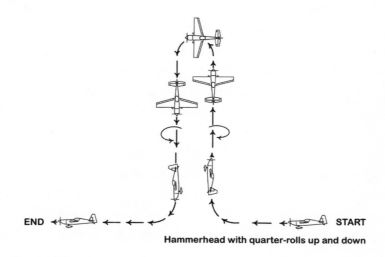

Hammerhead with quarter-rolls up and down

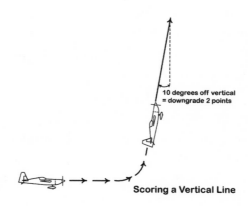

Scoring a Vertical Line

It's hard to know whether a loop is perfectly round from inside the airplane. The only way to learn how to fly better maneuvers is by getting feedback from people on the ground. A precise circle is difficult because you need to pull harder on the stick as the plane moves faster. And that's on a calm day. Wind changes the shape of the loop, and it's the pilot's job to correct for its effects so it looks perfect to the judges.

I may not have known how to fly an outside loop or double snap roll, but it turned out I was very good at eyeballing maneuvers, detecting when someone was a few degrees off vertical, or judging the crispness of a snap roll and giving feedback where Frank and Stu went wrong.

"You have a good eye," Frank said with rare approval. He was usually critical of everything, whether it was airplanes, maneuvers, or the state of affairs in Silicon Valley. He thought all the companies he did business with were full of incompetents, and went off on rants at the drop of an altimeter.

"That's great to hear," I said, pleased that these advanced pilots thought I could make a contribution to their flying.

"Why don't I go up in the Decathlon with you and show you a few things?" he offered.

I was delighted. That was exactly what I needed, even more than critique.

But once we'd been in the air for a few minutes, Frank began to list all the Decathlon's flaws. "The controls are sluggish, and it makes all the maneuvers look sloppy, no matter what you do. You need a Pitts."

"I wish," I said. I felt embarrassed to admit I couldn't afford one. It was annoying sometimes to socialize with people who made assumptions about how easy it was to spend money. If I kept going with this sport, it was going to be a continuing hazard. At least Stu was more on my level. A retired truck driver, he pinched pennies as much as I did, and could only fly because he'd built his own plane.

However, Frank had a point about Juliett Lima. One day its tailwheel broke off during a landing, making for an exciting, loud—and short— landing roll as the metal pole dug into the pavement on touchdown. I lost several days of practice and had to get a mechanic to fix it. Another time, a month later, Frank and I were flying a rolling turn when suddenly we heard a loud bang and the airflow in the cabin increased, whipping my hair around and giving me a few seconds of pure panic. It turned out one of the rear plexiglass windows had popped out of its frame and was now gone. Fortunately, we were flying over empty fields, and the plane was still able to fly, although with a little extra drag on one side.

"I've been telling you for weeks now, stop futzing around and get a Pitts," Frank told me. "All these maneuvers would be much easier, and you'd be safer."

But Pitts airplanes cost at least $40,000, most likely $50,000, $60,000, or $70,000—even used. They were not typically available for rent, since they were such specialized machines. Plus, the reputation of the Pitts frightened me. It was so unpredictable on landing that it had one of the highest landing accident rates of any general aviation airplane. Supposedly it was incredibly easy to get into an accidental spin as well. Curtis Pitts, the designer, optimized it for aerobatics and nothing else. Although I'd gotten better at that subtle and instinctive sense of feeling how the airplane reacted to the air, and was now comfortable landing the Citabria and Decathlon, both of them were relatively docile compared to the Pitts.

I shook my head at Frank. The Pitts wasn't within my abilities, financial or physical. I'd never flown a Pitts, and likely never would. I'd be flying the Decathlon, with all its limitations, for the foreseeable future.

But then one day I heard about a two-seat Pitts for rent at Santa Rosa Airport. Interestingly, it was available for solo checkout, but only to instructors. Since I was one, I decided to schedule a lesson. I desperately wanted to fly a Pitts in competition, and that required being able to solo.

It took a good hour and fifteen minutes to drive up north to the Santa Rosa Airport. I crossed the San Rafael Bridge and followed the 101 north. Up here, in Marin and then Sonoma Counties, everything was greener, cooler, and mistier. I turned onto the aptly named Gravenstein Highway and wound my way through apple orchards and farm buildings that looked like they hadn't been updated since the forties and fifties. The rural area brought back memories of my childhood days of working in apple orchards, and inevitably led to thoughts about my hopes and dreams. I'd had such big ambitions as a child, despite the discouraging environment both in school and in the community. My dad was certain I was destined for a great career as a scientist, that I would make discoveries no one else had, and make the world a better place. And yet, I'd dropped out of my PhD program, and whenever I thought about it, I felt ashamed and sad. I was a failure at something that mattered to me. I forced my thoughts away from the past and onto my hopes for flying my dream airplane in the future, and they consoled me.

When I finally reached the airport, I parked under a hawthorn tree outside the flight school. Outside my car, it was still cool—quite a change from the ninety- to hundred-degree temperatures at New Jerusalem.

My soon-to-be instructor, Louie Robinson, a scrawny and vibrant seventy-year-old with thin white hair, had sounded a lot younger on the phone. He greeted me with an unlit wooden pipe clamped between his teeth.

"It's too bad the owner won't let me smoke in his airplane," he told me as we entered the small neat classroom with a view of trees out the window. "My pipe makes for a very sensitive g-meter, because I can gauge the g-force by how much it pushes against my teeth."

I wasn't sure if he was pulling my leg. Would he really smoke his pipe while doing aerobatics? His expression was deadpan, but his eyes were twinkling. Later, after I got to know him, I would realize that he was likely telling the truth on both counts. One thing was clear immediately: There wasn't much about the Pitts, or indeed about flying, that Louie didn't know.

Our lessons over the next few weeks included subtle details of how to fly a plane notorious for being difficult to land, a plane so sensitive that accidental spins were common. But they also encompassed a flood of aviation history viewed from Louie's personal experience, expertise honed over a lifetime of flying and teaching in hundreds of different aircraft, including aerobatics, tailwheel flying, and aerodynamics. But for the first lesson, Louie concentrated on the Pitts.

He spent some time drawing diagrams of each of the maneuvers we'd do on the whiteboard. "For the hammerhead, you'll dive to a hundred and sixty miles per hour and pull to vertical. Hold the vertical upline until it's time to pivot a hundred and eighty degrees and transition to the vertical downline." He squinted at me. "Which plane have you been flying?"

"A Super Decathlon."

He smiled. "Ah, most transitioning Decathlon pilots pivot too early in the hammerhead."

I nodded, making a note to myself that I'd prove I was better than "most pilots." After a thorough ground briefing, we walked out to the aircraft.

Six Three Zero Zero Victor was a 1983 Pitts S-2A, the two-seat training version of the famous single-seat biplane designed for aerobatics. The picture of snub-nosed elegance, it sat, compact and gleaming, in a small portable hangar at the end of the field. Only seventeen feet long, white with red stripes, its two stubby, rounded wings spanned twenty feet, and it reached a mere six feet in height. It was small enough to fit in a living room. But this was the plane that had enabled the US to dominate world aerobatic competition in the 1960s and '70s. I fell in love at first sight.

I'd been dreaming of flying a Pitts for months, ever since I saw one close up at the Taft Contest and had admired the grace and precision with which it could execute aerobatic maneuvers. Even though my sensible mind knew it was beyond my reach, I'd spent many hours fantasizing.

Now, at last, I was about to fly one myself. The mere thought was terrifying. My new friends in the International Aerobatic Club (IAC), Chapter 38, had warned me about the reputation of the Pitts. It ate unskilled pilots for breakfast and was the epitome of the famous aviation saying, "Aviation in itself is not inherently dangerous. But to an even greater degree than the sea, it is terribly unforgiving of any carelessness, incapacity or neglect."

The Pitts did exactly what you told it, and if you told it the wrong thing, the costs could be dire. Pitts pilots were larger than life, possessing superhuman skills, the types of skills that I'd only recently dared to dream of attaining.

And now I was about to fly a Pitts. Thank goodness Louie had fifty years of instructing experience. Otherwise, who knew what terrible situations I could get us into?

Louie paid attention to details no one I knew had ever considered. He was the first instructor I'd encountered who took the time to meticulously measure my position in the cockpit, taking about half an hour (without charge) to seat me in the Pitts, having me get in and out several times while he adjusted my seating position with several one-inch and two-inch thick U-shaped custom-molded pieces of Styrofoam (affectionately known as "butt shims"). He said it was critical to raise the pilot's eye level to gain the information needed for safe flying and smooth three-point landings.

I was eager to fly, and worried that we'd run out of time for the lesson since we were spending so long on the ground, but he refused to be hurried. "If the plane isn't adjusted to you, you won't be able to land well. You might blame yourself, but it's your environment that's setting you up for failure."

Because I was five feet two inches, and the Pitts cockpit, as befitted a precision machine, was carefully designed for a pilot five feet ten, plus or minus four inches, it took a stack of about seven inches of Styrofoam cushions before Louie was satisfied. He had me gaze out over the front of the nose and off to the side, where I was to note exactly where the horizon met the cowling. This was "landing attitude," he informed me, and memorizing that "sight picture" was key to making perfect landings.

Finally, I was seated to his satisfaction and ready to strap in. First, the parachute: make sure its straps are not entangled with the seat belts. Next, the five-point aerobatic harness: two seat belts, two shoulder belts, and a crotch strap.

"Tighten the seat belts as much as you can," Louie said. "Use your left hand to feed in the lap belt while you sashay the other end of the strap back and forth with your right hand. You can get another inch or two that way."

He eyed me as though expecting an argument, but remembering my experiences in the Citabria and Decathlon and how insecure it felt to be the least bit loose in the seat belts, I said nothing. I tightened the belt.

"Good. Is it tight enough?" At my nod, he grinned. "Now tighten it some more."

The second seat belt, the backup safety belt, used a ratchet attached to the nylon webbing, the same assembly employed by haulers to strap cargo into place on trucks and container ships. It had to be strong enough, after all, to hold an adult in place under maximum g-loads, the body potentially exerting thousands of pounds of force on the nylon webbing and buckle. Louie supervised me closely as I tightened the ratchet, and he had me practice several times, constricting and releasing it. Finally, I secured the belt across my lap for the last time. He checked the tension with knobby fingers and smiled. "Good. You'll probably want to give the ratchet a couple more pulls once we get up to altitude."

Surely he was joking! The belt was already cutting painfully into my thighs. But I remained quiet. In under an hour, Louie had already shared more aviation wisdom with me than I'd learned in hundreds of hours of flight. I wanted to hear more.

He strapped in and gave me the signal to start the engine, and we taxied out to the runway. Even on the ground the infamous Pitts felt like a serious machine, a pulsating contraption far too eager to fly. I had the sense of operating a precision instrument, and at last I understood what Frank had said about slop in the controls of the Decathlon. A twitch of my foot on a rudder pedal brought an instant response. The plane lunged to the side, and I had to immediately correct with pressure on the opposite rudder, and then back to the first. It was a high-speed dance, even on the ground.

And it was a dance without sight. The pilot-in-command in the Pitts S-2A sat in the rear seat. With the plane sitting tipped back on its tailwheel, the nose completely blocked any view I might have through the windshield. The Pitts utilized a single overhead canopy rather than a door for egress, a giant piece of plexiglass that curved over both pilots' heads. When I glanced forward, I saw the top of Louie's head and his headset, and beyond that, a small triangle of struts below the top wing, framing nothing but blue sky. I had to taxi in a series of S-turns, winding my way back and forth across the centerline of the taxiway, turning alternately to the left and right to clear the blind spot in front of me. It felt disorienting and unusual not to be able to see where I was going unless I turned sideways.

On takeoff, I advanced the throttle and was astonished by the roar and thrust of the two-hundred-horsepower engine. The Pitts thundered to life under my touch, the stick becoming effective almost instantly. It vibrated in my hand as the propeller slipstream generated so much airflow over the wings that they were almost ready to generate enough lift and fly before the plane even started moving.

But first I had to keep the plane tracking straight on the runway. I had ridden on a motorcycle once, and it gave me the same sensation of mounting a powerful beast that vibrated between my legs, sensitive to every move and weight shift. More primal than driving a car, it lent me a sense of constrained power intimately connected with my physical body.

The Pitts was nimble and ferocious, a vibrating dynamo of power now at my tentative command. It swerved and bucked at my inexpert guidance, wobbled back and forth on the runway, until I shook myself and firmly took command. A quick jab of left rudder and another on the right brought it back to the centerline. Then we attained flying speed, and I eased gently back on the stick. The plane leaped into the air with an alacrity I'd never felt in any aircraft.

In the air, the Pitts came into its element. It transformed from an overpowered and difficult-to-control land creature into something like a mythical bird. It bit and slashed its way into the air. We ascended so quickly my ears popped.

Louie's voice came over the intercom, difficult to hear over the wild roar of the engine, directing me to the practice area. We were already at altitude. I'd never flown an airplane that commanded this much thrust. It was intoxicating to have so much power at my beck and call. When I banked for a turn, the lightness of the ailerons astounded me, as did the speed with which we got to 60 degrees of bank. Then the g-force slammed me into the seat with the might of a giant fist as we pulled around the turn. When I applied full left aileron for a roll, the plane gyrated on its axis. How could anyone call this a "slow" roll when it was over in about a second and a half? The power and maneuverability of this plane were unbelievable. Too much power, it turned out. I was about to find out why the Pitts had such a fearsome reputation.

Louie asked me to perform a hammerhead. I remembered what he'd said about transitioning Decathlon pilots pivoting too early, and my competitive streak surfaced. I was determined to show him I was better than all those other Decathlon pilots. I pulled to vertical, holding the wingtip at a precise 90-degree angle with the horizon. We rocketed up and up and up. I waited and waited and waited. I'd show him I wasn't going to pivot too early! A quick glance at the airspeed indicator revealed it was pegged at the slow end. Time to pivot.

I applied full left rudder and some forward stick, and then fed in a little right aileron as the plane tipped over on its back. The Pitts pivoted slowly, excruciatingly slowly.

From what seemed like very far away, Louie's soft voice said calmly, "Looks like you're entering a spin."

All at once, I realized that the plane was doing something unexpected, something that I hadn't told it to do—or so I believed. It tipped over on its back, sidled to the left, and then with a roar and a whoosh, we'd been slammed flat on our backs, whirling at full power, the nose tracking the horizon in a demented circle. Confused, I glanced at the altimeter, only to see I was losing altitude at a horrific rate. It hit me with a shock of adrenaline: This was the dreaded inverted flat spin!

I'd accidentally entered the worst kind of spin, the one that had killed hundreds of pilots since the birth of aviation.

For a couple of seconds I froze on the controls. Louie did nothing. Why didn't he save me? The ground rotated at a crazy rate. I was beyond disoriented, lost in a world which had become a complete blur. All I could think was: *This is how pilots die.*

Then my training came back to me. Emergency spin recovery in the Pitts: throttle to idle, hands and feet off the controls.

The instant I took action, the plane recovered; the wings snapped level and the whirling stopped. The plane settled into a steep dive, wings level and steady, nose pointed straight at the ground. We still had five thousand feet above the vineyards—plenty of altitude. Trembling, I slowly pulled back on the stick, bringing us to horizontal flight, and fed in throttle, breathing rapidly, my heart pounding faster than the Pitts's rotation rate, my hands tight and sweating on the controls.

Louie's voice floated back to me, calm: "Good recovery, though you waited so long I almost had to take over."

On the ground later, I realized that he had totally set me up for that spin entry with his warning comment about Decathlon pilots, playing on my ego, ensuring I'd hold the upline far longer than I should have. Setting up students to make their most dangerous mistakes while the instructor is still in the cockpit is one of the hallmarks of a great teacher. Throughout my thousands of hours in Pitts and other high-performance aerobatic airplanes afterward, I would be exquisitely sensitive to those first split seconds of an initial spin entry and would recover instantly, once as low as a few hundred feet above the ground. Thank you, Louie Robinson.

During the time I was his student, Louie taught me all sorts of subtle techniques to get the most out of the Pitts. To find the precise moment to apply full left rudder to pivot in a hammerhead, he advised me to "interrogate the vertical." What he meant by this was to delicately shake the stick back and forth, just a few millimeters, barely enough to feel the air pressure against the ailerons. As the plane slows down, the airflow past the ailerons lessens, rendering the stick forces lighter and lighter. That subtle "interrogation" enables you to sense the reduction in airspeed, and when it reaches the precise speed, you "kick," which means you apply full left rudder, opposite aileron, and forward stick. You'll pivot cleanly around the top as though someone inserted a pin in the fuselage of the airplane and you're revolving around it. This makes for a flawless hammerhead.

But it was my landings that improved the most with Louie. I'd accepted that sometimes my landings were good, and sometimes merely adequate. As long as they were safe, I thought everything was fine. Now I realized for the first time that there was a higher degree of precision in flying, that true expertise was possible, and it wasn't guesswork or luck. Louie had a set of guidelines to judge a landing. He'd developed a nine-point scale measured in small slices he called "increments," and he taught me to memorize the sight picture of each of those increments. We would use all of them as he taught me to land the Pitts cleanly every time.

Learning from Louie felt like the first day I wore glasses. As a near-sighted child, the distant world had been a blur to me as far back as I could remember. But one day when I was five years old, my mother took me to have my eyes checked, and I came home with glasses. It was a shock and a wonder to discover so much detail in what had previously been a big, sloppy mess off in the distance.

Before Louie, I'd never understood the minutiae of flying—how to judge height above the runway in inches rather than feet or to know the precise position of the airplane the way a dancer knows the exact placement of each limb. Much later, I'd use Louie's techniques in aerobatic competition, and other pilots would remark on the beauty of my flying.

Louie would teach me not only about the six different spin modes of the Pitts (normal, flat, and accelerated in both upright and inverted positions)—as well as his ingenious techniques for flying, landing, and performing aerobatics with flair and finesse—but also how to be an excellent educator. For the rest of my career as an instructor, I would use Louie's techniques to teach landings and spins to my own students. My flight instructor Hank was the first one who showed me that teaching mattered. Louie taught me it was possible to take instructional quality to an entirely new level. He was not merely an instructor but a mentor and friend. Along the way, he peppered his lessons with stories about his early days teaching pilots to fly in World War II, how to land and take off in a J3 Cub on a steep hillside, and how to handle any emergency.

We didn't only talk about flying. Louie had a youthful and creative mind, flashing over new ideas. It belied his appearance as a scrawny, slight man who walked slowly and with a stoop. Once he told me in a tone of wonderment, "I caught sight of myself in a mirror the other day. My God, I walk like an old man!"

He surprised me by how much he came to care about me—even about my problems outside of flying. Soon I had told him my entire life story, confiding in him my hopes, fears, and dreams. I told him I'd set my heart on flying the Pitts at the major California contest at the end of the summer in Delano. I told him I longed to complete my PhD and one day become a professor, but that I doubted it would ever happen. "No one's ever returned to the Berkeley program after such an extended leave," I said as we ate sandwiches at the classroom table during a break one day. "Even if I could reenter, the dissertation requires original research. I'm just not good enough."

He tipped his head to one side. "Are you sure about that? Maybe they simply haven't set you up with the right sight picture."

I snorted. "Besides, I could never afford to go back to school."

He was concerned about my financial status, the fact that I didn't have any retirement savings, and that I poured everything I owned into my passion for flying. "I have a solution for you," he told me one day. "You need to buy a triplex, rent out two units and live in the third. That way you'll have a nest egg, something saved for retirement. But make sure you never pay more than 6 percent on a loan, because once you sign on the dotted line, they own you."

I smiled because I didn't want to hurt his feelings, but inwardly I laughed. Retirement? I was still in my twenties, and the idea of retiring seemed farther away than the moon.

I loved him so much that when he died in early 1990, I cried for days. His wife found him dead in his car from a heart attack one evening outside their home in Healdsburg. He must have driven home as usual from the airport at the end of a day of lessons, slowed to pull into his parking spot, slumped over the wheel, and rolled gently into a tree. A quiet end for a man whose wisdom bettered the lives of many pilots in the Bay Area.

* * *

The insurance company required a ten-hour checkout in the Pitts before I was allowed to solo. It was eating through my funds rapidly, but it was more than worth it to spend that much time with Louie. One issue we grappled with repeatedly was the question of how I would be able to solo the Pitts. When Louie checked out my position in the cockpit, he noted that with the stick all the way back, jammed into my belly, my legs were so short that I couldn't quite get that crucial last half inch of extension on the rudder pedals.

"You need full travel on the rudders in a Pitts, or it could be dangerous. Without full rudder, you might not be able to exit a spin, or land safely in a crosswind. Do you really need to solo? You can get all the fun flying you want with a taller person along in the cockpit."

I shook my head. To fly the Delano Contest during Labor Day weekend that September, I'd need to solo the airplane. Besides, something inside me knew I had to take on the Pitts on my own.

I still had many hours left to fly with Louie to satisfy the insurance requirements, so in the meantime, on the long drives between Berkeley and Santa Rosa, I generated ideas and discarded far-fetched options. My legs were too short, but what if I wore shoes with thicker soles that could give me a few inches of height? I only needed an inch or two.

I called a number of shoemakers all over the city of Berkeley, but no one could sell them to me. "Elevator shoes" were apparently a specialty cosmetic item, typically designed for someone with one leg shorter than the other so that the lift was invisible to the outside eye. They were extremely expensive, a custom item that needed to be specially ordered.

One afternoon, I walked into a tiny, old-fashioned shop on Shattuck Avenue barely the size of a bathroom. The wizened old man behind the counter listened to my story and then grinned. "Shoot. You don't need no elevator shoes. What you need is some built-up soles glued onto a pair of regular shoes. That's a lot easier—and much cheaper."

I listened with dawning hope. "Could you make a pair like that for me?"

"Sure thing! Just buy yourself a pair of good leather shoes and bring 'em in next Monday. I'll have 'em built up for you in a day or two."

I left the shop smiling for the first time in days, bouncing on the tips of my toes down Shattuck Avenue. But I still had another problem to solve: the minimum pilot weight in the rear seat of a Pitts S-2A was 140 pounds, and it was designed for an optimum of 180 pounds. With a 100-pound pilot, the center of gravity of the plane (the CG, or point at which the airplane would balance if suspended there) would fall outside the authorized envelope. It's dangerous and illegal to fly an airplane outside of its CG range. Too far forward and the nose can become too heavy to lift, rendering it impossible to land. What this all boiled down to was I simply could not fly alone weighing just 100 pounds; 140 pounds wouldn't be ideal, either, due to the heavy stick forces, but at least it was legal and safe.

So, how could I increase my weight to 140 pounds? Sure, I'd have fun eating gallons of ice cream, but deliberately fattening myself was probably not the best solution. There had to be another way. I could wear weighted clothes, but what if they came loose in flight? Any type of weight in the cockpit was potentially hazardous if it became detached from its moorings. Some airplane owners attached a lead weight to the tail, moving the CG rearward. But obviously, I couldn't do that on a rental plane. No, any change I made had to be portable and unique to me.

A scuba-diving friend mentioned he wore a weighted belt to manage his buoyancy underwater. A belt with lead weights! This sounded like a terrific idea. I went to the local dive shop to check out the possibilities. Trying on a belt with four 10-pound weights threaded through it, my heart sank. Yes, the belt and weights would effectively increase my mass, but as soon as I rolled upside down, those big clunky weights would slide up my torso, probably hitting me in the head. Add in the g-force multiplier, and I'd get four 60-pound weights bashing my brains out.

Nope. Not gonna work.

Louie commiserated but suggested tentatively, "Maybe you should just give this up."

On the long drive home, a brainstorm hit me. What if I strapped the webbed belt to the airplane itself, rather than around my waist? The belts were strong and secure, and I could strap them tight around the metal bracing in the seat pan of the Pitts. It wasn't a permanent attachment to the airframe; the belt would only be in use while I flew. I'd place my Styrofoam cushions on top of the weights, adding yet another layer of safety, as the seat belts would secure both me and the weights.

I took the idea to Louie. He listened, at first dubiously, then with rising excitement. "Yes, it could work. Bring your shoes and belt to our next lesson, and we'll try it out."

That Saturday, I showed up with the brand-new shoes and a blue webbed belt linked to forty pounds of dive weights. Louie and I got the airplane set up. I clumsily strutted out to the ramp like I was wearing platform shoes from the 1970s. We each took a turn pulling the webbed belt as tight as possible around the seat pan, and double-checked the buckle. Louie confirmed that it was secure, and I stacked the Styrofoam on top and strapped in.

Once in the air, we rolled inverted and checked everything out. There were no problems pushing on the rudders, and I couldn't even feel the dive weights under my seat. I gave Louie a thumbs-up. We had a workable plan!

After we landed, Louie signed me off to solo in the Pitts. I was on my way.

Chapter 10

"Good vertical, nice pivot, two degrees negative on the downline. Maybe nine point five on the hammerhead. Good job." Frank's voice crackled over the radio as I flew the Sportsman sequence at New Jerusalem in my rented Pitts S-2A one hot August afternoon in 1988.

After the checkout with Louie Robinson when I was approved to solo the Pitts, I'd been practicing all day every Sunday with Frank and Stu at New J. It had been a couple of months now, and Frank's critiques had gone from scathing to cautiously favorable. In some ways, his quest for the perfect aerobatic figure reminded me of my father, who never stopped pushing himself—or me. In Frank, I found a kindred ambitious spirit. Central California's extreme heat ruled out contests during July and August, but on Labor Day weekend, the largest California contest of the year would be held in Delano, a small agricultural town a few miles north of Bakersfield. This was the contest, Frank told me, where we'd see the best flying of the year. Pilots had been practicing the sequences all summer, honing their skills in the hot California sun. I was anxious because it would only be my second Sportsman contest. I wanted to do well, but I only dared admit to hoping to place above the middle of the pack.

Competition aerobatics is extraordinarily demanding, and flying a perfect-ten maneuver is nearly impossible. No one in aerobatic history has ever completed a contest flight without a single mistake. Scores of ten on individual maneuvers are rare, even for the best pilots. It only takes a split-second error to overshoot a roll, underrotate a snap, or deviate from the precise circle required to fly a perfectly round loop. And every tiny error earns another deduction from the eagle-eyed judges on the ground.

Even so, I loved flying the Pitts S-2A. At last I understood what Frank and everyone else had been saying: the airplane was purpose-built for aerobatics. It *wants* to fly beautiful maneuvers. It's only the imperfect human at the controls who mars that achievement. This airplane would fly a flawless routine if I didn't get in the way. And it had become my goal to reveal those perfect maneuvers, one by one. As I flew the Pitts, it reminded me of something my dad had told me when I was thirteen or fourteen as we did math together: Michelangelo believed every block of stone contained a statue within, waiting to be revealed by the sculptor.

"There's an underlying structure in the world, a beautiful one," my dad had said. "And mathematics is the best way to reveal that structure."

"Not sculpture?" I asked.

"With pencil and paper you can discover the truth. But it's important to keep going until you find that underlying beauty. Don't give up too early."

"Aren't there times when it's just too hard to figure out?" I'd been wrestling with a particularly difficult math problem he'd set me. "When it's a waste of time to keep going?"

"I know you're good enough to solve this problem. Keep thinking. That cubic equation proof you were struggling with last week? I remember you complaining you'd never figure it out. But you did, and I knew you would. It's helpful, sometimes, to take some time and look back on what you've already accomplished."

I scowled but went back to work. It took me longer than I expected, but I eventually figured out the answer. When I brought it to him in triumph, he beamed and said, "My buttons are popping."

Now, flying the Pitts, I had to marvel over how far I'd come. What had happened to the klutz riddled by fear? to the INTF: Incompetent, Nerd, Terrified, Failure? I'd once wondered if it was even possible for me to solo a plane, any plane. But I'd improved so much over the past three years, and now I was flying my dream airplane. My progress fired me up to push even harder. If I'd accomplished this much already, who knew how much further I could go? I even had a sneaking suspicion that maybe a PhD wasn't as far out of reach as I'd once thought.

I practiced regularly in the relentless heat. At first, my new shoes felt heavy, especially during inverted flight. But after a few days of sore muscles, my legs strengthened, as did my biceps. It often took a hard, fast pull to satisfy Frank's demands for a crisp transition to vertical. My stick forces were exceptionally high even with the extra forty pounds of lead weight strapped to the seat pan, so it took both of my hands on the stick. I'd started lifting weights at home to build up my upper body strength. I bought a pair of bike gloves so my hands wouldn't slip off the stick and create a potentially dangerous situation.

"You're flying well," Frank told me one afternoon in late August. "I think you'll put on a good showing at Delano."

* * *

Santa Rosa Airport was cool and misty in the early-morning sunlight as I prepared the Pitts for its flight to Delano on Labor Day weekend. Getting an aerobatic airplane ready for travel is very different from prepping it for maneuvers. Aerobatic planes typically have little baggage space, so every available nook and cranny must be utilized if you intend to carry any cargo. Fortunately, I travel light. All I needed was a couple of extra T-shirts and sets of underwear, a small toiletry bag, my regular sneakers, a water bottle, of course, and my wallet and keys. That was enough for a four-day trip. For the airplane, I brought plastic quarts of aviation oil, the eighteen-inch wooden dowel I'd hand-calibrated as a fuel dipstick, rags, a knee board, and extra charts. It all got crammed into the meager turtledeck behind the pilot seat in the cockpit of the Pitts. An extra duffel bag sat under my thighs on the plexiglass floor panels.

I pulled on my stiff flight gloves, sweatshirt, and a jacket. It'd be colder at altitude, but the forecast read one hundred degrees at Delano this afternoon. It was maybe sixty degrees at Santa Rosa. Delano felt like a million miles away. I performed a final preflight inspection, strapped in, and taxied out.

I arrived at the Delano airport a little over an hour later, still chilled from the high-altitude flight. It was stiflingly hot as I descended into the traffic pattern. Once on the ground, I cracked the canopy to let a blast of superheated air into the cockpit. It was still early, but the temperature at Delano had already reached ninety.

Delano (pronounced Duh-LANE-oh, not like Franklin Roosevelt's middle name) is a small town at the south end of California's Central Valley known primarily for growing table grapes. The area is also famous as the site of the Delano grape strike, which began in 1965 when Filipino farmworkers walked off their jobs, demanding a pay increase to the federal minimum wage of $1.25 per hour. Cesar Chavez and his union joined the strike within a week, and news of the strike spread across the US, where even in Indiana my parents participated in the consumer grape boycott that lasted for five years.

In 1988 Delano's population hovered around twenty thousand, about the same as my old hometown in Indiana, and the area was known for agriculture and for being the site of the largest Voice of America broadcast facility in the US.

I stayed in the second cheapest motel at thirty dollars per night. Most of the meals I ate over the next four days were at a diner with no name except *eat* in all capital letters facing the freeway.

When I asked the local pilots about the major industries in town, they shrugged. "Farming," said one. Another added, "We're lobbying heavily for them to open a new prison in town."

The shock must have shown on my face.

A third pilot smiled. "It'd be great for the local economy."

Later on, I asked Tom Sumner, a farmer and one of the top Unlimited pilots at the event, about his work. His farm wasn't far from the airport. He was young, and many of the young pilots I'd met were eager to join the airlines to make a good salary. I asked Tom if his plans included this. He glanced at me incredulously. "No way. I can make tons more money as a farmer than I ever could as an airline pilot."

It was the first I'd ever heard that some farmers were rich. I always assumed they were all poor and struggling, based on the farmers I knew in Indiana and what I had seen in the media. It turned out that owning a farm could be an extremely lucrative profession. Many of the aerobatic pilots at the contest—90 percent male—were farmers, and their gleaming aircraft—Pitts biplanes and higher-end monoplanes like the German-built Extra and Russian-built Sukhoi—dotted the flight line.

When I entered aviation, it was the first time I'd met wealthy people. Although most pilots were middle class like me, in the upper echelons of aerobatic competition, significant amounts of discretionary income were required. Many of the people at those levels were farmers, airline pilots, business owners, or otherwise independently wealthy. Not for the first time, I was reminded I was getting in over my head financially. Even if I developed the skills to fly aerobatics well, could I afford this sport?

Delano Airport, though hot and dusty, possessed a long, well-maintained runway, much smoother than New J, where I often had to avoid potholes on landing. I taxied to the small terminal building, shut down the Pitts, and pointed it into the light northwest breeze.

I climbed out of the cockpit, shedding my jacket and sweatshirt with relief. Sitting on the boiling hot tarmac, I unlaced my elevator shoes and switched to my regular sneakers. I sighed with bliss as the hot, arid air hit my feet, drying my sopping wet socks.

A group of pilots clustered near the terminal. Some of them were checking their airplanes, waiting for the contest technical inspection to start. I got into the registration line and filled out the Sportsman paperwork. This was a typical five-category regional contest, with pilots flying the gamut from Basic through Unlimited. Basic and Sportsman pilots would fly twice, and Intermediate, Advanced, and Unlimited three times each.

"Is this your first time flying Sportsman?" a young man in a panama hat asked.

I smiled. "Second. But it's my first time flying a Pitts in a contest."

He glanced at my Pitts, white with its jaunty red stripe. "That's a nice S-2A. Did you just buy it?"

"It's a rental."

His eyebrows climbed his forehead. "Where can you rent a Pitts around here?"

"Santa Rosa. But only flight instructors can solo by insurance requirements."

"That's a weird-ass insurance requirement."

I shrugged. "Works for me."

He grinned. "Do you think you'll win?"

I broke into laughter, perhaps louder than I should have. "Of course not! I only started a couple of months ago. Who do *you* think will win?"

He pointed across the taxiway at a wiry man with a shining bald head, wearing a pair of immaculate gray suspenders and busily waxing a gleaming Super Decathlon. "Nick Burkett, for sure. He's won every other Sportsman contest this year, and he's hoping to make it a clean sweep with this one. He's an awesome pilot; been flying that Decathlon for twenty years." He pursed his lips. "He flies that plane hard. It's a good thing he maintains it himself, or it would have fallen apart by now, the way he punishes it."

"Punishes it?"

He shot me a sidelong glance. "You know, overrevs his engine, goes past redline—those sorts of things."

"Redline" was another word for the "never exceed" speed in all airplanes. I'd been taught exceeding that velocity was dangerous and could lead to structural failure or loss of control of the plane. My mouth dropped open. "Really?"

"How else are you going to get high scores in a Decathlon?"

"I always used to enter a loop at one forty and a hammerhead at one forty-five." I laughed, feeling a little embarrassed and naïve. "But I didn't score very well at the last contest."

He shook his head. "You need at least a hundred and eighty miles an hour to get a good vertical upline in a Decathlon."

"My instructor told me to keep the speed ten percent below redline to avoid damaging the plane."

He sent me a look of pity. "That's why you'll never do well in competition flying rentals. You need to own your own airplane."

There were nineteen pilots flying in the Sportsman category, the biggest category of the contest and the year. I asked a few of the other pilots about my competitors in the category. They'd flown aerobatics five, ten, even twenty years. Most were flying a Pitts, either a single-seat or a two-seat like mine. But there were a couple flying Extra 300s, sleek monoplanes that cost more than $250,000.

I was clearly out of my league flying a rental airplane in a contest after having taken my first aerobatic lesson only a few months ago. *But it doesn't matter*, I told myself. I was here to have fun and learn. I was going to talk about airplanes and flying all weekend and do the best I could.

When it was my turn to fly, I pushed my plane to the starting line, awkward in my special shoes. I strapped in and waited for the signal. Bill Larson put down the radio handset atop his beige 1970s Pontiac sedan and approached my cockpit. As the contest starter, Bill had a heavy responsibility to keep the planes sequenced and separated, as well as make sure that anxious pilots didn't overlook critical safety concerns. He'd volunteered for longer than anyone remembered at many US contests, flying out to multiple airports and paying for his own expenses.

"Harnesses and belts?" he asked in his gravelly voice, hoarse from decades of smoking.

I checked my seat belts and made sure they were secure.

"You got your sequence?"

I tapped the white card in the clear plexiglass holder on the instrument panel. "Got it!"

He leaned into the airplane. "Are you nervous?"

"Yes!" I squeaked.

He broke into a wide grin. "Then you're gonna fly well." He backed away and signaled with his finger to start my engine.

As I taxied out to the runway, I was so keyed up I could barely go through my checklist. I told myself to calm down, that it was just like flying in the practice box at New J.

But it wasn't. At practice, there weren't five judges grading every maneuver, watching every bobble, grading you against perfection. Performance was very different from practice.

Still, I forced myself to focus on routine, and on the procedures I followed every flight. I took off and circled in the holding pattern, rolling upside down once to check that my belts were secure and that my heavy shoes were pressed against the rudder pedals.

Then the panels on the ground went from red to white, and the call came over the radio that I was cleared to enter the box. The first Sportsman maneuver, as in the Basic sequence, was a spin, so I started high and slow, wagging my wings as I entered the box. I tugged the throttle all the way to the idle stop, slowly raising the nose higher and higher with the stick. The Pitts broke crisply into a stall, and immediately I pushed left rudder full to the stop and pulled the stick all the way back into my belly, and the plane entered a beautiful spin.

It felt wonderful. My movements had become precise and sharp, and somewhere in a distant corner of my mind, I noted that I was no longer scared of the spin but only nervous that my maneuvers wouldn't score well.

I recovered from the spin, moved the stick forward to push the nose down vertical, and shoved the throttle to maximum. Now I was roaring straight at the ground. I did a quick check of my left wingtip to make sure I was exactly vertical, and then I glanced over the nose. Now! A crisp pull off the downline, just like Frank wanted, and hard back to horizontal—six g's. I couldn't help grinning. A perfect spin.

I had plenty of airspeed for the hammerhead. Through the plexiglass panel between my feet, I caught a glimpse of the corner box marker coming up fast. Time to pull.

Wham! Back on the stick, soaring up again into a perfect vertical. *The hammerhead is my favorite maneuver*, I thought as I sailed straight up into the sky, the ground dropping away from me at incredible speed, then gradually slowing, slowing, slowing. I'd stopped "interrogating the vertical," as Louie had taught me, because Frank warned me that the judges could see the sunlight flashing off my wings and would mark me down. But it didn't matter, because I no longer needed it. I could now sense exactly when the plane had slowed enough to pivot.

Somewhere during the long hours of practice in the dry heat of New Jerusalem, I'd finally acquired that elusive "seat of the pants" feel and become fully connected to the plane. Now it felt like an extension of my body. The airplane vibrated like it was talking to me, telling me *"Now!"* When the controls felt right, I applied full left rudder, opposite aileron to keep the wings level, and a hint of forward elevator. I pivoted on a dime. Now I was pointed straight at the ground.

I was exactly vertical. I held it, held it, held it, then pulled back to horizontal. Yes! Another great maneuver. Who knew how well it would score, but I had fun flying it, and that was all that mattered.

I gasped, breathing hard through my mouth and nose. My muscles trembled from tightening my quads and abs during the pulls to keep blood circulating to my brain. But I no longer noticed exactly what my body was doing, because I'd entered a flow state.

In the air, it finally felt like I belonged. It no longer mattered that I'd spent so many years fighting to prove myself as a woman and Latina in math and software engineering. It no longer mattered that I got funny looks on the ground when I taxied past a row of men. It didn't matter that Don Schwartz had beat into me that I would always be an outsider, barely above subhuman. It didn't matter that my marriage was still shaky, and I hadn't told my parents I was flying. Air was the element I was born to live in. My wings trembled in the air currents like they'd grown out of the muscles in my back. This plane *was* my body. My body gleamed in the sun, a tiny bright being free of the confines of the earth. There was only the horizon, the wide sky, the box markers, and the singing in my heart. California was so beautiful, the Sierras to the east and the latticed fields extending into the blue distance. I'd found where I belonged. I never wanted to leave.

But eventually, the sequence came to an end with a final cross-box roll. I exited directly over the judges' heads, at the bottom of the box, wagging the wings enthusiastically, all the way to knife edge and back, three times. I was grinning as I entered the traffic pattern and circled for a landing.

It wasn't until much later in the day that the scores were posted. I'd been volunteering out on the line, assisting one of the judges in the Advanced category by writing down his scores on a clipboard. It was sweltering, and I'd already drained my water bottle. I was looking forward to spending time in the air-conditioned terminal.

As I jumped off the truck, my friend in the panama hat, sitting in the grass in front of the scoreboard, called out, "Congratulations!"

I looked around to see whom he was addressing.

Someone else said, "Are you Cecilia Aragon?"

When I nodded, he pointed at the scoreboard. "Congratulations. You're in first place."

I walked over to the board in a daze. *It can't be true. There must be some mistake.* But no, there it was in blue marker in the first column of the whiteboard. My name topped the list, flying aircraft N6300V, with 1121.5 points—84 percent.

And then there were eighteen pilots below me, all their names listed in a neat column. Nick Burkett had taken *second* place.

I couldn't believe it. People as surprised as I was came up and congratulated me.

"Who's this girl who came out of nowhere to beat all the top pilots who've been flying for years?" I heard someone ask.

Nick Burkett congratulated me, but said, "Remember, that's just the first flight. We still have another flight to go tomorrow!" He grinned, and I returned a shaky smile.

That night, I couldn't sleep. My heart was racing, and I felt suffused with joy. I told myself to relax, that I'd need to get a good night's sleep to perform my best the next day, but I was so incredibly excited that I tossed and turned in the narrow bed, listening to the rattle and whine of the aging air conditioner in the cheap hotel room.

* * *

My mind went back to a time I'd had the audacity to imagine I might take first place in a contest. During my senior year in high school, it looked like I might end up as valedictorian based on my GPA. My main competitor was a tall, blond boy who seemed to be a favorite among the teachers. I have to admit, he was polite, soft-spoken, and nice to everyone, including me. There were no weighted grades at my school, so an A in choir counted as much as an A in calculus. I noticed that my male classmate avoided the more advanced classes, while I'd taken every advanced class the school offered, including a couple that were notoriously difficult. Still, I received A's in every class. But on a senior English elective that was widely considered easy, I was shocked to receive my first B, even though I had earned all A's on my written assignments. The reason listed by the teacher on my report card? "Creates a disturbance in class."

Still painfully shy, I often went days without saying a word to anybody, and I *never* talked in class. The two girls who sat behind me were constantly chatting. Could the teacher have made a mistake? Or did he assume it had to be the Hispanic kid, rather than the girls whose parents and grandparents had always lived in Indiana? Either way, I didn't say anything and thought the whole thing was my fault. Because of this, I didn't make valedictorian.

* * *

Now, as I twisted in my sheets, I couldn't help worrying that I would do something the next morning to lose that first-place trophy. That's what was sure to happen, wasn't it?

I arrived at the field the next morning punchy from worry and lack of sleep. I was so afraid I'd botch my second flight, but as I taxied out, I reminded myself how much I loved flying, and how the sheer joy I felt in the air was what mattered.

I launched into the air, and all my worries dropped away as the ground disappeared beneath my wings. It was a beautiful flight, and I knew when I landed that I had flown another excellent sequence. Even though my score in the second flight was slightly less than Nick's, I managed to hang onto my overall lead.

I finished the contest in first place.

At the banquet, the contest director, Drew Eckert, called me up to the front. "And in Sportsman first place, a little gal who flies the big Pitts very well, Cecilia Aragon."

The big Pitts. I'd never thought of that seventeen-foot-long plane as "big." Nor of myself as a "little gal," but I didn't say anything. As I stood shyly in front of the crowd of pilots, Drew presented me with the most beautiful trophy I'd ever seen, an artist-made, three-dimensional wire sculpture of a Pitts. While second- and third-place winners received conventional plaques, first-place winners in each of the categories received one of these special creations that Drew had hired an artist to create. Pilots had been exclaiming over the unusually striking trophies since the contest began.

I set the trophy down on my banquet table, my heart still pounding with excitement and pride. GERRY MASSEY MEMORIAL AEROBATIC CONTEST. SPORTSMAN FIRST PLACE. SEPTEMBER 4, 1988, the trophy read.

Nick Burkett called me over from another table and said, "I've been waiting all year for this contest. This was gonna be the year I took first place overall. Then you show up out of nowhere and ruin my streak! And the worst part is this year they had the best trophies." He smiled like he was joking, but there was an edge to it. "I really wanted to take one of those special trophies home! And you ruined it!"

He grinned again to show me he was just kidding, but I wasn't altogether sure I'd want to meet him in a dark alley that night.

I'd won my first aerobatic contest, and it was a heady feeling. The thrill of winning had gotten hold of me and wouldn't let go. Against all odds, the awkward woman who couldn't operate machinery was unexpectedly good at aerobatic flying. But why? Did something about the precision and rhythm work well with my brain? It was a three-dimensional dance in the sky, art plus mathematics, science plus sport, requiring fast reflexes, rhythm and timing. Was I a dancer after all?

How did this happen? Didn't my driver's-education teacher sneer at my skills? Didn't my classmates laugh at me for failing to ride a bike until age eleven? Didn't I go through three instructors before I got my private pilot license?

How could I possibly win an aerobatic contest? Was it just that few people had ever believed in me before, and I'd finally learned to believe in myself? Was that the magic I'd been missing all my life?

The next day, I flew home, my heart still higher than my altitude. I made a perfect landing at Santa Rosa and taxied back to the hangar. As I unloaded my plane, a pilot in a brand-new pair of designer jeans walked over.

"Good-looking plane," he said. "Where did you fly?"

"I just got back from the aerobatic contest at Delano."

He gave me a once-over. I stood a full head shorter than him even in my elevator shoes, and he snorted. "A contest, huh? Where's your trophy?" A scornful smile played on his lips.

I popped open the turtledeck. I'd saved space for the trophy in the tiny luggage compartment by shipping my clothes home via UPS. I brought it out carefully. The wire sculpture gleamed in the afternoon sun.

Chapter 11

It was a sunny fall day at New Jerusalem Airport, and Frank and I were watching Stu fly. Frank lifted the cassette recorder to his lips. "Stu, you really bobbled that snap. You need to practice it a lot more. Remember to unload the stick during the snap." He turned back to me. "Stu's given himself a reputation of not flying Advanced very well. You don't want to do that. It's too soon for you to move up to Intermediate."

"I want to move up a category as soon as I win a trophy," I said. After winning the Sportsman contest on Labor Day weekend, I'd been practicing Intermediate because I wanted a new challenge, despite getting feedback from several chapter pilots, like Frank, that I should spend another year in Sportsman to hone my expertise at the foundational maneuvers. My goal was to fly Intermediate at the next contest in late October 1988 in Borrego Valley, California.

Intermediate was *much* more challenging than Sportsman, though. The number of figures a pilot had to master increased tremendously each time you moved up a category. Sustained inverted flight was required in Intermediate, as were rolls on a vertical and snap rolls on 45-degree lines. Additionally, rather than repeating the same sequence two or three times, the way Sportsman pilots did with their "Known Compulsory" flight, Intermediate pilots flew three different sequences: the Intermediate

Known Compulsory, a Freestyle, and an Unknown sequence. The Known for each category—a fixed sequence of maneuvers—was determined by the officials of the IAC at the beginning of each year. The Freestyle was custom designed by each pilot according to a set of rules for the category, and the Unknown sequence was revealed for the first time at the contest.

I had a lot of practicing to do in about five weeks. Fortunately, the Pitts made it all a joy. I couldn't believe how cleanly the airplane flew, how responsive it was to my touch, how precise my lines had become. It felt like moving up from sneakers to pointe shoes. At last, I had an artist's tool. I practiced and practiced until my rolls stopped crisply and on point every time. No more 5-degree overshoots. My favorite maneuver in the Intermediate Known was a hammerhead with quarter rolls up and down, the maneuver with the highest difficulty factor in the sequence.

At Borrego, slightly after dawn one clear October morning, over desert speckled with cholla cactus and sagebrush, surrounded by tawny mountains, I took off to fly the Intermediate sequence for the first time in a contest. The scorching summer heat of the low desert had passed. Circling high above the airport and off to the east, I waited for my turn in the box.

When the panels turned white, I began my approach for the spin. Exiting exactly at my target airspeed, I enjoyed the feel of the controls, firm under my hands. I checked between my feet through the plexiglass for the center box marker, then hauled back on the stubby black metal stick with both hands for the hammerhead, pulling six g's, clenching my abs and quads and breathing fast and hard through my mouth. My newly installed, star-shaped sighting device, mounted between the two wings of the Pitts, lined up perfectly on the horizon as I pulled sharply to the vertical and stopped exactly on the line as though I'd thrown a dart at a board. *Bam!*

As I drew the vertical line into the air, waiting for the right moment to pivot at the top of the hammerhead, I glanced back over my shoulder at the box markers on the surface of the Borrego desert. The plane slowed down and the controls softened, and the air felt quiet as a dream. I always loved this part of the hammerhead, just before the pivot, when it felt like I was floating fast and far, directly away from the earth, pointed vertically into the blue sky, fantasizing maybe this time I'd keep going, achieve escape velocity, and never have to return to the earth again. Wait, wait, wait ... then *now!* I applied controls for the pivot, shifting my gaze to the nose once again. My view out the windshield changed from bright blue to golden brown as the sky and earth swapped places and I pointed straight at the ground.

The hammerhead with rolls up and down was a gorgeous and complex figure, adding up to a high difficulty, or K-factor—thirty-two points, while a simple loop is worth only twelve.

When I landed, I was pleased with my flight. Intermediate was more fun than Sportsman. I pushed my plane back into the hangar and decided to take advantage of the beautiful weather by walking out to the judging line instead of waiting for the truck. I was assisting a judge in Advanced today, and I was looking forward to seeing all the different Freestyles created by the Advanced pilots.

After my stint out on the line, I hopped off the truck and eagerly ran to the scoreboard. Other pilots had gathered around, congratulating the top scorers. Unfortunately, I wasn't one of them. Overall, I ended up in the middle of the pack. I was crushed, but I was careful not to let anyone see how I felt. They'd think it was presumptuous of me to assume I'd perform well after only a few months flying competition. Although most of the competitors were friendly and helpful, there were a couple who had made it clear they thought I was an interloper.

"Girls have an unfair advantage in this sport," Carl, a fifty-something, heavyset man, had informed me when I taxied in after the first contest flight. "You weigh less than half what I do. They should handicap you with a hundred-pound weight to make it fair."

I didn't say anything about the forty pounds of lead I had to strap under my seat just to fly an airplane designed for men. All my life I'd been conditioned to stay quiet, even though I never liked it. This didn't stop my thoughts or my will, however.

Carl flew an Extra 300, a plane with a far bigger engine than my Pitts, which cost more than $250,000. Sitting on a lawn chair out on the tarmac, holding a beer, he turned to his neighbor and said, "I can't practice next weekend because I hafta take my wife out to our vacation home."

His comments made my competitive urge even stronger. I yearned to be the underdog who came from behind to win once again.

After the results from the third and final contest flight came in, I analyzed my scores. It turned out all my verticals were 5 degrees off. It became clear I'd made a critical mistake: I'd misaligned my new sighting device when I installed it on the wing strut. I told myself firmly that even though scoring in the middle of the pack wasn't bad for my first contest in Intermediate, I'd fix my sighting device and do better next time.

All through the California winter and early spring, I practiced. When it was rainy or foggy and I couldn't fly, I put in extra hours programming in the South Bay to save money for gas and maintenance costs. Taking on the challenge of flying had given me the courage to face other kinds of challenges. I took on multiple software clients at a time, and dove into learning new languages and new systems. Working as a contractor meant I often got stuck dealing with hand-me-down code, the software projects none of the regular employees wanted to tackle. I had to take over messy, buggy, uncommented code written by the guy who left and make it work on a short deadline.

"Sorry you've got to deal with Dominic's code," one coworker apologized. "I had to work on it once, and it's got to be the most frustrating and ugly software I've ever seen. It's a good thing he's gone."

But I enjoyed the work. It was like being thrown into a room and given a huge puzzle with no instructions and a lot of missing pieces. Kind of similar to flying an Unknown competition sequence. Things that only a few years ago I would have thought impossible, in both flying and programming, had become interesting brainteasers. My job as a software contractor involved figuring out how everything fit together, constructing the parts that didn't yet exist, and cleaning up the mess other people had made. I learned how to write efficient code rapidly and the importance of adhering to good software engineering practices such as writing useful comments, creating clean revision histories, and never "breaking the build" (the term for leaving software in a failed state), which could cause dozens or hundreds of team members to lose work.

The best part of contracting was less office politics—maybe the most frustrating part of working in software companies, and eerily reminiscent of my elementary school days. The averted glances in meetings in which I was the only woman and only Latinx present. The condescending remarks of surprise when my software was delivered early and performed efficiently. Why did everybody expect so little of me? The advantage of being a contractor was that I could perform the job, collect my paycheck and my employer's pleased evaluation, and move on to the next company where everyone needed my code.

Over the winter, Ben and I spent more time together because I wasn't at the airport as much. One afternoon, we were making bread in the kitchen, and I finally worked up the courage to talk about the bullying and some of the assaults I'd experienced as a child, and how flying was helping to heal these wounds. Even though I was now an adult, it was still painful to talk about these incidents. Perhaps it was because people, even close friends, had said to me dismissively, "That wasn't *so* bad." Or "get over it." Or, as my mother said, "They're only teasing you because they *like* you."

Ben hadn't been dismissive of me, but there were times when he hadn't wanted to hear what I had to say. He'd frequently change the conversation to a more neutral subject, like something tech related. To be fair, I didn't even understand the full psychological impact of my childhood experiences then, so it's not surprising that I couldn't explain it to him. But as we made bread together, I asked him to listen and not interrupt or try to analyze me. I explained how all those experiences had a silencing effect on me.

He stopped folding the dough and gave me a floury hug. "I'm so sorry you had to go through that."

Receiving his support made me feel warm all over, but our discussion wasn't complete. I still hadn't fully acknowledged then how much race had played into my childhood abuse. Those who've lived through racism as a child understand how corrosive it is, how damaging it is to be told you intrinsically have less value than others. In my experience, most white Americans have difficulty truly understanding the depths of this pain, and neither could my parents, who hadn't been victims of racism in their home countries. I've since seen this in other immigrants who've come to the US as adults to take technology jobs. Despite regularly experiencing discrimination on the basis of their skin color, culture, or accent, they often possess the kind of confidence that I had been missing, the confidence that comes from growing up with people around you acknowledging you as an equal. People of color who grow up in the US usually recognize that this corrosive lack of confidence is a result of internalized racism instilled from birth.

In addition, women everywhere also experience internalized sexism. This often manifests as imposter syndrome, the inability to believe that your success is deserved. In the tech world especially, even women sometimes accept worn-out excuses used to justify the continued exclusion of women, such as "There aren't as many women in technical jobs because you women *choose* to do other work—you're just more socially adept than us guys."

When I talked about flying and what it meant to me, Ben made a promise to back my decision to fly aerobatics. "If flying means that much to you, I'll support you. I love you more than anything. But if anything happens to you"—he looked away—"I don't think I'd survive."

This was a big step forward for him—for us. "Don't worry," I reassured him. "I'm probably the world's most cautious pilot."

That winter, Ben and I spent many peaceful hours at home in our living room. While he worked out equations on an engineering pad, I had my aerobatic catalog, lots of blank sheets of paper, and my calculator, as I played around with different maneuvers, trying to come up with a freestyle sequence that would showcase my skills and my airplane at their best. It reminded me of all the days I'd spent curled up in the window seat of my father's office, working on math problems while he scratched away with his fountain pen at physics calculations for his next publication. Solitary work was necessary for any creative career, but it always made me feel warm inside when I could do that work next to someone I loved. And creating a freestyle sequence, it turned out, was a mathematical challenge. I needed to optimize the numbers to maximize my score.

Freestyle performances were one of the exciting aspects of the Intermediate category that set it apart from Basic and Sportsman. In addition to creating their own Freestyles that conformed to the specific rules for the category, Intermediates also needed to perform a sequence never flown by the pilot and handed to them just eighteen hours before the contest. No practice of this new sequence in any airplane was allowed before the contest.

Flying a sequence I'd never flown was a huge challenge. The Unknown had been my worst flight at Borrego. The only thing I could do to prepare was practice it in my mind, visualizing myself in the airplane, going through the maneuvers in that aerobatic box, flying a perfect flight. I'd draw up a sequence card by hand and affix it to my dashboard.

The next spring, in May 1989, I planned to fly in the Taft Contest again, this time in Intermediate. To my surprise, Ben told me he wanted to accompany me to the contest. "I want to see what you're so fired up about," he said, fiddling with a curtain pull in our dining room.

I couldn't help beaming. Had those long winter conversations had such a positive effect? "I'd love to have you come along. You want to fly down with me in the Pitts?"

He shuddered. "No, thanks. I think I'll drive. I prefer to keep my lunch inside my stomach, thank you."

It was still early in the competition season, but I'd been spending several days a week out at New J with Frank and Stu. I was determined to do well at Taft. My secret goal was to win a trophy so I could move up to Advanced by the Paso Robles contest in June. I hadn't told anyone, though, because I was afraid of more comments about being a young upstart. I was pretty sure Frank, and probably Stu as well, would say I was overreaching. "Ambition" was another word like "selfish" that had been used against me. ("It's not ladylike to like math so much," one teacher said to me.) Also, as soon as I moved into Advanced, I'd be competing with Stu directly, something I wasn't looking forward to. Stu had been flying Advanced for years, but he had an unfortunate tendency to make mistakes at contests. He would roll the wrong way and earn a zero on a maneuver. On one disastrous flight, he ended up flying most of his figures in the wrong direction, resulting in a string of zeros.

It was clear that once I started flying Advanced, I'd be beating my friend. I didn't want to think too hard about how that'd make him feel. I felt guilty because I knew I was going to do it anyway.

"You're flying the Advanced figures better than I expected," Frank said as he handed me the mini-cassette recorder after a critique flight. He glanced at Stu, lying on the asphalt under his Eagle out of earshot. "And significantly better than Stu."

"So you think it's okay for me to move up to Advanced soon?"

He snorted. "You haven't even won a trophy in Intermediate. It's a big jump up to Advanced contest flying."

"As big as the jump from Advanced to Unlimited?" I asked.

"Of course not." He sounded annoyed. "Why do you think I've been spending two years practicing Unlimited before I fly a contest?"

My main problem with Advanced was the introduction of outside loops and other high-negative-g maneuvers in addition to high-positive g's. From the ground, there's not much difference between a regular loop, where the pilot's head points toward the inside of the loop, and an outside loop, where it's on the outside. In both maneuvers, the plane draws a circle in the air. But there's a significant difference in how outside maneuvers feel, as all your blood rushes to your head. The Air Force and Navy don't even allow their pilots to undergo more than one negative g. It's unexplored and risky territory.

When you pull positive g's, you need to tighten all your large lower-body muscles to enable your heart to keep blood flowing up to your brain. The heart has to work hard, pumping blood that now weighs six, nine, or even twelve times as much as usual so oxygen can continue to nourish your gray matter. To help it along, the pilot has to force the blood out of the legs and lower torso. It's extremely demanding physically, but well understood by aviation physiologists and military physicians.

Negative g's are the complete opposite of positive g's. When you fly an outside loop, it's like hanging in the straps, upside down, with the acceleration of gravity pointing away from your feet and toward your head. All the blood in your body rushes to your head and pools in your brain. If you tighten your muscles like you would for positive g's, the blood pressure inside the delicate vessels in your brain can become dangerously elevated. The first warning sign is bloodshot eyes because their tiny capillaries have burst under the pressure. You don't want that to happen inside your brain. (Although some might argue that all aerobatic pilots already clearly have some kind of brain defect!) Instead, you want to completely relax and allow your blood vessels to expand. This reduces the blood pressure inside your head.

You also need to build up a tolerance for negative g's. At the beginning of the aerobatic season, it's best not to push more than minus two or three g's. Every couple of days, you ratchet up the negative-g load. Nobody's quite sure which physiological changes take place inside your brain, but subjectively, it feels like the walls of the blood vessels are toughening up, and the negative g's become less painful with practice.

By the end of the season, you might comfortably be pushing six to nine negative g's without a problem. Of course, certain parts of your body don't ever develop a tolerance. Advanced and Unlimited pilots become accustomed to what appear to be permanent bruises on their thighs from the webbing of their seat belts digging in while they are thrust from their seat by a force of over a thousand pounds.

On the other hand, it also has some benefits. As a programmer, I sat for long hours at the computer and developed low back pain. It got worse when I started doing high-positive-g aerobatics. But as soon as I started practicing for Advanced, my back pain disappeared. I once read about an expensive treatment for slipped discs and other back troubles, involving a complex and costly machine that alternately applied and released traction to the spine. That's exactly what happens when you're flying an aerobatic sequence with negative g's. People also use inversion tables for the same reason: negative g's are good for the spine. I never had back trouble while I was actively flying aerobatics, but whenever I stopped flying and returned to a mostly sedentary desk job, it would flare up again.

* * *

In May 1989, I flew to the Taft Contest. Ben drove and joined me at the Taft Motel. Taft was so tiny that it was a short walk from the motel to the airport. Ben and I walked on a narrow residential street thick with potholes, passing small decrepit houses packed in tightly on either side. As we walked in the predawn light, a monotone voice rose from a house with sagging windows and a broken chain-link fence. "I hate you. I hate you. I hate you," it repeated, fading when we'd walked too far away to hear.

Ben looked at me with wide eyes. "Are all the places you fly this depressing?" He dutifully waited for me in the air-conditioned terminal during the contest, but he refused to help out on the judging line, saying only, "Too hot."

My competition flying was workmanlike but not excellent. I finished fifth out of ten in Intermediate, slightly better than middle of the pack, but far away from even a third-place trophy. Still, it lifted my heart to have Ben at the contest. He handed me my water bottle after the flight and said, "Congratulations!" even though he had no idea how well I'd flown.

He even attended the banquet in the terminal hangar, though he rolled his eyes when his plastic fork snapped while cutting his meat, and made me leave early after the food fight started. But overall, it had been a good contest.

However, as I continued to practice Advanced as well as Intermediate back at home, a severe problem with the plane was becoming apparent. Although the Pitts S-2A was technically rated for Advanced, and able to handle positive and negative g's equally well, the situation with my low body weight made flying negative g's particularly difficult. Since my lead weights and I together tipped the scales at only 140 pounds, I had to fly the airplane in its extreme forward center-of-gravity condition, making the control stick very heavy. I'd been lifting weights at home to build my upper body strength, but it wasn't enough. The stick forces were so high, in fact, that under normal conditions it was beyond my strength to pull or push at the limit.

The plane did have an aerodynamic power steering device called a trim lever that could reduce the stick forces. But unfortunately, it had to be adjusted before each transition from positive to negative g's. In other words, for the stick not to be punishingly heavy during a positive-g pull, I needed to move the trim lever aft. But as soon as I rolled inverted and pushed negative g's, I simply didn't have the strength to apply sufficient pressure to the stick. So I found myself having to quickly shove the trim lever forward before each push, and then move it back for the next pull.

This was dangerous. If I ever missed adjusting the trim while heading straight toward the ground, I might be unable to move the stick and pull out of the dive. I'd end up losing too much altitude—or possibly even hit the ground.

It was becoming clearer and clearer that if I was going to fly competition seriously, I'd need to move to a single-seat Pitts that could be better adjusted to fit me.

But it was still too much money. I had to come up with a new idea for raising funds.

* * *

"Are you my Pitts S-2A instructor?" asked a tall, elegant man in a buttery-smooth British accent one sunny spring morning in 1989. He stood peering in the door to Lou Fields's hangar as though looking for someone else.

"I'm afraid Lou's not available today, so I'll be flying with you," I said, getting up from the folding chair where I'd been waiting. It was my first instructional flight in the Pitts, and I felt apologetic. I was definitely lacking as a replacement for the highly knowledgeable Lou.

Damon Whittington-Smythe had a touch of distinguished gray at the temples and was a long-time member of IAC Chapter 38. He was one of the senior pilots whom everyone respected as he performed well in competition and had been doing so for years. He owned his own single-seat Pitts, but was interested in checking out in a two-seat Pitts to give the occasional ride to a friend.

As we made small talk in the hangar, he remarked, "I sold my business to Apple a few years ago, and ever since, I can't spend the interest fast enough."

Intimidating much?

After my win at the Delano contest and my less-than-stellar performances in Intermediate, my enthusiasm for flying the Pitts had only increased. But the expense of aircraft rental was mounting rapidly. If I wanted to do well in aerobatic competition in Intermediate and beyond, I'd need to own a Pitts. Of course, I couldn't yet afford the approach other pilots recommended—buying a single-seat Pitts—but after a few hours of number-crunching, I'd realized that if I bought the S-2A, instructed in it, and rented it out, I could significantly cut my costs.

I scraped together all the funds I could for a down payment and made the owner an offer of $40,000. He accepted, and I got another loan and added a new line to my aviation business, that of competition aerobatic instructor. After all, I now possessed the impeccable credential of 1988 Delano Sportsman Aerobatic Champion, and people who had never noticed me before were now calling up to ask for aerobatic competition advice.

I moved N6300V to Lou Fields' hangar at Oakland and started renting it out. The only instructors authorized to teach in my airplane were Lou Fields and me. Nevertheless, the imposter syndrome had hit me hard again, and although I was comfortable flying the Pitts, I doubted my ability to teach advanced aerobatics.

Trying to be a conscientious instructor, I dutifully checked out Damon's logbook as a prelude to giving him ground instruction in Lou's hangar. It was daunting. He'd logged about five thousand flight hours, almost ten times as much as I had, and had far more aerobatic and competition proficiency than I was likely ever to lay claim to. And I was supposed to be checking *him* out in the airplane?

I asked him basic questions about the flight, and he was polite in his understated British fashion and answered every question correctly. We preflighted and strapped in, and I continued to be impressed with his handling of the plane as he taxied to the runway and performed a gossamer takeoff.

Once in the practice area, he executed each of the maneuvers so precisely that I was left in awe and once again embarrassed to have been placed in the role of instructor. Clearly he knew much more than I did, and it felt ridiculous to be charging him money for this flight, when he was the one demonstrating how to do the maneuvers so exquisitely.

At last, we returned to the airport and entered the traffic pattern. He was comfortable on the radios, elegant on the controls, and I was just along for the ride.

Embarrassed to ask him to demonstrate multiple landings, I planned to just have him come in and land once, and then sign him off. He flew a flawless pattern, and at the end of the final approach, when he should have been descending the last few feet to the runway, he rounded out about six feet in the air.

This was unusual.

And potentially dangerous. You needed to perform the flare, or transition to the correct nose-up pitch attitude for touchdown, within a couple of feet of the ground so that when the stall occurred, the landing gear could absorb the impact. Ideally, you rounded out only a few inches above the ground.

If I'd been flying with anyone who hadn't demonstrated such consummate mastery in the air, I would've taken the controls, or at the very least warned them they were too high.

But something about his presence and confidence stopped my tongue. I was too intimidated. Besides, maybe he was simply demonstrating a new type of landing I wasn't familiar with.

We floated along, gradually losing flying speed. If he didn't do something soon, the plane was going to stall and we'd crash. We were looking at certain damage if he didn't do something.

If *I* didn't do something.

The wings started to give up their lift. We were barely beginning to sink, prelude to a devastating crash. Damon did nothing. And still nothing more.

Someone had to do something.

At the very last instant, I grabbed the controls and jammed in throttle. The increased thrust of the propeller accelerated air over the wings, lending them just enough lift to slow our descent. We were sinking like a rock, but the burst of power cushioned our landing. Just. Barely.

It was the hardest landing I'd ever experienced, even worse than that first one with Jack Springer. I felt it in the base of my spine as we hit the ground.

Did we damage the plane? At least we were alive and uninjured. I was shaking and stunned. How could this have happened? Since I was sitting in the front seat, I couldn't see Damon's face, and he was silent over the intercom, making only the required radio calls.

We taxied back to the Old T's, where we shut down, and I hopped out of the plane to inspect the landing gear and propeller. Fortunately, every-thing seemed okay. Curtis Pitts designed this little airplane to be super strong. It looked like my last-minute intervention was enough to save us. But I was still shaking as I checked the propeller to make sure that it didn't strike the ground during landing.

Damon turned to me. "I'm sorry about that," he said in his gentle accent.

I spun to face him. "What happened?" I demanded. "You were flying so beautifully."

Was he blushing? "I'm sorry," he repeated. "I misjudged our height above the runway, and I thought we had already landed."

I stared at him. "You couldn't tell we weren't on the ground?"

"I thought I'd greased it on in an incredibly smooth landing, and we were rolling on the runway. I had no idea we were still up in the air."

It shocked me that this man lacked even the most elementary feel for the airplane and was unable to tell whether it was in the air or on the ground. In an instant, I realized two things. First, I had a better feel for the plane than even a highly experienced, superconfident, double-named British pilot. And second, I'd made the mistake of allowing my own social discomfort to get in the way of what I knew was right.

What I'd learned after flying with Jack Springer was how to have confidence in my own official title of flight instructor. What I learned after flying with Damon was something more important. Self-confidence wasn't a static state of mind. It wasn't something I could acquire once and then possess for the rest of my life. Instead, it was a dynamic process, something I had to actively nurture and grow. I had to stop making passiv-ity my default, relying on social roles and job titles to guide my actions.

Chapter 12

"Want to come with me to the next contest?" I asked Ben.

He shot me a look. "You're asking if I want to spend four days in the broiling sun in the middle of nowhere, culminating in a 'banquet' where we eat hamburgers off paper plates in a hangar because the coffee shop where they held it last year didn't invite them back after the food fight?"

I couldn't blame him. Contests were pretty boring for nonpilots. But it wasn't going to stop me from pushing forward. I'd decided to save up for a single-seat Pitts, and to that end, I started working longer hours as a programming consultant and banking all my savings. I also volunteered to do all the night checkouts in the flying club so that I could put in extra hours there too. Perhaps fortunately, Ben's company had been bought out, and his new employer demanded incredibly long hours, so I didn't feel too bad about not being at home with him much. However, even with all my extra work hours, the numbers still weren't adding up to buy my dream airplane. But then I got some unexpectedly good news.

It turned out my Pitts S-2A had appreciated in value. Demand had grown for two-seat factory-built aircraft. In less than a year, it had gone up by nearly 40 percent. A little sadly, I put it on the market, and it promptly sold for the astonishing sum of $55,000. I walked away with a substantial profit. After adding in my savings, I could pay off my loan and still have enough to make a hefty down payment on a used Pitts S-1T. With a much smaller loan on the S-1T, I could afford as much as $40,000 without renting it out. I broke open *Trade-a-Plane* once again. After many hours of searching and calling everyone in an ever-increasing circle around San Francisco, I found an airplane that appeared to meet all my criteria—in Oklahoma.

It's a little nerve-racking to buy an airplane halfway across the country. What's more, it was a single-seat airplane, so I couldn't rely on the "training wheels" of an instructor to catch my mistakes. From everything I'd heard, the Pitts S-1 was even more unpredictable and difficult to manage than the S-2. It had taken me a full ten hours in the Pitts S-2A before Louie Robinson pronounced me safe to land it and checked me out in the plane. I'd never flown an airplane solo without completing a checkout flight with an instructor.

I'd be flying without a safety net from the very beginning.

Everything I had learned, every principle of safety I had absorbed, made it clear it was a mistake to fly an unfamiliar plane without sufficient training. Accident reports often listed the cause of fatalities as "unfamiliarity in type." I'd be violating one of the safety policies I'd followed religiously ever since I'd begun flying. The statistics of crashing in a small airplane were ten to one hundred times worse than in an airliner. But I'd always told myself, even prided myself, that I held higher safety standards, that I would beat the statistics.

On one of the long commutes home from my consulting job, I debated whether I was doing the right thing. The thought of buying a single-seat Pitts gave me an incredible thrill. For the first time, I'd be buying an airplane not as a business decision, not to give flight lessons, but purely because *I wanted it*.

If I went through with the purchase, I'd be spending a huge amount of money on something that would be fun for me. It wouldn't earn me money. It wouldn't be a good investment. It wouldn't make the world a better place. No, I was just buying it to convert irreplaceable fossil fuel into noise while drawing circles and lines in the sky.

It was incredibly *selfish*.

And that gave me even more of a thrill. It was either delayed rebellion, or a really early midlife crisis. Throughout my childhood, I admit to having been kind of boring. I didn't take the usual stupid adolescent risks. In school I always did my homework. I followed my parents' rules. If I rebelled, it was usually against my classmates, who called me disgusting for getting 100s on tests, who called me a freak, a goody-goody, a spic. After Don Schwartz, for instance, told me that maybe he and his friends "would go easier" on me if I didn't do quite so well on tests, I'd redoubled my efforts. Ha!

So maybe flying was a form of rebellion against my parents and the rest of the world. Flying was the one thing I knew for certain they'd consider too dangerous. But I'd finally come to the point where I wanted to tell them. I didn't want to mention anything about the aerobatics, though. Better to break the whole flying thing to them slowly.

"You better not tell your father," my mother said when I told her over the phone.

Just then, my father picked up the extension.

"Cecilia, are you going to tell him?" my mother asked.

"What? Tell me what?"

"Dad, I'm taking flying lessons."

"What? You're crazy!"

"See! I told you not to tell him," my mother chided.

Soon after that, she started clipping newspaper articles about plane crashes and mailing them to me. She warned me that I needed to think of others rather than just myself.

The word "selfish" hung in the air, unspoken.

As a child, I desperately wanted to make my mother happy, so I hid all my selfish inclinations from her. I pretended I was good, but I was secretly afraid that I was an evil person. My favorite characters were the villains, particularly female villains like Catwoman or the evil Queen Achren from Lloyd Alexander's fantasy series *The Chronicles of Prydain*. These badass women lived life on their own terms. They demanded what they wanted. They did all the things I never dared. Most of all, they had *fun* even though they were doomed to come to a bad end, just like I would if anyone were to find out what I was *really* like.

I never spoke of the appeal villains held for me to anyone until communication on the internet became widespread and I discovered that I was far from alone in my affection for the bad guys. Our society often defines "good" in females to be well-behaved, passive, and giving—actually, kind of boring. If a woman wants to do something interesting, break out of societal norms, or worst of all, become powerful, she's often relegated to villain status.

Wanting to buy an airplane purely for the fun of it, a single-seat plane that only I could fly, was still my guilty secret. As I sped along the freeway in the left lane, though, something inside me, a part of me that had been crumpled up for many years, seemed to unfold and breathe deeply for the first time.

I was going to do it.

I laughed a full-throated, badass laugh.

* * *

After many phone calls, and airplane photos and copies of logbooks arriving in my mailbox, the seller and I agreed upon a price of $40,000 and a date for me to fly out to Oklahoma to inspect the airplane.

There was a well-known aerobatic flight school, Munson and Denny (M&D) Aviation, located not far away in Houston, Texas. I arranged for the seller, Doug Waldron, to fly his Pitts there so the M&D mechanics could inspect the plane, and Daniel "Doc" Munson, a well-known pilot on the national competition aerobatic scene, could give me some additional instruction in his two-seat Pitts in preparation for flying a single-seat airplane.

It was hot and humid when I arrived in Houston, and the air held a slightly sour odor with an almost metallic tang. I decided not to inquire too strenuously about what was being spewed into the atmosphere from the local factories.

Doc met me at the local airport for my lesson. I'd introduced myself to him over the phone as an Intermediate pilot looking to start flying Advanced, and that I'd just sold my Pitts S-2A to buy an S-1T. He greeted me like an old friend. With silver hair brushed back from a wise face and penetrating eyes, Doc had a wry, understated sense of humor. He was a local doctor who ran the flight school with his partner, Marge Denny. In his spare time he was an aircraft designer and Unlimited aerobatic competitor. I met Marge, who also flew Unlimited, later in the day. She had a Texas accent and was relentlessly cheerful and almost aggressively down-home. She possessed that hard edge I'd noticed some veteran women pilots seemed to acquire over time. Although I admired her tremendously, she intimidated me, and I was never quite sure how to act around her. She soon dubbed me "Granola," since I hailed from Berkeley, which bothered me immensely, but of course I said nothing. I was pretty sure she meant it affectionately—pretty sure.

"Are you gonna try out for the US Aerobatic Team?" she asked. The Olympic team of aviation, consisting of the ten best aerobatic pilots in the United States, was selected every two years at the US National Aerobatic Competition to represent the United States at the World Aerobatic Championships. Marge and Doc were contenders for the team. I certainly wasn't.

"I'm only flying Intermediate," I protested, not sure if she was teasing me. "I just started competing a year ago."

She scratched her ear but said nothing.

Doc, however, was so kind and encouraging that I felt instantly at ease. There are a lot of egos in this business, especially among top-ranked pilots, and given how famous he was, I wasn't sure what to expect. Normally, I was very closed and a little prickly around strangers, but within a few minutes of meeting Doc, I'd found myself opening up about my hopes and fears.

"I'm worried about flying a single-seat airplane," I told him in the closet-like instruction room in the back of the M&D lobby.

He leaned back in his chair. "You're already flying a Pitts S-2A. You already know what to do. I'm not quite sure why you want to fly with me."

"I want to be sure I'm completely safe landing a Pitts," I explained. "I thought you could give me some extra tips, and check that I'm super current before I get into the S-1."

"I'm happy to fly with you, but I'm sure you'll do fine."

The new plane, N521MS, had been in their hangar all morning

getting a thorough inspection. We walked over to check it out. It was tiny, and up close I could see all the small imperfections in the paint scheme that hadn't been visible in the photos. Doc eyed it critically and frowned as he checked the tailwheel. Still, I couldn't help feeling a quiver of excitement that I might soon own this beautiful plane.

"I think the owner went to get some coffee," Doc told me. "Why don't we go flying now?"

The flight in Doc's two-seat rental Pitts went smoothly. We stayed in the airport traffic pattern and practiced landings. Doc gave me tips on how the S-1 might differ from the S-2, and he pronounced me more than ready to solo the S-1T.

When we returned to the hangar, the owner, Doug Waldron, had just shown up. He wore a cowboy hat and answered every one of my rapid-fire questions in a laid-back drawl.

"Have you had any problems with the supplemental fuel tank?" I asked. The tank was an ungainly, homemade-looking welded hunk of metal that fit over the top wing in a rough airfoil shape and was designed to increase the plane's range on cross-country flights. Translucent yellow tubing hung down from it and attached to a specially designed port.

He scratched his head and squinted at it. "You're not supposed to fly aerobatics with it on," he said after a long pause.

"How can you tell when it's time to switch tanks?" I prodded.

He shrugged. "When the engine quits, I hit the boost pump and flip the switch." He laughed. "'Course, if you're nervous, you can watch for bubbles comin' into this clear plastic tube here. That's a sign the tank's gettin' a little dry."

This S-1T was originally built by the Pitts factory, but Waldron had the certification switched to experimental so he could modify the plane without going through the standard FAA certification process. This world of experimental aircraft was another new venture for me. Everything I'd flown up until now had been factory-certified, giving me the security of knowing it complied with rigorous testing and the exacting legal standards laid down by the Federal Aviation Administration.

Not so with this S-1T.

I checked the plane over dubiously. There were a number of homemade-looking additions, like a small metal cylinder to the right and under the seat pan in the cockpit.

"That's an accumulator," Doug said. "Sometimes the oil pressure dropped on a long vertical upline, an' the prop would bog down."

"What?" I asked, not understanding.

"The prop revs slow down when the plane don't know if it's upright or inverted," he explained. "I lost power on hammerheads, which ain't too good during a sequence." He grinned at me, his shoulders loose and relaxed as he talked about a situation that would have terrified me. "But I put in the accumulator, an' it solved the problem."

The reason I picked this plane out of all the other S-1Ts for sale around the country was precisely because Doug had flown in Unlimited competition. I figured he'd already found all its weak spots and addressed them with additions like this accumulator. Hopefully, my logic was sound.

Doc Munson's mechanic pronounced the plane in good shape for a 1984 Pitts S-1T. He warned me, though, that the plane had been "flown hard, but it's strong and can take it."

I probed Doug further. "How long do you plan your flight legs for?" The airplane had a small main fuel tank, and even with the extended tank installed over the wing, I wouldn't be able to fly very long before I needed to refuel. It was over 1,900 miles to my home airport—definitely the longest cross-country flight I'd ever flown—and I was hoping for tips, for reassurance.

Doug drawled, "I dunno. I jus' fly along till I see bubbles in that little tube, then I start lookin' for an airport."

Was he pulling my leg? It was kind of hard to tell with that weathered, deadpan face of his. Okay, my meticulous, maybe even a little obsessive-compulsive approach to flying might be just a bit abnormal. Apparently, a lot of people took flying far more casually than I did.

I tried to make more small talk with Doug as we finished up the inspection. "What kind of work do you do?"

He tipped his hat further back on his forehead. "I work in a bank."

"What do you do there?" I pressed.

He looked away. "Aw, a little of this, a little of that."

Guessing he was probably embarrassed about being a janitor or something, I didn't push further. Later, I'd find out he was the bank president.

Even later, I'd hear from other pilots more harrowing tales about Doug's escapades, like how he departed aerobatic contests by flying low over the runway until he built up speed, then pulling vertical, with that tank still mounted on the wings, and doing a full vertical roll before capping off and flying away, despite all the rules not to fly aerobatics when that wing tank is attached. Doug, it seemed, wasn't a guy for rules.

The plane was pronounced satisfactory. I handed Doug his check, and he headed off. He didn't appear noticeably happy, the way an airplane seller was supposed to act, but I couldn't read his facial expressions anyway.

I was now the proud owner of a red-white-and-blue single-seat Pitts S-1T.

Doc Munson gave me a verbal checkout before I took the plane up for the first time, leaning over the cockpit and pointing out little details to me as I nervously hung on every word.

Eventually, I couldn't avoid it any longer; it was time for me to get into the airplane and fly. The best news was I didn't need my elevator shoes or my forty pounds of lead weights. The plane would fly fine with me just the way I was.

I decided to spend lots of time taxiing the plane around the airport, memorizing landing attitude, imagining what it would be like to land. Better to be cautious. Yep. The plane was incredibly responsive. Actually, it was squirrelly. The lightest tap on a rudder pedal sent the nose careening off in first one direction, then the other. I felt like I was balancing on top of an overinflated beach ball, always on the edge of losing my balance and falling to the ground with a splat. I caught a few swerves in the nick of time, before the plane pivoted too far and started to enter the dreaded ground loop. I was getting more and more nervous. If it was this hard to taxi, how was I ever going to land? More newspaper headlines flashed through my mind: BERKELEY, CALIFORNIA, WOMAN CRASHES PLANE ON FIRST TEXAS FLIGHT. "Well, she ate granola, like all those other left-coasters, so what do you expect?" Marge Denny would tell the reporters.

Stuffing down my overactive imagination, I did a few fast taxis on a long, deserted taxiway. Then I taxied around slowly some more. A crowd had gathered in front of the hangar, watching the spectacle of the "little gal" flying a single-seat airplane for the first time.

That was it. I screwed up my courage, taxied to the runway, did a final pretakeoff check, then a second one. At last, I made a call over the handheld radio tie-wrapped to one of the cockpit spars and advanced the throttle.

Oh. My. God. The plane accelerated like crazy as the engine roared, and the sleek metal beast reared up on its wheels with ferocity. If my S-2A was a thoroughbred horse, skittish but bred for the racetrack, this S-1T was a sinewy tiger, a wild animal. With me hanging onto the controls for dear life, it started to veer crazily toward one side of the narrow runway, but by then I'd gained flying speed. I yanked it off the ground and was airborne.

It flew like a rocket ship, like nothing I'd ever handled before. *I've got a tiger by the tail*, I couldn't help thinking. Two hundred horsepower and under a thousand pounds gross weight meant it was overpowered as hell. We were at altitude almost before I exhaled for the first time after takeoff. The runway lay so far behind me that it was scary to look over my shoulder at it.

Just a caress of my hand on the ailerons and we swung into a wild bank, the plane pirouetting at my touch. It hummed with satisfaction at finally being unleashed into the sky, cavorting into the wild blue like an animal on steroids.

I'd been instructed to try a few stalls and gentle maneuvers and then come back in for a landing before doing aerobatics, but I couldn't help myself. My hands sticky on the controls, I rolled and spun, flying Immelmann turns, point rolls, hammerheads. I almost couldn't stop, it was so exhilarating.

This was it. This was the dance I'd always dreamed of, the plane barely getting between my mind and my body. I'd tightened the seat belts, ratcheted them down as tight as I could, like I was welded into the airplane, like it was a part of my body. Of course, I was now joined with an overpowered, crazed monster about to tear off out of control.

It was *spectacular*.

I glanced at the ground again to get my bearings, and suddenly realized

I couldn't see the airport any longer. My pulse accelerated. Back home, I was intimately familiar with the terrain and knew exactly where I was at every second. But here, I was disoriented. What if I couldn't find the airport again? What if I ran out of gas? I'd jammed a Houston sectional chart under my thigh and took a few seconds to wiggle it free. I flew in aimless circles, peering this way and that, until I finally spotted a few landmarks and my breathing settled. Thank God. I wasn't too far away from the airport after all. Better head back. At least I didn't embarrass myself by making a radio call admitting I was lost.

I flew a tight pattern and headed on in. My palms were damp with sweat and my heart was hammering. Next step: Could I land this thing safely?

I made my position report over the radio, checked for other traffic in the pattern, and began my final descent to the runway. I reduced the throttle nearly to idle with the runway in sight, green fields all around. On high alert, all senses quivering, my hands and feet jittered on the controls.

With the throttle at idle, the Pitts glided like a free-falling safe. The plane wasn't designed to be aerodynamic. To fly powered aerobatics, you needed plenty of thrust accompanied by plenty of drag. This gave you the ability to essentially start and stop abruptly in the air. It made for incredible flexibility when performing aerobatic figures, but unfortunately, it wasn't so good for landing.

I was sinking—fast. I had some experience with the S-2A, but this unfamiliar, smaller, wigglier airplane possessed even more of the infamous Pitts characteristics than the two-seat version.

Okay. Deep breaths to keep from panicking. *I can do this. Keep the end of the runway steady in the windshield.* I could glide to that spot.

But it was coming up awfully fast. If I didn't do something soon, I was going to crash for sure. Now I was on short final descent, only a few dozen feet above the ground. The nose blocked my view of the runway completely, but I needed to line it up exactly with the strip of pavement, while at the same time keeping track of exactly how far I was above the runway—in feet and then in inches. It sounded impossible—landing without seeing where I was going—but flying had taught me the human body and mind were incredibly adaptable.

There was plenty of sensory information my brain could use while landing. In my peripheral vision, both edges of the runway rose to meet me. Also in my peripheral vision, the runway centerline appeared in the plexiglass window between my feet. The stick slackened as the airplane slowed down, an excellent airspeed indicator. The whoosh of air rushing past the fuselage lessened. Finally, the closer I got to the ground, the more pungent the scent of the earth and asphalt became. Some Pitts pilots claim they land the airplane by smell alone.

I couldn't help remembering that landing accidents make up a large part of crash statistics. And as I'd learned in the Citabria checkout, tail-draggers always wanted to swap ends in a ground loop. The Pitts, of course, was significantly faster and more unstable on the ground than a Citabria.

The riskiest part of a landing is always immediately after you touch down. *Ahhh! I've made it onto the ground without crashing! The hard part is done*, you think. Unconsciously, you relax on the controls. In a nosewheel aircraft like a Cessna, this isn't a problem; its inherent stability will keep the airplane tracking straight on the runway, no matter what you do. Not so in a Pitts.

Further, the plane I'd just purchased had been retrofitted with an experimental tailwheel without a steering spring. Although I'd noted it on preflight, I hadn't realized the full extent of its effects. I was about to learn a big lesson.

I touched down in a three-point landing attitude and tapped the rudders to keep the airplane straight. With the tailwheel in the locked position, it was supposed to be fairly stable. But to my shock, as the plane slowed down, it veered to the right. I'd been dreading the possibility of a ground loop during the entire flight. With this fear filling my mind, I kept hearing the words an old-time pilot had said one day in the hangar. "If you ever get into a ground loop, you just need to hang on and go along for the ride."

This turned out to be terrible advice. I bumped along the runway, stick all the way back into my belly. It was hot and muggy on the ground, and the sun glared through my windshield as I fought the unfamiliar airplane and my own burgeoning panic.

The plane swerved further to the right. "Hang on and go along for the ride," echoed in my head, and I made the critical mistake of letting my feet relax. Of giving up, and becoming a passenger, not a pilot. To my horror and dismay, the plane did something I'd never seen before. It bumped off the edge of the runway and into the soft earth, where it gradually slowed down, and then slowly, excruciatingly slowly, tipped forward onto its nose and buried itself into the ground with its tail in the air.

I'd gone along for the ride, and now I sat, thrown uncomfortably forward into the straps, staring through the windshield, not at the sky, but at the loamy earth and yellow-green weeds at the edge of the Texas runway. The engine abruptly stopped as the propeller bit into the soft ground. Reflexively, I turned off the ignition and pulled the mixture to stop fuel flow to the engine.

Then I sat there, shame pouring over me in waves. I'd done the unthinkable. Wrecked my new Pitts on the very first landing. I was devastated. I couldn't move because of the flush of humiliation suffusing my face and skin. I was INTF—Incompetent, Nerd, Terrified, Failure. A bad pilot. Every criticism I'd ever heard came back to me. "Women just don't know how to handle machines." "They're terrible drivers, and rotten pilots." "Amelia Earhart didn't know how to land, and neither do you." "You fly this thing?" "What's a little girl like you doing in this man's world?" "Rod-REE-kezz, you freak."

Dimly, I saw out of the corner of my eye that several people had emerged from M&D Aviation and were rushing to the runway. Doc Munson was the first to reach me. He ran to the tail of the airplane and yanked it down. Now the plane was back in the familiar three-point attitude, and my frozen brain started to click along again. What had I done? I'd given up my control of the airplane. I thought I'd learned that lesson before, but apparently, I needed to keep on learning it.

Doc Munson came to my side. "What happened? You never deviated from the centerline when we flew together."

I bowed my head, unable to say anything through my mortification. I climbed out of the airplane and sat on the grass.

"Is the plane okay?" I finally asked. One of the M&D mechanics was checking the propeller and the undersides of the lower wing.

"I don't see anything obvious, but let's get it back in the hangar," said Doc.

The five witnesses to my disgrace and I pushed it back along the taxi-ways. Running the gauntlet, we walked past rows of spectators.

A big guy called out, "What happened?"

I certainly wasn't going to answer, and I was slightly comforted that neither Doc nor any of his staff said anything.

Finally, we got to the relative safety of the hangar, where I sank down onto a stool while the others inspected the airplane. Doc checked the propeller.

"You're lucky the ground was so soft, and you were going so slowly," he said with a relieved breath. "No damage at all to the prop."

"What about the wings?" I asked.

"Did you drag one?"

"I don't really remember."

He straightened from his examination. "I don't even see any grass stains. I think you got lucky. No damage at all to the airplane." He walked around the aircraft, and then bent to examine the tailwheel. "Uh oh."

"What is it?" I asked, worried that I'd done something worse.

"I've never seen a Haigh tailwheel with this much play in it." He wiggled the tailwheel and the plane shook from side to side. "No wonder you couldn't keep it straight. Don't blame yourself." He put a hand on my shoulder. "You came out okay. You didn't ground loop; you didn't put a speck of damage on the airplane. Just a little runway deviation because there was a problem with the tailwheel."

They replaced the tailwheel, but I knew that despite Doc's attempt at reassurance, the problem wasn't defective equipment. Doug hadn't had any difficulties landing the plane. It was because I was a defective human being. It was my fault. It always was my fault.

That night in my hotel room, I couldn't stop going over and over again what could have happened during that landing, what I could have done better. I could have been more aggressive with the rudders. I could have refused to "just go along for the ride." The air conditioner in the room rattled and whined, and when it stopped, water plopped onto the linoleum flooring. Drip, drip, drip. I twisted myself up in the sheets and shoved the pillows from side to side, but couldn't get comfortable.

There was an ache in my chest, a hot ingot of shame just under my ribs. I'd given up my authority over the airplane for a split second, and that had been enough to lose control of it. I'd allowed the words of others to worm their way into my soul once again.

It took a long time to fall asleep in that dark and muggy hotel room.

The next day, I returned to the airport, still ashamed and subdued. The M&D mechanic installed a new tailwheel on my Pitts as I watched, and I could see for myself what a difference it made. I knew I'd have to get back in the cockpit and fly again. My shame was like a cattle prod goading me over my fear. I preflighted and strapped in again, taking lots of deep breaths.

But I needn't have worried. I flew the Pitts several times around the pattern, landing perfectly each time. The new tailwheel *did* make a difference. I started to feel a little better.

Later that day, I said goodbye to my new friends at M&D Aviation, and took off in my very own single-seat plane heading west. Ahead of me lay 1,900 miles of terrain I'd never seen and at least four or five fuel stops at airports I'd never visited. I was flying an unfamiliar airplane with, as was typical for a Pitts in those days, no electrical system, no working navigation instruments, a compass that pointed in the wrong direction, no portable GPS, nothing but a stack of aviation charts shoved under my thigh and the wide world below me.

As I flew over thousands of miles across Texas, New Mexico, Arizona, and California, over mountains and deserts, through the Tehachapi Pass and into the Central Valley, the color of the earth changed from green to brown, and the scent of the air shifted from agriculture and farms to creosote and sage. For hundreds of square miles, not a single human walked the ground below me.

I was alone in that single-seat airplane, alone with my judgments, my decisions.

The hours passed slowly. Cool, thin air blew in through the vents. I had plenty of time to ponder what had just happened. Once again, I'd let old instincts from my childhood take over. Deep underneath, I still believed there was something wrong with making my own decisions, with acting, with taking power in the world. That it was better to be a passenger than a pilot. That it was shameful to take action.

But that little Pitts had taught me something new. It was up to me now. I'd never give up control of an airplane again. I'd keep flying, no matter what. There was a difference between control and selfishness, between the wide world and the constriction of my own old beliefs.

As I flew, the landscape unrolled beneath me. The flat central plains of Texas morphed into the folded and wrinkled high desert of New Mexico. In a jet, one flies too high to get a sense of the human scale of life on this earth. And when you drive, you can't see anything at all beyond the road signs and the gas stations and shops lining the highways. It's sometimes hard to get exactly the right perspective in a constantly changing world.

But the earth was beautiful, and my little airplane was carrying me over it at just the right altitude. Being the only person at the controls of my life wasn't selfish. It was necessary. I was a pilot, not a passenger, and I too could be badass.

Chapter 13

"Nice airplane," contest organizer Harry Beecham said after I taxied up to the Paso Robles terminal in my new S-1T one hot June morning in 1989. "Did you just buy it?"

Paso Robles was our chapter's home contest. The airport boasted a huge V of two runways in the middle of Central California with its Mediterranean climate and forests of live oak trees. Harry, a longtime chapter member and Advanced pilot, had asked me to arrive early to help set up the contest. It was an important volunteer role that involved laying out the box markers, sweeping out the hangars, and making sure everything was ready for the onslaught of pilots that Thursday.

"Are you flying Intermediate this weekend? You flew Sportsman last year, didn't you?" Harry asked as we walked into the neighboring vineyard to check out one of the box markers.

"Yes, but I'm practicing Advanced." I was going to compete in Intermediate, but it wasn't unusual for pilots to practice sequences in the next category up in preparation for competition. Frank had been practicing Unlimited without entering a contest for two years. On the other hand, Stu was still trying to fly in Advanced despite not being competitive.

Harry raised his eyebrows. "You don't want to move up a category until you thoroughly dominate it. You should win first place at all four of the major California contests. Do that next year in Intermediate. Then you can move up."

I thought to myself, *Is he afraid of the competition?* Out loud I said, "Thanks for the advice." I was going to ignore him and do what I wanted. This was heady stuff! I'd vowed to myself that I was going to fly well enough in this contest to win a trophy. Of course, I announced to everyone else that I was sure I'd come out somewhere near the bottom. Sadly, I still felt safer denigrating myself in front of others. Other pilots (mostly male) could brag about how well they were doing, but I didn't yet dare.

Entertaining such ambitions was a big step for me. During my childhood, whenever I felt proud of an achievement, someone outside my family would criticize me, or say I had a swollen head, or try to sabotage my work. Only my parents were consistently proud of me. "Your brain works better than anyone else's," my father frequently told me. "My buttons are popping." And then there was the shame I felt if I didn't do something perfectly, like the bungled landing in front of Doc Munson and the M&D mechanics, which I only partially accepted was not my fault. Even now, my childhood conditioning still made me look over my shoulder whenever things were going well.

By 1989 I'd set my sights on competing in the Unlimited category by 1990, less than two years after I'd started aerobatics. It was unheard of for someone to move up that fast. Many pilots told me it was too difficult to learn the maneuvers and procedures in such a short time. But I was determined. Paso Robles was just the first step.

I flew my beautiful, brand-new airplane that weekend through three grueling sequences in the blistering central California sun, and when it was all over, I'd managed to snag a third-place trophy in Intermediate at Paso Robles. And, as I'd promised myself, once I won any trophy, I'd move up a category. Next step: flying Advanced in competition.

From June through September of that year, I practiced Advanced and flew in several regional contests. Despite the caveats I'd gotten, I did well from the start, winning a couple more trophies, including a second-place win at Pendleton, Oregon. By the end of the 1989 competition season, I headed out for the first time to the National Aerobatic Championships in Denison, Texas, to compete in Advanced at the national level.

At the premier contest in the US that September, I joined over a hundred pilots from all over the country to compete for the title of National Champion in each of the five categories. Thirty pilots were vying for honors in the Advanced category, and I'd only been flying it for three months. It was intimidating and exciting, but I was touched by the kindness and friendliness of many of the veteran pilots, who took time to welcome me to the national level of the sport. The competition was tough, but I surprised myself by flying well—especially in the Unknown, where I'd had problems before. At the end of the last day, I stood at the whiteboard in the hot Texas sun and watched the scoring director hand-write the results.

Despite my inexperience, I snagged fourth place out of a field of thirty-one of the top Advanced pilots from all over the country, all of them far more experienced. I'd scored 6619.2 points, less than a tenth of a percent behind the third-place winner, a veteran Advanced flyer who took home a trophy nearly as tall as I was. I could hardly believe it.

With my fourth place at Nationals, I was now ranked one of the top Advanced pilots in the country. I was going to move up to the Unlimited category, the pinnacle of competition, the category only world-class pilots even attempted because the maneuvers were so dangerous, and so hard on the airplane and on the body. I'd be pulling as many as ten positive g's, making my one-hundred-pound body weigh nearly ten times as much, or one thousand pounds, as I strained through the high-g corners at the bottom of a loop or a pull to vertical. I'd be flying outside or inverted maneuvers, pushing so hard I pegged my g-meter in the negative direction, leaving my eyes bloodshot and spreading massive yellow and green bruises across my thighs. There would be rolling turns, tailslides, and the infamous four-minute Freestyle, the airshow routine where nothing was forbidden. I'd seen other Unlimited pilots make up their own figures, fly crazy gyroscopics such as lomcovaks, terrifying maneuvers that rely on using the gyroscopic effect of the propeller to cause the airplane to tumble nose over tail like a somersault or cartwheel and then resume flying moments before the plane would otherwise hit the ground.

To fly Unlimited, I'd need to get serious. I'd need to train like an athlete. I'd need to practice every day.

My current software contract had me working from 9 a.m. to 6 p.m., Monday through Friday. I needed the income from that job to pay for rent and food, make the monthly loan payments on my airplane, and for insurance, taxes, hangar, and gas. But I couldn't fly my new airplane after 6 p.m. because it had no electrical system and no lights.

I came up with an idea, and approached my boss. "What if I take a four-hour lunch every day, and come into the office from nine a.m. to one p.m. and five to nine p.m.?" I asked. "That way I could make morning meetings and synchronize with everyone else, and then spend four uninterrupted hours in the evenings getting more software written."

He hesitated but then said, "As long as you keep on being such a productive member of the team, it's fine. But remember, we've got a big deadline coming up in November."

"I'll make it," I promised. Inside, I was grinning. I was way ahead of schedule on my part of the project.

Now I'd have time during daylight to make the forty-five-minute drive out to Livermore Airport, where my Pitts was hangared. In that four-hour break, I'd have enough time to get the plane ready, practice my Unlimited sequence in the area near Tracy, land, wipe down the plane and push it back into the hangar, jump into my car, and arrive back at the office in time to start my next four-hour shift.

It was possible. And perhaps even more important, I was now forcing myself to go out and practice each day. There was something about daily practice that helped me make the biggest improvements yet to chip away my fear.

Even when it made me sick to my stomach to think about getting in that scary little airplane, I'd do it. Day by day, I was becoming less fearful and more skillful at making the plane do what I wanted. And I needed this relentless practice. Just as Frank had warned me, the jump from Advanced to Unlimited was even bigger than moving from Sportsman through Intermediate to Advanced.

Marge Denny had mentioned it when I first bought my Pitts, and now I was finally acknowledging it out loud: I was going to try out for the US Aerobatic Team at the next opportunity at Nationals. I wanted to represent my country at the World Aerobatic Championships. In 1992 the best pilots in the world would come together in France, and I, the "little granola gal" from California, was going to try to be one of them. I had two years to get good enough. Two years in this man's world. Two years until the next team tryouts in Denison, Texas, in September 1991. I'd have to fly a lot of Unlimited regional contests for practice before then.

*   *   *

A tall, sun-bronzed man in a white mesh shirt and baseball cap greeted me when I landed at the airport in Ephrata, Washington. "Hey, are you Cecilia?" There weren't many five-feet-two women flying single-seat Pitts in the entire country, so I guess it was kind of obvious I was the one who'd called in advance asking if there'd be an Unlimited category at Ephrata this year.

I wasn't used to being recognized, and it made me a little nervous. After years of remaining invisible so my classmates wouldn't notice me, I found myself hunching my shoulders as if expecting a blow.

I shook the man's hand, and he introduced himself as Myron Richardson, the chapter president. The contest director was inside the terminal, meeting with the registrar and dealing with paperwork. Myron told me everyone was pleased to have another Unlimited pilot show up. It's a long flight from California, so usually only pilots from the Pacific Northwest fly here.

"Evan Jenkins is getting way too cocky," he said. "He tells us we should just engrave his name on the trophy before we even fly."

I raised my eyebrows and he laughed.

"Problem is that he's right," Myron said. "He's taken every Unlimited trophy at the Pacific Northwest contests the past few years. Kind of hard to beat that beautiful Extra 300."

He gestured at a gleaming German-built composite aircraft parked on the ramp not far away. I took a moment to admire it. It was huge, more than twice the wingspan of my Pitts and about twice as long. The cockpit itself was almost as big as my entire fuselage. Brand-new, it had come from the German factory that year. I sighed a little. A truly professional airplane, the Extra had won several world championships already. All the aerobatic pilots I knew dreamed of buying a plane with such incredible amounts of horsepower, clean lines, high-tech composite airframe, and super-strong wings. My Pitts, parked on the ramp next to it, looked almost shabby with the patch on its wing and the slight discoloration of its dark blue fabric stretched between wooden ribs.

Of course, the Extra also came with a $250,000 price tag. It was so far out of my league that it wasn't even funny. Not like my $40,000 Pitts that I'd had to take a loan out to buy. *But I can look, can't I? And I can drool.* Myron noticed my expression and laughed. He clapped me on the shoulder. "Don't worry," he said kindly. "Evan doesn't bite ... too hard." He chuckled as he walked away.

Oh well. I came here to practice, not to win. I thought. *Every time I fly in a contest, I learn something new.* I reminded myself again of my goal. *I'm not here to win, but to learn.* But I didn't really believe that. I wanted to win. I wanted to smash the competition, prove that my old-fashioned little US-built Pitts could defeat that modern, sleek, state-of-the-art European technology, prove that I could fly better than a man twice my size. I wanted to show the world that you didn't have to be a tall, confident man to win. I wanted to show my teachers it was okay for me to be number one, and I wanted my dad's buttons to pop.

* * *

My competitive streak went back a long time, and it had always been both a blessing and a curse. It gave me the discipline to push myself to do better, but it also caused me difficulties in my social life. As a girl, I observed that when boys or men competed with each other, it ended up being a bonding experience, but if women competed against men, it fractured their relationships.

Many years ago, our family was on vacation at a hotel that had a Ping-Pong table, along with several other families we hadn't known well before. All the kids played, but the two best players were a thirteen-year-old boy named Michael and me. We played ferociously. Sometimes I won, and sometimes Michael did.

Then a tall, blond girl arrived. She was a lousy player, but Michael started spending all his time in endless, slow volleys with her. He was no longer interested in playing with me.

Bewildered and hurt, I asked my mother, "Why does Michael play with her?"

"Maybe it's because she lets him win. You should try it."

I crossed my arms and frowned. Never.

*　*　*

When I won first place for my first flight in an Advanced contest, the only woman placing ahead of five men, I was flushed with pride, but like the Ping-Pong incident, it was quickly taken away.

A pilot named Will Haas stood beside me at the contest board, watching as the scores were written out. He'd been flying aerobatics for thirty years, and other pilots respected and liked him, saying he was one of the kindest men they'd ever known. He'd placed last. He was facing away from me when he said just loudly enough for me to hear, "Last again. I'd fly much better if I was willing to be *selfish*. To take time and money away from my loved ones. But I have a family to take care of."

I knew his words were directed at me, and they stung, especially because Will was reputed to be so nice. Was I selfish to be pouring so much effort into my flying? No one called Leo Loudenslager, the seven-time National Aerobatic Champion, selfish for focusing on his practice, for becoming the first pilot to win Nationals so many times. No one called my father selfish for dragging his wife and children halfway around the world every year or two so he could build his career. Was it only selfish for women to focus on their work or achievements? It took all the joy out of my flight. If someone as well-respected as Will Haas called me selfish, maybe it was true. I didn't fly as well on the second and third flights, and someone else took home the first-place Advanced trophy that contest.

After that, though, I became even more obsessed with aerobatics. I flew every day, and when I wasn't flying, I was thinking about flying, dreaming about looping and rolling in my Pitts. I read compulsively about aerobatics, buying every book I could find, poring over my copy of *Sport Aerobatics* magazine from cover to cover as soon as it arrived each month and talking to my fellow chapter members about aerobatics for as long as they'd reciprocate. Even Ben started to pick up more aerobatic lingo as he patiently listened to me go on and on. By now he knew the names of all the aerobatic maneuvers and could help me plan a Freestyle—a sign of true love if there ever was one.

"Whatever matters so much to you is important to me as well," he reasserted one evening at dinner.

Each weekday I made use of my four-hour lunch breaks, drove out to Livermore and flew a half-hour sequence. On weekends, I joined Frank and Stu at New J. It felt good to have friends who shared my obsession. There were no complaints about selfishness from Frank or Stu. Frank claimed that being selfish was good, and if Stu's wife of forty years minded that her retiree husband spent his weekends with his homebuilt Eagle and two crazy friends on a patch of asphalt in the middle of the Central Valley, we never heard about it from him.

I was so obsessed that I couldn't wait for the California contests that summer of 1990. I'd been practicing Unlimited that spring, and I was eager to try out my skills in competition. When I heard about the May contest up in Ephrata, Washington, I decided to fly north to the Apple Cup on May 17, even though it would be a long and uncomfortable flight in my Pitts, which was not designed for cross-country travel.

"Are you sure it's a good idea to fly that far?" Stu asked me one afternoon at a critique session. "It's an expensive trip. Lots of gas. I couldn't afford it in my Eagle."

He was right that it probably wasn't the sensible thing to do. I couldn't help but feel a pang of fear that I was going to blow my budget for the year. But I felt desperate to fly a contest after the long winter.

I put in a request for time off work, loaded up my airplane before dawn that Thursday, and rolled my hangar door shut just as the sun spilled a molten band of light over the Altamont Pass east of Livermore.

I knew my Pitts so well now. It fit like a spacesuit designed exactly for me. I'd put away my elevator shoes and my dive belts threaded with lead weights. I still needed custom-carved Styrofoam cushions to see out of the airplane, but at last I could modify the plane instead of me. I'd attached a five-pound lead weight to the tail post, shifting the center of gravity aft to lessen the control forces and make the plane more maneuverable. Now, it performed snap rolls crisply, and flicked off a horizontal line with a touch. It was magnificent.

I had my prep routine down. It took me less than ten minutes to get the plane ready. I slid the canopy back and stepped fluidly onto the wing walk. One leg up and over the side into the cockpit, right foot on the parachute harness, then left. Then I grasped both struts in front of the windshield and slid down into the seat.

I slipped my car keys and all the contents of my jeans pockets into the small zippered pouch attached to the inside of the cockpit. I double-checked every pocket, my fingers tracing the seams. Then, I checked again. It was important never to climb into an aerobatic airplane with anything in your pockets, even loose change. An inverted roll is like someone turning you upside down and shaking you. Every little thing in your pockets will fall out. You might not notice that coin sliding out of your pocket behind your elbow. And then the next day, that quarter will slide down the fuselage into the tail section, where it may rattle around innocently for many flights.

But then one day, it'll get wedged just inside the elevator control, and the next time you pull, to your surprise and dismay you'll find your controls are blocked. You can't pull the stick back all the way. If you're lucky enough to be flying level when this happens, it's not too bad. You'll have time to shake the obstruction loose, or figure out a way to regain control. If you can't, you climb to altitude, slide open the canopy, and jump. Yes, you've crashed your $40,000 airplane because of twenty-five cents, but hey, you're still alive.

If you'd been unfortunate enough to be screaming out of a downline, heading straight for the earth at low altitude, you might not be able to escape hitting the ground. Friends of mine, superb pilots, have died this way. Bart Rogers, for one, a brilliant Unlimited pilot, top-notch flight instructor, a sweet guy and a careful pilot.

Bart told me one day at Nationals, "You can't ever skip a single item on your preflight checklist. It could kill you." The next week, I got the news he had flown straight into the ground on an instructional flight with a student, a long, full-power dive from near vertical. Witnesses said they saw the plane appear to make an aborted pull then push.

The sign of jammed controls. Was it a quarter his student hadn't bothered to remove from his pocket?

Twenty-five cents can seem trivial, like nothing. Sometimes you get funny looks. "Why are you such an obsessive jerk?" "Who the hell cares about less than a dollar?" "Let's just go fly." But would you rather be polite or alive?

Once, when taxiing, I found I couldn't pull the stick all the way back. I returned to the hangar. There, I unscrewed the inspection plate at the tail and found … a slightly bent nickel, with a sharp crease on its surface where my elevator attachment had jammed straight into the metal. How did that nickel get in there?

Because the Pitts is such an unusual airplane, it's a magnet for spectators. People bring their kids out to the airport, and it's fun to show them the cute little biplane with its single seat. But sometimes a father will lean over the cockpit, and a stray nickel may fall out of his shirt pocket as he gestures to an instrument or to show off to his child. Maybe he heard it fall, or maybe he didn't.

If I hadn't caught that nickel on taxi, I might not be writing this today.

So, I'm careful and obsessively so. Whenever anyone goes near my airplane, I spring to alertness. This is one arena where my life might depend on being a detail-oriented, obsessive-compulsive jerk.

So, anyway, emptying my pockets and placing the contents in my zippered pouch was now part of my routine. Next, earplugs in my ears, headset on, headset wires threaded through my belts—two sets, tight, excruciatingly tight, pressing hard into my bruises. Finally, ratchet the second belt down even further. Every elite athlete learns to ignore pain or use it.

Every time I flew, I performed a couple of extra pretakeoff checks to psych myself up for that frightening moment when I'd commit myself to the air. When I trusted the plane was mechanically sound and that my piloting skills hadn't become rusty, I'd double-check the weather along the route and at my destination and once more trust or pray that this flight wouldn't be my last. This time I wouldn't crash and die. My imagination overrevved, my fears rose up in me, and I pushed them down again firmly. Every time.

But now, I was finally ready. I taxied onto the Livermore runway for departure to Ephrata. I still found every single takeoff terrifying but also thrilling. I don't think I'll ever lose that thrill, and to be honest, I don't really want to. I advanced the throttle, and the Pitts leaped forward onto its main gear, quivered, and bounded into the air. The ground fell away.

I was flying and it was a beautiful day. The blue sky enfolded the tawny, golden mountains, and I was embraced between them.

It was going to be a long flight north. I'd bundled up with several layers under my flight jacket and gloves. The chilly early-morning air bit into my lungs as I sailed past the four-thousand-foot peak of Mount Diablo. Two hours until my next fuel stop, and I was already freezing and cramped, jammed into the tiny cockpit with two duffel bags scrunched under my legs and my flight bag lodged in a narrow slice of space just under my left elbow.

I scanned the instruments, checked that the hum of the engine sounded right, and made a note in my flight log, settling in for the trip.

Cross-country flights in a small airplane are said to be "hours of bore-dom interspersed with moments of pure terror," but for me the terror never quite goes away. Other pilots say they've sometimes fallen asleep on long flights, and one even told me he brought a paperback to read on those interminable flights over the desert with no one else around.

I was incapable of relaxing when flying. Every sense was keyed up. I listened for the slightest stutter of the engine that might presage a failure or problem. I constantly scanned the ground for potential landing sites, just in case the engine quit. Maybe I was just a little more neurotic than the average pilot.

The aromas blasting through the vents shifted as I flew over rice fields, then vineyards, then lakes ringed by old-growth redwoods. The air started out dry and dusty—the California Central Valley in summertime—then sweetened as I flew north, growing moist with the scent of pine needles. Flying was a small miracle, a hint of the divine, and these glorious days always reminded me of that.

It was about seven hundred miles to Ephrata, a little more than two flight legs of about three hundred miles each. I'd planned two stops, one at Redding and the second at Bend, Oregon. Three legs, with two one-hour breaks. I'd land at each stop, put fuel in the tank, stretch my legs, go to the bathroom, grab something to eat, and then take off again. This plan would land me in Ephrata in the late afternoon. I couldn't fly after dark because my plane had no lights, so I intended to be on the ground well before sunset.

On my last leg, I planned to run the overwing tank nearly dry, so it would be empty at my destination. Otherwise, it would be way too heavy to remove from the wing when it came time to do aerobatics. But it didn't have a fuel gauge, so I had to time it. It was a little nerve-racking. Unlike Doug Waldron, the former owner of this plane, I was about as far away from a cowboy pilot as you could get. I obsessively planned everything, and I liked the safety and security of a fuel gauge to let me know how much gas there was in the tank. I didn't want the engine to quit in the middle of the air.

The wing tank was a big homemade hunk of metal that did its job but no more. No-frills flying, here. The only way to know when the tank was empty was when bubbles appeared in the clear plastic tubing that curled down through the open vent.

But when those bubbles showed up, it would be almost too late. Doug had said, "When the wing tank starts bubbling, I'll play a few games with the plane, tilt it this way and that to get the last few drops of fuel to the engine. Don't wanna waste any gas!"

"But won't the engine quit?" I asked. I'm sure my eyes had gone wide, betraying my shock.

"It starts right up again when you hit the boost pump," he informed me with appalling unconcern.

Today, when my timer told me the tank was about to run out, I watched the tube closely. As soon as I saw the very first bubble, I immediately flipped on the boost pump and switched over to the main tank. It was okay if I wasted a few ounces of gas to prevent the engine quitting.

When Ephrata Municipal Airport was finally in sight, I circled to the west to avoid the commercial Grant County International Airport, possessor of one of the longest runways in the world. I monitored the tower frequency, just in case. Not a peep over the radio. Stiff with cold, I flexed my fingers and toes before taking a firmer grip on the stick and planning my approach.

The Ephrata airport was shaped like a giant letter *A* nestled amid a russet-colored desert lit up by the late-afternoon sun—two long runways meeting at the top, a telltale sign of a former military airfield. A shorter, narrower runway joined the two arms of the A, and after calling in and announcing my approach on 122.8 megahertz, the Unicom radio frequency for non-towered airports, I carefully checked out the box markers on the ground to the east of the field, parallel to this small runway.

The town of Ephrata, a quiet community of around five thousand people at the time, is tucked to the southwest of the field. A notable event occurred here the previous year when Steven Spielberg filmed parts of the movie *Always* at the Ephrata airfield, parts involving aerial firefighters flying surplus World War II bombers in 1943 to fight forest fires.

A pilot I met at the Reno Air Races the year before flew the scenes for the movie. When I first started flying, it was kind of cool running into semifamous people, actors, and other folks out at these tiny airfields. The aviation world was small, and pretty soon you knew everybody, including all their foibles. When Harrison Ford called me to ask for advice on an aerobatic aircraft purchase, he paused after saying his name as though expecting me to react. Too shy to say anything, I instead politely spent time explaining the basics about the plane he was looking to buy.

I circled Ephrata to the south, determined wind direction, and entered the traffic pattern. Landing a Pitts always requires focus, so I snapped myself awake, sat up straight in the plane, and curved in for a landing. The air was hot, dry, and dusty.

As I slowed down, a wide high-speed taxiway opened up to my left, and I headed off the runway and bumped over the ancient tarmac. The field looked like it was paved in 1940 and had only ever been patched since then. I slid the canopy back and warm air gushed over my face and shoulders. Although I was still trembling with cold from the cross-country flight at altitude, I was soon sweating under my layers because it was a hot day in Ephrata.

I made careful S-turns across the ramp, heading for a chain-link fence where a couple dozen brightly colored planes were parked facing into the wind. There were biplanes (Pitts and Great Lakes), single-wing planes (Decathlons, Citabrias, and Van's RVs), and higher performance mono-planes (Extras and Sukhois). Across a neatly trimmed green lawn sat a two-story clapboard building with wide windows on the second floor and faded letters spelling EPHRATA on the roof. It was the only building in sight, so it was probably the terminal. I guessed it must be contest head-quarters, judging from the small crowd gathered there. Far to the north towered a huge, World War II–era hangar with a rounded top, perhaps thirty feet tall at its bulbous apex. That hangar would most likely be dedi-cated to overnight aircraft storage for the contest. You could pack a lot of little Pitts and Citabrias into a hangar sized for an airliner.

There were four pilots registered for the Unlimited category: Greg, Evan, Lloyd, and me. When our turn to fly arrived, we'd push our planes out to the starting line. Greg would fly first in a Stephens Akro, a sleek monoplane he built himself from a kit that cost $80,000 for the parts alone. Then came Evan in his huge, gleaming Extra 300. Lloyd flew a brand-new factory Pitts S-2B, the newer version of the S-2A I used to own, redesigned and with a bigger, throatier engine. Finally, there was me, "tail-end Charlie," in the rear with my little S-1T.

I felt inadequate. But hey, *I'm just here to fly and learn* was the mantra I repeated in my head. It didn't matter if I came in last. It didn't matter that I'd just overheard a guy in a faded flannel shirt saying, "A woman flying an airplane is like a dog riding a bicycle. You don't expect they can do it well. What's amazing is that they can do it at all."

But I wanted to *win*. I wanted it fiercely and completely and furtively.

Friday morning, the official contest began. The coffee shop was full at six o'clock with pilots eating big breakfasts. Aerobatic flying was physically demanding, even at the Sportsman level. Pulling g's put a strain on every muscle—actually, every cell in the body. It was probably one of the most efficient calorie-burning exercises ever. I usually found that a big omelet, hash browns, and a chocolate milkshake gave me enough fuel to start the day. At one point I was certain that the secret of my flying success was those chocolate milkshakes. Something about the combination of sugar, carbs, protein, and fat always did the job to get me fired up for a competition sequence.

The contest briefing was held at the airport at seven a.m. Attendance was required. The contest director called the roll, and anyone who didn't answer wouldn't be eligible to fly in the contest, even if you had registered, paid your fees, and flown seven hundred miles to get there. This was why I always set two alarms.

The competition might appear friendly on Thursday, but by Friday, the gloves were off, and the fierce rivalry began in earnest. Evan Jenkins sidled up to me during the briefing, checked me over from head to toe, and offered me his hand to shake. "I hear I might have some competition this year," he said.

I gave a self-deprecating laugh. "I'm just here to fly for fun. I only started flying Unlimited last October. How long have you been flying?"

He scratched his cheek and twisted his mouth as though counting. "Lemme see. I believe it's nine ... no, ten years." He raised his eyebrows and gave me a slow smile. "That is, in Unlimited. I've been flying aerobatics for nigh on twenty years, but at first I thought all this competition stuff was silly."

"I flew my first contest in 1988," I offered, trying to be friendly. "In Basic, at Taft."

"Taft? You from California?"

At my nod, he gave me a mock frown. "Just make sure you don't move up to Seattle anytime soon. We don't need any more Californians coming in and driving up our housing prices."

"Don't worry about it." I scoffed. "That's the one city I'd never move to. I can't stand rain."

"Just make sure you keep it that way, and we'll get along fine." He grinned and moved off to greet another friend.

After he left, I replayed the conversation in my head. Did I sound too arrogant, implying I'd moved up more quickly than he had? I didn't want to appear rude or unfriendly. I was the newcomer here in this group, and I couldn't help feeling a little shy and intimidated. I watched all the other pilots greeting each other, catching up after the long rainy winter, seeing each other for the first time in months. I desperately wanted to make a good impression. I wanted them to like me.

When it came time for Unlimited to fly, several of us sat under the wing of a Decathlon to get out of the sun. We all watched intently as the first pilot up, Greg, in his blue-and-white Stephens Akro, pulled to vertical and flew up, up, up into the cloudless sky.

The pilot unlucky enough to draw the number one position in the order of flight is affectionately dubbed the "wind dummy." The winds at altitude are frequently different from those on the ground. Watching the pilot flying ahead of you is one of the most effective ways of gauging the wind for your turn in the box. And correcting for wind is one of the most important skills a competition aerobatic pilot can master.

"Looks like a lot of crosswind and not much headwind," commented Evan laconically. I glanced at him. That wasn't what I was seeing. I lifted my thumb to the sky and watched as the plane was blown south. The wind drift was especially noticeable as the plane slowed down just before the hammerhead pivot. Was Evan getting it wrong, despite all his experience?

I was about to correct him when I reconsidered. I'd heard Evan was infamous for playing the psychological game with competitors, like in chess tournaments. Could he be trying to psych me out so I wouldn't make the proper wind corrections when I was flying? I felt inexplicably honored. Part of me was buoyed by the knowledge that someone considered me serious competition.

It made me even more determined to fly well and stay in the box. It would involve lots of math to estimate the radius of each figure, count how many seconds I was blown out of position, and calculate my starting and ending points. I also had to elongate certain arcs and compress others.

It meant doing a whole series of calculations before I flew and again in the air. It required split-second timing. Every good Unlimited pilot had to do it.

At a roll rate of 200 degrees per second, one one-hundredth of a second too long in the roll would cost fifteen points. It was simple math.

I sized up the "wind dummy." The wind was manageable, and I'd practiced in conditions similar to this. If I stayed focused, I'd keep all the maneuvers in the box. I could do the math.

My turn. I waved to the other pilots, took a last swig from my water bottle, and pushed my Pitts to the starting line. I strapped in rapidly, placed my headset over my ears, and brought the microphone close to my lips—close enough to kiss.

The contest starter Bill Larson approached and propped his meaty forearm on my canopy rail. He didn't smoke out on the line because of safety issues, but he reeked of burnt tobacco. I kept myself from wrinkling my nose. I liked Bill.

"Harnesses and belts?" he asked in the familiar refrain.

"Check."

"Sequence?"

I tapped my hand-drawn diagram, secured in a custom plexiglass holder mounted on the dashboard. "Ready."

"You're flying south to north," he told me, and I nodded.

I closed the canopy and made an S-turn down the parallel taxiway. The solitary taxi out for takeoff was always one of the most nerve-racking parts of competition aerobatics. I'd practiced hours, days, months, years for this moment. I'd risked my life numerous times, and spent thousands of dollars in preparation.

And now everything would be decided in the next six to eight minutes. I'd be making thousands of tiny corrections, gasping for breath under crushing g-loads, and putting my body through forces that no human body was designed to withstand. One split-second error would mean the difference between triumph and despair. Would I humiliate myself this time? I breathed deeply and went through my calming mantra. The important thing, I'd learned, was to skate on the surface of my fear, keep it from turning into panic. Panic translated into rough and hurried maneuvers, lack of elegance, error.

But if I were too calm, if I focused only on precision, I'd lose flair and beauty in my figures. I'd fly more like an automaton. Although the judges were supposed to grade solely on precision, they were still swayed by artistry. I had to fly without errors, make all those mathematical computations for the wind, but in addition, I had to put excitement in my flying.

If I could put all my emotion, all my agony from a lifetime of discouragement, all of my anguish and joy into my flying, the judges might sit up and take notice. And their scores might reflect their enthusiasm.

Would I achieve it this time? Would I make an error? It only took a split second to fail.

The call came over the radio. Time to fly. I closed the canopy and zoomed up into the sky. I pulled hard for the first figure, checked the position of the box markers, compensated for the wind. Pause. Roll.

I had to "crab," or turn the nose, about 2 degrees to the left. Not enough for the judges to notice, but enough to keep me on centerline with this amount of crosswind. I needed to make major corrections for the headwind, extending my upwind lines and rushing the downwind maneuvers to avoid a penalty for going outside the box.

I breathed hard. Was my timing right? Nervousness used to make me perform badly, but now it gave me energy, put an edge on my flying. My snap rolls came out crisp and precise. I took more deep breaths as I roared along the bottom of the box at two hundred miles per hour, timing the final pull for the last figure just right. *Yes!* I thought as I exited the sequence and enthusiastically performed my wing wags.

I'd done it. Flown the sequence precisely and well. I hadn't made any errors. But had I been successful at putting my excitement into my flying? I wouldn't find out until the judges' scores were posted. But as I made a perfect landing on the Ephrata runway, I felt good about my flight.

That afternoon, I called up my parents and told them I was flying in an aerobatic contest. Much to my surprise, they weren't as upset as I'd expected. Maybe they'd already expressed all their worry when I first told them I was flying. My mom reminded me to be careful, and I assured her I always was. I waited to hear the echo of the word "selfish," but it never came.

Instead, she said, "I love you, Cecilia."

My father said, "I'm sure you'll win that contest."

"The scores aren't out yet," I told them.

"You're my daughter, aren't you? My buttons are already popping."

That evening, I ran to watch the scores being posted on the whiteboard. When they appeared, I squealed with joy. I'd taken first place, just barely ahead of Evan.

And I maintained my level of performance throughout the competition. I ended up winning all three flights of the contest, and snagging my first Unlimited championship.

After the final flight, I was sitting on the floor of the hangar, wiping the belly of my plane with a rag when a shadow fell over me. I glanced up—and up—to see Evan Jenkins standing beside my plane. I hadn't realized how tall he was. He wore a sleeveless shirt that exposed well-developed biceps. His face was impassive. I swallowed.

"Hi?" I squeaked. I couldn't help looking around the hangar for witnesses. How seriously did he take his defeat? Below my belly, my body twinged with remembered pain.

"I wanted to congratulate you," he said.

I scrambled to my feet, exhaling with relief. "Thanks. It was a good contest," I said, holding out my hand.

He shook it and gave me a level stare under his baseball cap. I essayed a timid smile.

All at once, he broke into a grin. "I watched your sequences. You fly well—crisp but with style and heart. You deserved to win."

Something inside me that I hadn't known was clenched suddenly relaxed. "To tell you the truth, I wasn't expecting the psychological warfare."

He threw back his head and laughed. "You haven't been flying in Unlimited long. You're going out for the US Team, right."

It wasn't a question. I gave a tiny nod.

"Get used to it," he said, still laughing.

"The flight was really close," I countered.

His face turned stern. "It sure was. Don't count on winning next time."

I grinned. "You want there to be a next time?"

"It'd be an honor to fly against you again. Just one thing though, California gal—tell all your friends it rains too much up here." I glanced out at the cloudless sky, and he smirked. "Here's my card if you ever want to talk flying. It's been real."

As I watched him saunter out of the hangar, unexpected happiness flooded my belly. Wow. Were pilots simply different from my classmates back in middle school? Or had something changed inside me? I shrugged and went back to polishing my airplane.

In the end, I made a bunch of new friends in the Pacific Northwest and flew home with another trophy in my turtledeck.

On the flight home, I reflected on how only four years prior, I'd been a timid grad school dropout. Now I was a woman who flew with confidence and had overcome her fear not by ignoring it but by learning to work with it and use it. I was a successful software consultant, valued for my technical contributions. It had become surprisingly easy to make friends, something I'd once thought nearly impossible. I was talking to my parents regularly. Ben and I had reconnected, and he even told me he thought competition aerobatics was pretty cool.

"I'd like to get more involved," he told me one evening at dinner. He'd asked me about the kind of software contests used, and had ended up even contributing code to the official US competition scoring program.

Behind me lay the many miles of terrain I'd traversed to get to this point, the emotional barriers I'd crossed, and the financial struggles and physical limitations I'd overcome.

Ahead of me lay the airfields still to come. The US Team selection at the National Aerobatic Championships in September 1991 was just fifteen months away. There had been few women on the team, and not a single Latina. But perhaps even more important was that no one without significant financial resources had ever made it onto the team. If I made it, I'd be doing it in a plane worth $40,000 rather than $250,000. It still seemed like an impossible goal, but now, with this Unlimited win behind me, I was one step closer.

Chapter 14

"The fabric under the wing sort of billows out when I fly," I said to my mechanic, Jim, when I brought in the Pitts for its annual inspection. "Is that a problem?"

"What?" Jim's eyes bulged. He ran around the plane and tapped on the underside of the top wing, then did the same on the other side. I watched, puzzled and upset at his obvious concern.

"You've got a real problem. The stitching has failed along the entire inner third of the wing on both sides."

"I've got the Borrego contest next week. Can it wait to be fixed until after that?"

He winced. "Uh, Cecilia, this is an unsafe condition. The fabric is coming loose from the wing spars. It's a major problem. You can't fly *at all* until it gets fixed."

"But ..." I sputtered. Not fly the contest? I'd been counting on practicing every day for the next few weeks. It was now October—less than a year until US Team selection in September 1991—and winter was coming on, with its bad weather and limited opportunity for flying.

Then an even worse thought hit me. "How much is this going to cost?"

"You're going to need to get the wings completely re-covered. It's labor-intensive, so I can't give you an estimate right now, but I'm afraid we're talking thousands of dollars."

"No!" I cried. I didn't have that kind of money. There was nothing left in my budget, and if I hoped to have a chance at Nationals, I needed to be banking money rather than spending it so profligately. I clenched my fists, and tears came to my eyes.

Maintaining a custom aerobatic airplane cost much more than I'd ever expected. Fuel and oil were only the beginning. I'd already spent over $5,000 on repairs this year. Shaking that plane around multiple times a week, the heavy vibration and g-loads played havoc with both the engine and aircraft structure. I'd had to replace the engine shock mounts several times, and when I'd gotten my cylinders checked during a routine inspection last year, a couple of them were cracked and needed to be replaced. It seemed the plane developed problem after problem, and all of them cost a lot more to fix than I'd projected.

And all of these repairs were absolutely necessary. Not paying attention to them could be life-threatening. One day I slid into the cockpit to be greeted by a pungent gasoline odor. Instead of flying, I pushed the airplane to Jim's hangar. He bent into the cockpit and within a few minutes discovered the culprit. One of the fuel pressure lines was rubbing against a strut under g-loads, and the chafing had left only a paper-thin skin of metal over the fuel line.

Jim wiped his face, leaving a streak of grease across his forehead. "Good thing you decided not to fly. The next time you did aerobatics, it would've worn through that fuel line and you would've had gas spraying all over the cockpit. Engine fire for sure."

I shivered. I'd finally found something my overactive imagination and fearful nature were good for: Keeping me safe in this dangerous sport.

Still, that incident led to another $1,000 repair bill. Something had to be done. I couldn't go on this way. Even working two jobs, I was barely making enough money to pay for both my living expenses and my flying. Plus, it was hard to count on a steady stream of income from either flight instruction or contract programming. I'd been let go in the middle of a programming contract with less than a day's notice only a few weeks prior. Fortunately, it hadn't taken me long to find another contract. What I wanted, however, was to find a way to fly more aerobatics *and* earn more money.

Was there a way to combine the two? Airshow performers were paid for their flying. Unlike the strict amateur rules of competition aerobatics with the single goal of precision flying graded by judges, airshows operated on an entirely different principle—one based on entertainment for the general public.

I loved attending airshows, but I'd never imagined myself as a performer. They were highly staged, almost like a circus, and airshow pilots performed one gimmick after another, such as wing walking, night shows, low-altitude inverted ribbon cuts, or "the flying dog" (where a dog appears to be sitting in the cockpit alone when the plane takes off). They flew comedy routines like the one where an old farmer gets into an airplane and ends up "accidentally" bumping the throttle and lurching about in the air. Shows were a lot of fun, but my kind of flying wasn't like that. It was like the difference between Olympic figure skating and the Ice Capades.

Still, I mused, if I could come up with an interesting airshow routine, maybe I could finally earn enough money to pay for my flying. And it could even be fun. I loved watching little kids get excited at the shows. And, to be honest, I couldn't deny it'd be an ego boost having tens or even hundreds of thousands of people gathered at an airport watching me fly. Okay. That would be super cool. The thought of all that approval, even if only for eight minutes, was seductive. So I started researching how to become an airshow performer.

It wouldn't be easy though. There was a lot more involved than just flying. I'd need to join an airshow organization and attend their yearly convention in Las Vegas. I would have to develop an airshow routine, something flashier than a competition sequence. I'd need to get an "airshow card," a low-altitude waiver of FAA regulations stating that I was qualified to perform aerobatics below the legal minimum of fifteen hundred feet. Of course, as an Unlimited aerobatic pilot, I'd already been flying maneuvers down to three hundred feet, but that was only in specially waivered airspace for competition or practice. Airshow waivers in front of spectators were held to a different and much higher standard.

If you messed up at a competition and crashed, it was unlikely you would take out any spectators for the simple reason that there *were* no spectators at competitions—at least not usually. In fact, there had never been a fatality at any aerobatic contest in the history of competition flying.

Not true at airshows. A number of infamous crashes, especially in Europe, had resulted in strict laws requiring all airshow routines to go through an approval process. In the US, no flight maneuvers involving a vector toward the crowd were allowed. If pilots screwed up and lost control of their planes, momentum shouldn't send them crashing into the spectators. It was an ironclad rule, and for many decades, airshow crashes in the US had only resulted in performer deaths.

I now had to design a set of maneuvers that appeared death-defying while staying perfectly safe. In competition aerobatics, everything was strictly prescribed and planned in advance. Competition was focused on that perfect-ten figure. It was one of those mathematically precise scaffolds I'd found so useful in overcoming my fear. I knew exactly what I had to do at each moment during the flight, and I could rehearse it beforehand.

Airshows and competitions were poles apart. Instead of trying to fly each maneuver to an exact standard so a trained judge could score me well, I could choreograph my flight however I wanted. What looked flashy and impressive? Audiences often had no idea of what made a "trick" difficult. If it sounded and looked scary, it was good.

One drawback was that I was shy, and now I'd have to become a marketer for my performance. This wasn't exactly an area I felt comfortable with. I'd also need all the trappings. I'd have to hire a videographer and an announcer. It was the announcer's job to make you sound impressive to the crowd. "From Berkeley, California, flying the unique and powerful Pitts S-1T, it's aerobatic star Ms. Cecilia Aragon!" It made me cringe a little, just thinking of it. And then I'd have to package this entire show and sell it to producers across the country by buttonholing them at the airshow convention, telling them what an awesome pilot I was and how they should hire me for their show.

Ouch.

But I needed the money. So I went for it. I didn't realize at the time that I was overlooking a key danger, a fundamental reason why more pilots died in airshows than in competition. I didn't realize how vulnerable

I would be to the simple weakness of wanting to impress others. It didn't occur to me I'd end up putting my life at risk in my very first show.

I decided to forgo the gimmicks. I was simply going to fly a precise and beautifully choreographed dance in the sky. Of course, it took an investment to get started. I gritted my teeth and opened another credit card. Since my Pitts would be in the shop for two months getting its wings recovered, I couldn't fly aerobatics, so I worked extra programming and flight-instruction hours to raise funds. My bank balance started to go up. I was able to hire an announcer and professional videographer to film my routine. The next step was to contact airshow producers and talk them into hiring me for their show.

Eventually, I designed, printed, and sent out glossy airshow packages, made dozens of phone calls, flew to numerous airports in my newly repaired Pitts, and talked enthusiastically to airshow promoters for weeks and then months.

Nothing.

Nobody wanted to hire a first-time airshow pilot. It was understandably risky. New airshow pilots killed themselves in accidents at an alarming rate. Nobody wanted to deal with a splashy crash by a newcomer at their show. I accumulated lots of rejections that winter and spring.

Finally, the producer of the Watsonville Airshow agreed to take a chance on me if I discounted my airshow fee from $1,500 for a weekend to expenses only. Not a promising start for a lucrative flying career. But I was so desperate to break into the field that I agreed. I sent out my freshly printed airshow contract, and he signed and returned it. I held the signed piece of paper in both hands, almost shaking with excitement. My first airshow contract!

* * *

The Watsonville Airshow, held every Memorial Day weekend since 1964 at this small agricultural town twenty miles north of Salinas, California, had a long tradition of showcasing historic civilian and military aircraft on the ground and in the air.

I flew over California's beautiful Central Coast early on a Friday, landing at Watsonville along with many other small aircraft all flying in for the
show that weekend. Sunlight glittered on the tarmac while a brisk wind
from the northwest extended the windsock to its full length. A guy with
an orange flag tried to direct me into the general public fly-in parking area,
and it gave me a little thrill to radio him that I was one of the performers.

I was directed to a large hangar at one end of the field, greeted with
tremendous respect by a young volunteer, and handed an official packet
of materials. My ego felt all puffed up. They issued me my very own rental
car, gave me a map to a local hotel, and politely asked if I'd be willing to
talk to the press later that afternoon.

Wow. Talk to the press? Me? I shot a glance behind me to make sure
they weren't addressing someone else. My pulse raced like crazy, and I had
to suppress a goofy smile. "Sure! I'd be happy to."

The desire for fame had been one of my guilty secrets for years. Like many
children, I craved more attention, but whenever I drew it to myself, I was
scolded by adults or hit by other kids. As a result, I developed a set of contra-
dictory desires, wanting both to stand out and to hide. In childhood, I even
once held the altogether inappropriate dream of becoming a movie star. Luckily, my realistic self had always kept me in check. *Don't be such an idiot! Nobody
would ever be interested in you. Besides, you're the least photogenic person on earth.*

My defense mechanism was to keep it buried. But the problem with
refusing to admit you want something is that you deliberately turn away
from opportunities to get it. I'd avoided most activities that might have
prepared me to perform onstage. For example, I'd deliberately chosen to
remain ignorant about fashion, makeup, or personal appearance as part
of my childhood rebellion against traditional femininity. That, however,
would have to change.

I turned to another member of the local chapter of the Ninety-Nines,
the association of women pilots, for help. She always managed to look
fashionable and well-put-together, even on the wind-blown airfield.

"First, you need to buy a flight suit and get your name embroidered
on it," Jane informed me. "Wearing jeans and a T-shirt all the time just
won't cut it anymore."

I groaned. "I'll feel like an idiot with my name plastered all over everything. And I hate one-piece flight suits."

The male pilots I knew loved them. But for a woman, the suit made it awkward to use the bathroom, because you had to unzip the thing all the way down. Anyone who's hung out at small airstrips knows it can be difficult to find an outhouse. Wearing a flight suit ruled out my usual habit of sneaking behind a bush.

Then Jane threw her hands up over my hair. It was a frizzy mess. "I've got no idea what to do with it," she moaned.

I was clueless myself. I'd tried tying it back in a ponytail, but big hunks of hair always sprung free all around my face. My mother had occasionally taken me to the beauty parlor in my small hometown in Indiana, but the hairdressers there had no idea what to do with my coarse black "ethnic" hair. After a disastrous attempt at "thinning," and another failure at "conking" (a type of chemical straightening), I'd become grouchy and stubborn whenever anyone suggested doing anything about my hair. I'm afraid it didn't help my airshow career. An acquaintance once informed me, "You look like you've been rode hard and put away wet."

At least at the Watsonville Airfield, due to the stiff breeze that day, most of the other pilots' hair was being blown all over the place, so mine probably didn't seem that bad in comparison. In any event, the reporter just asked a few questions and moved on to the bigger stars. A friend later told me that on the local evening news that night I looked "like a deer in the headlights." I was just glad it wasn't worse.

The next morning, the airport was packed with tens of thousands of spectators. I had to drive in the back way and park my rental car in a special lot. They held the airshow briefing at one of the local businesses at the airport in a large room lit by banks of fluorescent tubes. All our credentials and airplanes were inspected by stern-faced FAA officials. I watched the other airshow performers—famous pilots I'd watched at previous airshows and admired from afar, like Eddie Andreini or Julie Clark—out of the corner of my eye and tried to imitate them. I couldn't quite mimic their joking and laughing, but I was able to smile and talk about how excited I was—in a professional and safe way, of course. I'd come a long way from being completely shy, but there was still so much further to go. Yes, I insisted to myself, I was a professional, while a little voice inside my head said, *What if they find out I'm really a total amateur who isn't even being paid for this?* Somehow I made it through, and then it was my turn to fly.

I suddenly realized I wasn't prepared after all. I'd assumed that because I'd flown competition aerobatics, I was qualified to perform in an airshow. But the routine was different, and the change in procedure threw me off. There was no starter for instance. Instead, a sheet of paper at the briefing listed our timetable in detail, from the flour-bombing contest, the antique flybys, and the parachute jumpers opening a huge American flag to, finally, the pilot performers. Each routine was timed to the minute, with specific windows for launch and recovery. I had to taxi out and take off on schedule. Gaps between flights gave the audience time to buy hot dogs and airshow memorabilia.

My turn to taxi out was scheduled during the helicopter comedy act. As soon as I started my engine, the booming voice of the announcer disappeared under the roar, and it began to feel more like my typical routine. Well, as normal as it ever got, considering I was about to launch into a series of absurd gyrations in the sky and risk my life in a profession known for the short lifespan of its practitioners. Adrenaline rinsed my body in its customary cycle, and I went through my checklist as I had a hundred times before.

I took off as I saw the helicopter landing—right on schedule. I dove into the long, skinny aerobatic zone for my first maneuver, flipping the switch on my smoke tank. Immediately the cockpit filled with the strange, sickly sweet smell of Corvus oil, the EPA-approved, paraffin-based "concrete form-release oil" that's vaporized in engine exhaust pipes. It produces a dense white smoke that hangs in the air as a visible marker of the plane's path and then dissipates. It's certified nontoxic, but I couldn't help wondering about the concentrated exposure I was getting in the cockpit. But, like wearing makeup and a flight suit, it seemed to be an inescapable part of performance.

My aerobatic card was a beginner's—unrelated to the Basic through Unlimited categories in competition—and I was only allowed to descend to five hundred feet during my performance. More experienced airshow performers possessed ground-level cards that allowed them to perform right "on the deck," making inverted passes to within a few feet above the runway. Obviously, that's far more electrifying for the spectators. A plane at five hundred feet looks pretty small from the ground.

Nevertheless, I dove right to five hundred feet at redline airspeed, and my flying wires screamed. Then I pulled hard to vertical, pegging my g meter somewhere past nine, and launched immediately into a torque roll, a maneuver that always especially scared me. I flew straight up into the sky with full left aileron, rolling and rolling and rolling. Eventually, my plane slowed down as it ran out of thrust, still rolling about its axis, with smoke billowing all around it and rushing into the cockpit. At last the plane slid backward through the column of smoke, still rolling, until it swapped ends dramatically and I was thrown against the belts, completely losing vision for a moment.

Then I emerged from the smoke. I breathed in the fresh, briny air in deep gulps as I hung a couple thousand feet in the air, pointed straight down at the runway below me. I shoved the throttle forward and waited as the speed built up, keeping the controls centered on my vertical dive at the earth. I waited and waited. The ground rushed up at me, faster and faster. At the last possible moment, I tugged hard on the stick, zooming along at five hundred feet above the ground, and then pulled up for a "knife-edge Cuban eight," a figure I'd invented only a few months before.

It was on the next pass back toward the crowd that it hit me. There were tens of thousands of human beings down there, all looking at me. All that concentrated attention slammed into my head with a rush. Wow. They were here to watch *me*. Surely, they deserved the best airshow I could give them. Surely, they deserved something more exciting than what I had originally planned with all my tentative, safe maneuvers. Maybe I could fly just a little lower, do a few more rolls closer to the ground to show that I really was a death-defying airshow pilot and give them their money's worth.

I was going to do it. I dove for the next maneuver, excitement building in my body. I'm an airshow star now, right? *Um, not really*, the little voice said. *You're just someone the organizers talked into flying for free because it would be good "exposure." Don't you realize this is how airshow pilots die?*

I shook myself, alone up there in the airplane. I was pilot-in-command. It was up to me to make the right decisions, and pushing myself to be more and more daring wasn't *always* the right thing. Sometimes fear wasn't bad. My exuberance and agitation tapered off a little, and I took a deep breath.

I flew to exactly five hundred feet, just like I'd planned, and performed all the figures exactly the way I'd practiced, taking a firm grip on my eagerness. The flight went well, even though maybe it wasn't as thrilling as it could have been. I'd survived my first airshow flight.

Back on the ground, I taxied up in front of the announcer's stand, popped the canopy, and stood upright on my seat cushion, raising my arms above my head. And then I heard it. The crowd cheered and shrieked. Little kids jumped up and down, screeching, their parents waved, and hundreds of cameras were clicking. I'd never encountered this kind of adulation before. It was addictive. Electrifying. And obviously dangerous.

Breaking free from fear was complicated. I once believed that all I had to do was ignore my terror whenever it welled up deep inside me. Was I going to survive an airshow career? I'd almost made the kind of split-second decision that had killed so many pilots. I needed to find a way to earn more money, but was this worth the risk?

Chapter 15

By September 1991 I'd spent two years on relentless practice, flying airshows on weekends, practicing competition sequences on weekdays, and steeling myself every day to climb into the airplane and overcome my fear. Each day, I made myself drive out to the airport, perform the preflight, and go through the ritual I'd made a habit. Each day, I told myself I was going to fly no matter what, even if I didn't feel like it. *Build the structure, day by day and cell by cell. Follow the principle of induction.*

I spent four hours out of each day to get a forty-five-minute flight out of Livermore Airport. On the drive there, I listened to books on tape, went over sequences in my head, and dreamed of winning a spot on the US Aerobatic Team—a dream I still hadn't confided to most of my friends. It seemed too pretentious to proclaim such a lofty goal. Too big a dream for me.

But I've learned this about having a dream: It doesn't matter if you tell anybody or not. What matters is that you make some progress in that direction every day. Seeds don't know they will one day become trees, but they spend each day pushing out roots to gather nutrients, and sending tiny green shoots up toward the sunlight. This kind of pushing forward includes not only plant growth but the evolution of life in general as well as human development and the formation of human society. These are classic examples of what Nobel Prize–winning scientist Ilya Prigogine called dissipative structures, where "dissipative" refers to trading energy for growth. People have choices to make every day. Do we want to push forward into the unknown, or do we want to retreat? Life is an open system, a system that exchanges elements with its environment. Systems grow, remain static, or decay. Growth is always a little more difficult than stasis.

But in the end, the unrelenting persistence of growth is what has made a difference in human history. Life is relentless, and if you allow yourself to be fully alive, you too will become a force of nature.

I was going to push forward and fly two thousand miles to Denison, Texas, to try out for the United States Aerobatic Team. All my efforts, all my years of struggling to overcome my terror, the thousands of dollars I'd poured into this sport—it would all come down to a few minutes in front of seven judges I'd never met, out on the dusty flats of Texas at an old military airport about an hour north of Dallas.

On September 7, 1991, I loaded up my Pitts and took off from Livermore, heading southeast to Lawrence, Kansas, where I'd spend two weeks with a trainer before I competed in the Lawrence Aerobatic Contest, my final competition before the tryouts. First stop: Barstow, California. I fueled up quickly in the blazing desert sun, filled my water bottle, and jumped back in the plane. My next stop was Gallup, New Mexico. East of here, I loved the terrain—the red rocks and finely carved canyons of the high desert, fringed by the deep green of the mountains. At the end of the first day, I landed at Amarillo, Texas, after flying 1,300 miles in 8.2 hours. I slept soundly in a cheap motel and woke up early the next morning for a relatively short, 400-mile flight to Lawrence.

On Friday, September 20, I flew to Grayson County Airport in Denison, Texas, site of the US National Aerobatic Championships, and joined 120 pilots from all over the US. We came together to find out, at the culmination of the aerobatic season, who were the very best pilots in each of the five categories, and in Unlimited, who would be chosen to represent our nation in the Olympics of aviation, the World Aerobatic Championships, to be held in France in July 1992.

No one was allowed to practice in the aerobatic box before the contest, so I found a hangar on the field, unloaded my bags, and headed off to practice a few miles to the west. I planned to get in three practice flights a day for each of the following three days, so I'd be super sharp by the time the contest started on Monday.

The fields around Grayson County Airport spread out in dark green swaths below me, and an acrid, artificial scent hung in the air above the crops. Perhaps there was a refinery or factory upwind. I never found out.

It was a very different terrain, and culture, from California. Driving back to the hotel with a group of pilots after a day out on the airfield, we saw a spotted white dog, dead, in the middle of the highway. As we slowed to drive around him, I saw that the spots were large beetles feeding on his corpse. By the side of the road, a small creature scuttled along. It was brown and hairy.

"Is that a tarantula?" I asked, feeling sick to my stomach.

Phil Brown, a top-ranked Advanced pilot, called, "Stop! I want to collect him." He grabbed a widemouthed jar out of his duffel bag, scooped up the monstrous spider, and bore it triumphantly back to the car. I cringed while the other pilots made jokes.

"Sure wouldn't want to find that fellow in my Pitts during a flight," said John Michaels, an Intermediate pilot I'd just met.

"If I find a passenger like that, I'm jumping," said Jake Rogers, a large, garrulous mechanic who'd served as one of the maintenance crew at the US Nationals for over ten years. I wouldn't want to fly aerobatics with a tarantula on the seat beside me, although I thought bailing out of a $40,000 plane simply because of a spider might be a little extreme. I owed Jake a huge debt for finding out that the spinner backing plate of my propeller was cracked the previous year at Nationals. Jake donated a good two hours to pulling the prop, finding a replacement backing plate, and reinstalling it on my Pitts. He then refused to take any payment other than for parts. Without his efforts, I wouldn't have been able to fly in the contest at all that year.

His kindness as well as the support of many of the other pilots repaired a part of me that had been broken since childhood. As I worked alongside other pilots on my journey to the Unlimited Aerobatic Championships, I was also rebuilding the part of me that was damaged and distrustful and had been unable to give and receive help, friendship, and love. It deepened my relationship with Ben, and our marriage became stronger as we learned to support and respect each other as independent people.

* * *

Monday was a hot and humid day. A long lineup of pilots waited in the Unlimited category. They were twenty-eight of the best pilots in the country trying out for the ten top slots. Five of the slots would go to men, and five to women, since international competition was segregated by gender at the time. Some of the men complained, saying it was easier for women to make the team because there were far fewer female pilots in the sport. It was true that there were fewer women trying out; however, the top female pilots consistently scored better than the men as a group. As a matter of fact, the women's average score was higher than the men's.

No one pointed that out, though.

Similarly, I'd been told multiple times that the only reason I was doing so well in Unlimited was because I weighed one hundred pounds. It couldn't possibly have anything to do with my skill. It was true that weighing less gave me an advantage. The better your power-to-weight ratio, the easier it was to fly certain figures. But the sad truth was that my airplane—a stock (which means unmodified) 200-horsepower Pitts—was at a tremendous disadvantage compared with those of my wealthier competitors, many of whom were flying airplanes that had 300 or even 350 horsepower and had been highly modified and customized at great expense.

The fact was that everyone had advantages and disadvantages, as a group of us decided over cards and beer one night in the hangar, and in the end, it really did come down to who flew the best, and who was able to rise above their personal disadvantages and make the most of their advantages.

Phil said, "The only exception might be if the contest organizers deliberately designed a sequence to eliminate the lower-powered airplanes."

I scoffed. "I can't believe they'd do that."

"I haven't seen it in regional competition, but this is Nationals."

Little did I know what was about to happen.

Team selection in Unlimited would be based on three flights—the Known Compulsory, Freestyle, and Unknown—each about six to eight minutes long. I'd been flying the Known Compulsory all season and could handle it in various types of wind and at different air temperatures, field elevations, and levels of humidity. Heat, humidity, and high altitude cause wings to generate less lift and engines to produce less thrust, lowering the overall performance of the plane. Competition pilots need to make constant adjustments based on these changing factors. It's another math equation.

Freestyles were designed by individual pilots to showcase their own strengths, but each routine had to adhere to specific constraints. The difficulty factors of the maneuvers had to fall within a precise range, and certain figures such as a tailslide, rolling turn, or spin had to be included. I'd been tweaking my Freestyle for a couple of years. One of my specialties in math was a technique called combinatorial optimization, and creating an ideal Freestyle was exactly this type of problem. Combinatorial optimization allowed me to take the many required variables, the strengths and weaknesses of the airplane and the pilot, and juggle and arrange them into a sequence that expressed artistry while maximizing the potential scores for each figure. Certain maneuvers were known to be more prone to subjective grading from the judges. For example, it's difficult for an unaided human to judge a 45-degree angle by eye, the judges didn't use external aids, and the flights were not filmed. As a result, most pilots minimized the number of 45-degree lines in their Freestyles.

But there were many more subtle variables to optimize. For example, the Pitts, unlike the more expensive monoplanes like the Extra, was notorious for "flopping the wrong way"—in other words, swinging its wheels up instead of down or vice versa—during a tailslide and earning a zero. A zero on any figure was the kiss of death at the higher levels of competition. You had to score on all the maneuvers to win or place. To make certain my Pitts flopped in the right direction after a tailslide, I needed to enter the slide at a minimum of 180 miles per hour. Fortunately, that simply required setting up the figure beforehand to make sure I ended up with at least that much. You could adjust most high-speed maneuvers to exit at any desired airspeed, as long as you were willing to give up some altitude.

It merely required a lot of planning before the flight as well as during the sequence. And luckily, planning—and combinatorial optimization—was my strong suit.

Just like in the regional competitions, the Unknown sequence is revealed to the pilots trying out for the team a mere eighteen hours before flight time. In my early days in the sport, the Unknown frequently tripped me up. Although I could practice and prepare the other two sequences for as long as I had time and money, there was no way to prepare for the Unknown. In a way, it mirrored my social development as a child. For years, I was poor at casual conversation. Writing was fine, because I could always revise, and I was okay in situations where I could practice beforehand. But free-form conversations, where I had no idea what was going to happen, often flummoxed me. The comments of my classmates passed above my head, as they made references to cultural norms I had no clue about. To handle a conversation requires an ability to move fluidly among the topics in a kind of verbal dance. It had taken me well into adulthood to learn how to participate in a group conversation.

I had learned, over months of relentless practice, to produce that kind of instant response in flying, that kind of extreme flexibility in the Unknown. I'd learned to dance in the air. I'd done it despite my fear of imminent death, a fear that was burdensome—and rare—among top-ranked competition aerobatic pilots.

I asked Phil Brown one evening over gin rummy if he ever felt afraid while flying aerobatics. He took some time to respond and finally said, "Well, there was this one time when I was flying with my ten-year-old son in a two-seat Pitts over mountainous terrain. I looked down at those craggy mountains and realized if the engine quit, there was no place we could land. That gave me a twinge." He shrugged. "But other than that, no. It doesn't bother me, and I've never been afraid."

I couldn't help thinking of all the emotional energy I expended on dealing with my fear—energy and time I could have used to work on my flying. But I didn't want to lose my fear completely, because fear does have its benefits. It helped me make the right decisions and kept me alive. The extra spice and thrill it put into my flying led to higher scores from the judges.

They often remarked on the underlying excitement and vitality they saw in my routines. But still, I wished my fear wasn't quite so overpowering.

* * *

Late Wednesday afternoon, I walked back over the wide expanse of cracked white concrete to see a crowd clustered around the scoreboard in front of the terminal. Despite the heat and humidity, I ran to the board, almost tripping over an exposed cable on the tarmac. I'd flown a clean and sharp Known Compulsory on Monday, and my carefully designed Freestyle earlier that morning had felt good. But it was always hard to tell from inside the cockpit how well you were flying. It all depended on what the judges noticed.

I stood at the back of the crowd, my view blocked, nervously shifting from foot to foot. I didn't want to be rude and push my way through, but I couldn't help wishing I was a little taller.

At last, Jake noticed me standing at the back and gave me a thumbs-up. "Great job!"

What does that mean? Let me see the board already!

"Give her some room," he said, and a small gap opened up beside him. I squeezed through.

I skimmed the long list of twenty-eight pilot names and scores on the whiteboard, searching for mine. When I saw it, I yelped out loud. I'd made it into seventh place overall after the first two sequences! I couldn't believe it. I only vaguely felt Jake pounding me on the back.

"Congratulations!"

I checked the numbers again. Yes, the judges had liked my Freestyle. With that flight, I'd even improved my position over the Known Compulsory. I'd scored third place in the Free among all the women.

It finally felt real that I might have a chance to make the US Aerobatic Team. It was within reach. Now it would hinge on my performance in the Unknown.

The Unknown would be a challenge for me, especially since my plane was relatively underpowered. You can use extra horsepower to muscle through mistakes in the figures. But I didn't have that option. Out of the top twenty pilots, I was one of only three flying a stock Pitts. Most of the other airplanes cost at least twice as much as mine—in some cases six times as much. The pilots were all aerobatic veterans, extremely skilled and experienced. Several of the pilots were independently wealthy and spent all their time on flying. Others were airline pilots making $200,000 a year, doctors, lawyers, securities brokers, or business owners. I realized at one point that if I were to produce a graph or visualization, like I did at work, of the demographics of the pilots competing here, I'd be notable as an outlier. It'd been less than five years since my first solo as a pilot. My income level was half that of any other competitor. I was the second-youngest pilot trying out. I was also the only Latina competing in Unlimited, and I'd later realize that no Latina had ever made the US Aerobatic Team.

Thursday, September 24, was a humid day with temperatures in the nineties. A gritty haze topped by a thin overcast hung above the field. The air felt like a wet rag. Despite this, the morning started out with some excitement when Jake Rogers found an all-too-familiar, but empty, wide-mouth glass jar on the seat of his airplane when he went to roll it out of the hangar.

Phil was laughing so hard he could hardly stand straight. "Of course I didn't leave a spider in your plane!"

"Where's your tarantula?" Jake demanded. "I want to see it."

"Sorry, I let it go yesterday."

Jake practically turned his airplane upside down inspecting the interior. Finally, he announced to Phil, "If I'm flying my sequence, and I feel a hairy leg on the back of my neck, I'm jumping, and *you're* paying me forty thousand dollars for a new airplane."

It was three in the afternoon when the Unlimited Unknown sequences were handed out to the pilots. At first, I was eager to see the routine that would be so critical to all the pilots in our category. Then, as I read through the sequence, I felt lightheaded. I read it through four times, my stomach twisting more tightly with every pass. If there had ever been a sequence designed to weed out lower-powered airplanes, this was it. It was basically unflyable for a stock Pitts like mine. It contained a rolling turn in the center of the box, followed immediately by a tailslide at the upwind end.

No! I'd need 180 miles per hour after the rolling turn to avoid flopping the wrong way in the tailslide and zeroing the figure. But my Pitts *always* exited a rolling turn at 140. It was a limitation of physics and aerodynamics.

In a monoplane like the Extra, it'd be no problem. You'd exit the rolling turn at a fast cruise, well beyond 140 miles per hour, and have sufficient power to pull up immediately for a tailslide. It was easy to make a monoplane flop the right way. No problem.

This is so unfair! I wanted to wail. Although I was currently in third place among the women, a zero in the tailslide would wipe out my entire lead and put me well out of the running. It looked like my dream of making the US Aerobatic Team would remain a dream. At least for this year.

Perhaps over the next two years, I could save money, work more hours at my jobs, bank all my income, and maybe afford a used four-cylinder Extra. It would cost at least twice as much as my Pitts, which already stretched me almost beyond my limit financially. Some people were saying the two-hundred-horsepower, four-cylinder monoplanes would be obsolete by the following year, and six-cylinder monoplanes would be required for world competition.

Maybe this was all just an impossible dream, and I should give it up. A friend of mine had already counseled me that it was a mistake to pour so much of my energy into flying at this point in my life. "You're young; you have plenty of time to fly. Why don't you start a company and get rich instead, and then come back to flying once you've retired with a few million? That's a much easier path." Easier to get rich than make the US Aerobatic Team? I'd seen friends and acquaintances get rich in Silicon Valley. But thinking about that path only depressed me. Subsuming everything else in order to make money didn't feel right. Despite working as an engineer and software developer for many years and loving it, what I enjoyed was the artistic and intellectual thrill of building software, and the creative joy of designing a beautiful and effective algorithm. I was an engineer and a mathematician but also an artist. And flying was my art.

It was how I needed to express myself. It was how I needed to push forward to become the person I knew I could be. I needed to learn to overcome my fear and my early childhood experiences. Flying gave me an accelerated crucible to make that possible. Every lesson I learned in my push to become one of the best aerobatic pilots in the world resonated deeply in my core. To grow as a human being, to be truly alive, I needed to overcome the life-destroying fear inside my heart. And of course, I wanted to win.

Sitting in my dim hotel room that night, I bent over the Unknown sequence once again. There was nothing I could do about the physics or aerodynamics, nor anything I could do about the weather or the limitations of my aircraft. But I could apply my mind, my skill at math and combinatorial optimization, to maximize my potential score on this Unknown.

What if I could somehow find a way to exit the rolling turn at a slightly higher speed? For example, what if I flew the entire maneuver with a slightly downward inclination? Technically, I was supposed to maintain altitude throughout each maneuver, and I'd get scored down if I didn't. But I'd watched many pilots fly rolling turns, and based on my own experience on the line, I thought I could slightly angle the nose down throughout the maneuver without it being visible to the judges.

I did a quick back-of-the-envelope calculation. Although I'd never tried it, I guessed that I could exit with at least ten extra miles per hour, maybe twenty. So that would get me to 150, maybe 160. But I needed 180.

Hmm. Pilots were supposed to fly all the lines between maneuvers absolutely horizontal. You lost a point off both the previous maneuver and the following maneuver for every 5 degrees of deviation from horizontal. But if I pointed the nose 5 degrees down, although I would lose those points, I'd gain airspeed. What if I maintained a 5-degree nose-down attitude until I reached 180 miles per hour? I would get penalized for descending, and also for exiting the box, but then I could fly the tailslide without flopping the wrong way and getting a zero. Yes, my score would be reduced, but I would lose far fewer points than if I blew the tailslide.

I ran the numbers quickly with my calculator. Yes. That was the best possibility. It wasn't optimal, but it was optimal for the only plane I had to compete in. If I flew well, even with the downgrade for diving and the box penalty, my overall percentage would be respectable.

I spent several hours that night going over the sequence in my head, visualizing each maneuver, one by one, imagining myself in the airplane, feeling, smelling, hearing everything going on as I flew. I'd have to fly a damn near perfect flight, other than my planned downgrades, to stay in the running. Could I make it work?

Friday morning, September 25, dawned as another hot and humid day. The winds were light, which was both good and bad for me. Good because I wouldn't need to compensate much for the wind and distort my maneuvers. Bad because it meant that my dive for the tailslide would almost certainly take me well out of the box.

I pushed my airplane to the starting line. Sweat was already running down my face, and my white T-shirt was drenched. The sun shone like a disk of dull brass in a yellowish sky. The air slapped my face like a wet towel. I shoved the tail of my aircraft to move it into position, the cotter pins on the flying wires digging into my palms.

I took a last drink out of my water bottle and jogged a few thousand feet to the outhouse by the side of the runway.

When I came back, it was time to strap in.

"Harnesses and belts?" asked Bill Larson.

"Check!" I gave him a thumbs-up.

Bill leaned close. "Good luck," he said. "I expect to see you on the team, young lady."

I grinned and closed my canopy. Soon I was airborne. The air smelled even more like a sweaty towel at altitude. I circled in the holding area, scanning the box markers one more time, picking out landmarks and checking them against the hand-drawn sequence diagram on my panel.

The markers on the ground below went white. It was time to fly.

I dove into the box, wagged my wings, and pulled for the first maneuver. Although I'd never flown this sequence before, it seemed familiar after all the intense hours of visualization. I pulled, rolled to my landmarks, and checked the box markers. Breathing hard, I used all my strength to spin and flow through the routine I'd been living and imagining for the past eighteen hours.

I entered the rolling turn, remembering to keep the nose slightly below the horizon as I rolled and turned, like rubbing my stomach and patting my head at the same time. I had to maintain a constant radius along the horizon while at the same time rolling with a steady beat. It was one of the most difficult aerobatic maneuvers I'd ever done, but it felt good. Lowering the nose by 5 degrees increased the control forces slightly but also gave them more crispness, and I felt it was going well. On exit, I flicked a glance at my airspeed—155 miles per hour. *Yes!*

I dropped the nose further, and the airplane accelerated—160 miles per hour.

The upwind box markers sailed away beneath me. Thirty-point penalty for an out-of-the-box exit—*Let it go*—170 miles per hour ... 180. *Go!*

I pulled hard, nine g's, to soar into a perfect vertical up and up through the soggy air and into the murky sky. At the very end, I tipped the nose forward just a few degrees, barely enough to nudge the tailslide and flop the right way. I powered down to idle.

It's always strangely quiet in a tailslide. With the engine at idle and almost no airflow past the cockpit, most sources of noise are absent.

Would the plane fall in the right direction? I held my breath.

So much was waiting on this fragile aerodynamic moment. So much of my life hung on this one instant.

The plane stood still, suspended in the air at the top of its upward thrust, immobile, only its propeller rotating slowly.

There was nothing I could do but hope. Like a twig balanced on the end of a fingertip, the plane paused, its nose pointed straight in the air, the controls slack in my hands, waiting for gravity to tip it one way or another.

Then the plane began to slide backward. I kept the controls centered, my feet braced on the rudder, and both hands gripping the stick.

It had to slide backward a visible amount, but if it slid back too much, it could gain too much speed, potentially damaging the airplane or making the flop so violent that the controls might get torn out of my hands.

The backward slide continued. It was one of the longest I'd ever experienced.

All I could do was hang on.

There was a loud rattle, and a violent rushing of air, and the plane suddenly swapped ends, the nose swinging through a dramatic arc that threw me hard against the belts.

Wheels up, as specified.

Yes! I did it! I sucked in a great gulping breath of relief, shoved the throttle full forward, and concentrated on flying the rest of the sequence. Figure after figure, one at a time, I focused on completing each one with precision and flair. It all went well. My plan had worked.

When I landed, I felt oddly at peace. No matter my standing in the contest at the end, I knew that I had done the best possible job within the limitations of my airplane. If I didn't make the team, it wouldn't be because of another personal failure.

Now came the many hours of waiting until the scores came out. I wiped my plane down, fueled it for the flight home, and pushed it back into the hangar. I got on the truck heading out to the judges' line, where I was an assistant judge in Intermediate, the next category flying.

It was hot out on the line in the dusty Texas fields but tranquil after the tension of my earlier flight. I finally relaxed. I joked with the other judges, enjoyed the highly skilled Intermediate pilots flying their Unknown, helped the judges score the maneuvers, and drank several bottles of water.

At the end of the day, the truck brought us back to the terminal. We all jumped off and made a beeline for the competition whiteboard. The scores were posted.

And there it was. I had done well enough in the Unknown to place twelfth overall in the competition, and fourth among the women. Fourth out of the five team members.

I had made the US Aerobatic Team.

Chapter 16

On the Saturday morning after the competition, I pushed my airplane out of the hangar and performed the final preflight inspection for the two-thousand-mile flight home. The weather briefing was encouraging for at least the first six hundred miles, so I was good to go. Other competitors were packing up their airplanes and taking off, and the quiet Texas morning was occasionally pierced by the roar of a departing airplane.

More people had shaken my hand in the space of a few hours than usually did in weeks. There had even been an official photographer on hand to capture images of the brand-new US Aerobatic Team. My body felt lighter than the hot-air balloons that had floated by at dawn. I'd made it! After all the training, all the obstacles, and all the fears, I'd actually won a spot on the national team. I still couldn't quite believe it.

I was inspecting the tail of my Pitts, when a tall, skinny man with one eye larger than the other approached me. It was Alan Erickson, a former US Aerobatic Team coach. He'd critiqued me and given me a great deal of helpful advice over the past month as I got ready for the Nationals. I respected him tremendously.

"I just wanted to offer you my congratulations," he said, holding out his hand to shake. "Nice-looking Pitts."

I wiped the oil off my hand with a rag and smiled. "Thanks."

He looked over my airplane, frowning. "You got a modified engine?"

"Completely stock," I said proudly, wondering if he was going to congratulate me for doing so well with an unmodified Pitts.

He exhaled loudly and clasped his hands behind his back. "You know, I've spent many years coaching the team, and I've got to tell you the age of the biplane is over." He walked around my plane, eyeing it critically. "In Europe, a plane like this just isn't competitive. Don't take this the wrong way, but … maybe you should think of getting a monoplane."

Stung, I answered, "Gary Rogers and Dan Lynnwood are flying biplanes."

"Highly modified super biplanes, not stock Pitts. Dan's plane's got almost four hundred horsepower." He squinted. "How much does this one have?"

He knew as well as I did that a stock Pitts S-1T had a two-hundred-horsepower engine.

"I'm not trying to criticize you," he hastened to add. "You flew that T-model about as well as it could be flown. But I'm trying to think about the good of the team. You're going to be representing the United States now. It's not just about you."

"I can't afford a monoplane," I blurted.

There was a long pause. Then he pressed his lips together. "I don't know, Cecilia. Is it really worthwhile for the team to spend the time and effort training you and getting your airplane all the way to Europe if it isn't competitive at the world level?"

I stood frozen, my hands clasped over my chest.

"Well, I'm not telling you what to do. I'm just saying you should think about it. Think hard about what it means to represent your country."

He walked away, and I stood immobile, my oil rag gripped tightly in my fist. I'd had to take out a loan to get my $40,000 Pitts. A new Extra 230 cost over $200,000, the Extra 300 nearly $300,000.

On the long flight home, depression won over elation. I even got stuck behind a thunderstorm for a couple of days in Winslow, Arizona, so I lay in my motel room, listening to the rain pound on the thin roof, and wondered if my future was as bleak as the sky outside.

Back home in California, I pored through *Trade-a-Plane* and called everyone I could think of. Maybe some of the wealthy competitors who flew four-cylinder monoplanes would be trading them in for the six-cylinder versions. Perhaps they might be willing to sell their cast-off airplanes for a price I could afford. But no luck. Even the four-cylinder airplanes, obsolete as they were, were going for $150,000 or more.

Sunk in gloom, I attended an IAC Chapter 38 meeting at the Livermore Airport terminal one evening. During the break, as I waited in line to buy a soft drink from the vending machine, one of the chapter members, Nick Jefferson, congratulated me on winning a spot on the team.

"Thanks, but it looks like they may not even take me," I said. "I need a monoplane, and I can't afford the crazy prices of the Extra or Sukhoi."

"You should talk to Andy Benson," he said and took a swig of Dr Pepper. "You know, the aircraft builder down near Bakersfield? I heard he's upset because he was building a super monoplane for a pilot, Henry Morrison, who changed his mind at the last minute. Andy retooled his whole shop, even hired staff to build the plane, and now he's stuck. Maybe he'd ask Henry to sell you the project at a bargain price."

Andy Benson was an old-time craftsman, building one-of-a-kind precision aerobatic machines in his tiny shop on a private airstrip near Bakersfield. I'd heard of his exacting craftsmanship, and I'd met him in passing at a contest or two. Everyone said he was honest and a meticulous aircraft builder.

I was nervous, though. I'd never bought an airplane that hadn't been made in a factory, and I had heard plenty of stories about homebuilt aircraft that concealed deadly errors beneath a glossy surface. Factories had quality control and oversight and an established reputation to protect.

Some individuals did great jobs building airplanes in their garages. Most of them did, in fact. But all it took was one mistake, one poorly welded seam, to lead to a structural failure. And I wasn't just flying from one airport coffee shop to another. I was going to be stressing it under high positive and negative g's. To win at the world level, I had to fly the plane hard—incredibly hard.

I had already seen some of the stresses on my factory S-1T as I practiced Unlimited. I'd racked up all those maintenance bills to prove it. But the biplane structure was strong, with many fail-safes built in. Even though I'd snapped flying wires and pulled the stitching out of the wings, the plane kept on flying. And that airplane had been solidly tested by the previous owner before I took it over. So the failures, though expensive to repair, hadn't been life-threatening.

Still, it was worth at least talking to Andy. I found his number and gave him a call. I could tell from his voice on the phone that he was eager to find a buyer for the project, dubbed the Sabre. But true to his reputation for honesty, he cautioned that it might not be the right airplane for me.

"Henry wanted a plane with a big cockpit, since he's such a big guy. He weighs nearly three hundred pounds. He told me he wanted heavy control forces. And he's already got a wing—a big heavy wood wing, nice and solid."

I could hear the doubt in his voice. Heavy control forces? I was look-ing for something more like an Extra, known to be very light on the controls. Even after my regimen of weightlifting, my arms still had their limitations. To pull the stick hard under a 9-g load took quite a bit of physical strength.

Still, I called Henry to talk about the project and find out what he was asking for it. He said he'd just started a new business and was pouring all his energy into that, and he didn't have time to fly, so had decided not to go ahead with the airplane. But Andy had told me he thought Henry just didn't like the way the plane was turning out.

Henry didn't say anything about that, but he did say he would sell me the project for $30,000. Still too much.

I'd asked Andy how much it would cost to finish the project in his shop and get it to flying status. He hemmed a bit. "Say about fifty. But Cecilia, this is a big risk. This is a new design. It's never flown before. It's possible we'll get it together, and it won't have the characteristics you want."

I got off the phone discouraged. $80,000 was still twice as much as I could afford. This was my only option, and it didn't look all that good.

* * *

Throughout that fall, I continued working and flying. I wrote software, instructed students, practiced Unlimited in my Pitts, and flew more airshows. But as the weather turned colder, and California's rainy season approached, I felt more and more like I was simply going through the motions. It seemed increasingly unlikely that I was going to be able to make it to the World Contest. No one had told me outright that they wouldn't accept my stock Pitts on the team, and it would be difficult for them to blatantly refuse me membership simply because my airplane was obsolete. But what Alan had said to me still rang in my head. I had a responsibility, now that I was a representative of my country, not to expend our resources sending up an airplane that simply wasn't competitive at the world level. It would be actually selfish—unlike the "selfish" I'd been called for wanting to achieve my dreams. I couldn't do it.

I spent the long drives between work and various airports feeling bitter and railing about my lack of money and the unfairness of it all. *Why should rich people be the only ones allowed to represent the US? Shouldn't talent count?*

Both the Russian and the French governments supported their teams, providing aircraft, professional trainers, fuel, and maintenance costs. They even paid their pilots a salary.

No wonder both countries had been trouncing us in the World Competition for many years. Even with the fall of the Berlin Wall in 1989 and the subsequent breakup of the Soviet Union, all the former Soviet countries still managed to find enough money in their budgets to pay for their pilots to train and attend international competition.

It was so unfair! I whined to my friends until they got sick of me and refused to listen. So instead, I turned it all inward and walked around feeling sorry for myself.

In October, I flew the Salinas Airshow. I was still a novice performer, but at least I was paid for my work this time. I psyched myself up to act cheerful, since I knew it wasn't right to be a grouch to my clients and especially to all the young kids who showed up at the airshow and asked me—*me*—for my autograph.

I sat at a row of card tables behind a rope separating us from the flight line. Families had formed a long line to get autographs from all the performers. I came right after Lulu the Wonder Dog, the Amazing Flying Labrador, and before Gertrude, the "little old lady from Nebraska," who won a Cub ride at the show and "inadvertently" engaged the throttle while waiting for "her pilot." I still hadn't come up with the gimmick that I'd been told was required for airshow success.

Frankly, the whole airshow thing still made me feel like I was pretending to be something I wasn't. I wasn't glamorous or Hollywood. But I didn't think I was the granola girl from Berkeley either.

I sat at the airshow trying to pretend I was a star, thinking the kids were mostly lined up to pet the Labrador, but when they came up to my table to get their programs signed, I was delightfully surprised. The pages flashed in the sun as I signed away with my Sharpie.

A man and woman without a little one in tow approached my table. As I signed the woman's program, she pointed at her husband and said, "Devin is an author, and he based a character in his latest book on you."

Flummoxed, I looked up at him, unsure of how to respond.

He smiled gently and shook my hand. "I'm Devin Goffman, and I write techno-thrillers. I just published my second book this year. I'd read an article on a certain Berkeley computer programmer in *Pacific Flyer* last February, and it inspired me to create a minor character based on you."

Maybe I made him a little uncomfortable with my staring because he added, "Of course, I'm sure she's nothing like you, and I haven't told anyone else about the genesis of this character."

"Oh … no, that's really cool! What's the book called, and where can I buy it?" I asked, shaking myself out of my reverie.

"I'm sorry, it doesn't come out until December."

His wife said, "We just wanted to make sure that we stopped by and let you know we were huge fans."

The thought that someone might read about me in the paper and want to base a character on me was discombobulating. I expected nobody would ever care. I gave them my best gracious smile and thanked them both.

Later that month, Devin sent me a nice letter along with an advance copy of his book. He also noted that both he and his wife, Laura Wiggins, were private pilots, and they were interested in taking aerobatics lessons with me out at the Nut Tree Airport, where I was now teaching.

I met Laura for her first lesson soon afterward. She was an exuberant, tall woman who announced to me that she was on one extreme of the extrovert scale. All that confidence and vibrancy vanished, however, when she got into the air, and she was hesitant to move the stick, to bank more than 30 degrees, or to push the rudder.

I'd rapidly been gaining a reputation for being good with fearful students. Since I understood all too well, from personal know-how, the roadblocks a pilot could encounter while learning aerobatics, I knew how to coach them through their difficulties.

Over the course of ten aerobatic lessons, Laura and I became friends. She thought it was exciting that I was a member of the US Aerobatic Team, and I eventually explained my conundrum to her, wondering bitterly if I wouldn't even be allowed to participate in the World Contest simply because I didn't have enough money.

Laura was bewildered. She had just seen me enthusiastically coaching her on the best way to get over the fear of spins. "You overcame some intense fears, yourself. You succeeded at everything you set your mind to. Why don't you raise the money you need?"

I laughed sourly. "Who's going to give me any money?"

"I coach nonprofits how to fundraise. This is what I do for a living. Why don't I teach you?"

"I couldn't afford your fees."

"Silly, I'm offering to give it to you as a gift. That can be the first donation to the World Contest Fund for Cecilia Aragon."

Laura coached me step-by-step through the process of raising money, starting with setting my budget, creating a list of potential donors, and how to approach meetings with supporters. It turned out there was a particular procedure and even a script. "You must set up a specific time to meet with them, even if you see them every day."

"Do I have to do it face-to-face?" I cringed at the thought. "Can't I just send out a letter like the ones I get all the time?"

"I know you're shy, but mass mailings have a success rate of about one percent," she said. "Do you want to raise the money or not?"

And so it began. Perhaps the most important gift Laura gave me was a lifelong attitude shift to embrace being part of a community. She started by teaching me that I had to stop being resentful of others, because it only ended up making me miserable. People weren't going to donate money just because I needed it and they had it. They were going to give because they wanted to feel they were a part of something bigger than themselves, and that my success would also be their success.

"But I'll feel guilty if people give me something for nothing."

"They're getting more than they're giving," Laura explained. "They're sending a local pilot, an extreme underdog, a good friend, to the World Aerobatic Championships. They're personally supporting a representative of the United States. That's an opportunity that doesn't come along very often. It's exciting!"

I thought to myself, *But that means I won't be able to bitterly demand they give me money because they have more than I do.* And then I laughed. My attitude *had* been pretty ridiculous.

I started making appointments with friends and acquaintances, one by one. At first, I was unsure and worried, but I followed Laura's detailed scripts. She coached me by phone after each meeting, and I discovered she was right. I wasn't a supplicant, and it was thrilling and moving to share my passionate excitement about the goals of the US Aerobatic Team and have it reciprocated. I found that I loved talking with every supporter, and donations large and small poured in. One friend even organized a "Cecilia Aragon Day" at the Nut Tree Airport, proudly presenting me with a giant glass jar stuffed with twenty-dollar bills and checks.

Until that year, I'd still believed, in my secret heart, that no one liked me, that people were basically cruel, and that I had to keep myself completely barricaded at all times. That was the year I realized I was wrong—not just intellectually, but in the deepest part of my being. Of course, I still had setbacks.

"Laura, someone gave me one dollar. It's going to cost me more than that to write them a thank-you note. Do I still have to send one out?" I asked her.

She nodded firmly. "You always send a thank-you note. Always." Laura taught me to say thank you seven times before you ask for anything. This was a good philosophy for life in general.

Under Laura's tutelage, I went from being grouchy and miserable to feeling an astonished kind of gladness, the feeling of being held up by my community. It was wonderful. I wrote excited newsletters describing how I felt, giving updates on my fundraising, and talking about my experiences as I prepared for the World Championships each day. Friends helped me stamp and mail out hundreds of newsletters each month.

At first, I felt guilty for filling my newsletters with what I thought was useless fluff, but then people told me they looked forward to them every month and read them from cover to cover. My journey was exciting, and as I saw the exhilaration in the people around me, my own enthusiasm and joy were magnified. It was thrilling to be chosen to represent my country. It was an honor, and I was going to give it the very best I had.

Within the first few months, I raised $50,000. (Thank you, Laura!) I checked over my budget. It still wasn't enough for a $200,000 Extra, but I could afford $75,000. I called up Andy Benson. "I want to see the Sabre project," I told him. "If I buy it, will you be able to get the airplane finished so I can fly it in France next July?"

"I'll do my best," he promised.

* * *

True to his word, Andy delivered a beautiful plane in late 1991. The building of the airplane had weathered numerous setbacks, including the Sierra Madre earthquake in June 1991, but it stayed on budget and was true to spec.

I took the train down to Selma Airport to fly it for the first time on a sunny day that winter. It was a work of detailed craftsmanship, a long and elegant midwing monoplane with a red fabric-covered fuselage and a deep-blue wooden wing. It felt strange climbing into an airplane no one had ever flown.

Andy leaned over the side of the cockpit. "You're a test pilot now," he told me. "You need to follow a careful set of procedures to make sure the plane is aerodynamically sound before you begin any aerobatics. For today, I want you to go up to altitude, keep the plane slow, try some gentle turns and then some steep turns. Notice if the controls start to pull into the turn. Then try pitching the nose up and down. Do it all in

five-mile-per-hour increments. Again, note if the airplane is aerodynamically stable in all three axes, or if it develops instability at any airspeed. It's
best to do a series of short flights and come down and make notes on what
happened in each flight in between."

I nodded as though I understood, but inside, a voice was wailing, *A test
pilot? Me?* I was once scared to fly a Cessna 152. How could I be test-flying
an unproven airplane? It was ludicrous. But I'd created the structure for
this day. I wanted to fly in the World Contest, so I needed a monoplane.
True, it was untested, but it was also designed by Roger Blum, one of the
top people in the business, and built by a well-known aviation craftsman.
It was a combinatorial optimization problem, and I'd optimized it.

All I had to do was get in the airplane, take off, and go through the
steps Andy had laid out. If I did one, I could do the next. Mathematical
induction.

I flew several flights that day, and by some miracle, I didn't crash. As I
went deeper and deeper into the testing program, the steps Andy told me
to do became more and more terrifying.

"Now we'll test for aileron flutter. Go to altitude, start at a hundred
and twenty miles per hour and go up in five-mile-per-hour increments.
Bump the stick hard in one direction. If it starts to vibrate uncontrollably,
that's aileron flutter. You need to pitch up immediately and slow down."

"What if it vibrates worse?"

"If it keeps fluttering, and you can't get it to stop?" He shrugged.
"Jump. You've got a fresh repack on your parachute, right?"

"Jump?" I squeaked.

"I'm sure it won't come to that. You need to test it to ten percent past
redline airspeed."

"You want me to fly it past the never-exceed speed?"

He gave me a look. "Of course. You always test past redline to make
sure there's a safety margin on the airplane."

I swallowed. Of course, I knew that, but somehow it hadn't seemed
real that a human being, a test pilot, was the one who actually provided
those safety margins. Now it was my job. There was nothing to do but
follow the procedure. I had to trust it.

Chapter 17

Within two weeks, the test flights had been completed, and the Sabre had passed with, you might say, flying colors. It flew beautifully, was aerodynamically stable at high airspeeds, and recovered smoothly and easily from all six types of multiturn spins. I was excited to have completed the test flights and eager to start practicing aerobatics.

But there were problems. The previous owner, Henry Morrison, had wanted the control forces to feel solid and heavy, and they were. But the pitch forces were *extremely* heavy, which meant I needed both hands on the stick to enter a snap roll, and the wing tended to wallow and mush rather than making a clean break for the snap, even when I pulled the stick aft as hard as I could and jammed in full rudder. The roll forces were also extremely heavy, and it took two hands and a lot of arm strength to execute a slow roll.

I longed for the feel of my Pitts.

At one of our New J practice sessions, Frank told me it was only to be expected. "That's what people say about transitioning to a monoplane. The Pitts is more fun to fly. The monoplane is all business. It's a serious airplane, for the serious task of winning at the World Contest. You're not the first to think that the monoplane isn't as much fun to fly."

But it was more than that. Although I didn't confess to anyone my growing despair, the truth was that I could barely fly the plane in Sportsman. It was simply too heavy and wallowing to fly the higher aerobatic competition maneuvers.

I heard Andy's voice in my head as he had warned me throughout the building of the airplane: "I have no idea how it will fly. Henry wanted a big elevator to have a solid, heavy control feel."

One of the former US Aerobatic Team trainers was running a coaching session in Arizona. I flew out there that winter, and he watched me fly. When I got down after the first flight, he rubbed his brow. "Cecilia, those snaps look like Decathlon snaps. If you can't fly any better than that, they're not going to take you to Europe. It'll be a waste of team resources."

I'd done everything I could, sunk every last dollar of my own and everything I could raise into this experiment. Now it couldn't fly? I sat in the hangar staring glumly at my big lug of an airplane. It didn't look too different from an Extra, and everyone said *those* flew beautifully. But there was something missing, some magic that Curtis Pitts had lent the biplane, some elusive element in the subtle details of the shape of the control surfaces, the horizontal and vertical stabilizers.

Was there a way to improve it aerodynamically? I called up Roger Blum, the aircraft designer, but he said, "I'm sorry, but I designed the plane for Henry, and that was what he wanted. You bought Henry's design, and that's it."

Increasingly desperate, I called more and more people in the aerobatics industry. No one was impolite, but no one had any ideas for me until one person suggested I call Leo Loudenslager.

"You mean, the seven-time national aerobatic champion?" I asked.

"He designed his own airplane, and there's probably no one who knows more about monoplane design than Leo," this person told me.

Would someone that famous take a call from me?

At first, I decided not to. What if he refused? Then, I thought about the humiliation of being unable to fly at the World Contest with so many people depending on me. So I picked up the phone.

Not only did Leo take my call that Saturday, he also listened closely to my explanation of the problems. "It's difficult for me to diagnose an aerodynamic problem sight unseen," he said. "But listen, I'm going to be in Guthrie, Oklahoma, this Wednesday. If you can get your airplane there by then, I'll fly it and tell you what's wrong with it."

Pause. I had a job, flight students—my calendar was full. Wednesday was only four days away, and Oklahoma was 1,700 miles across the country. It was impossible. I opened my mouth and blurted, "Sure! Where should I meet you?"

He gave me directions, and when I got off the phone, I was in a fever of agitation. I canceled all my appointments, asked my boss for time off, grabbed my aviation charts, and planned the flight.

The Sabre had even fewer instruments than my Pitts. No electrical system, the compass didn't work, and the auxiliary tank was a bullet-shaped cylinder that strapped under the belly of the airplane and was necessary if I wanted to fly longer than twenty minutes. I'd never flown the Sabre anywhere near the distance to Guthrie. Fortunately, the weather forecasts across the Southwest and on into Texas and Oklahoma were good for the next couple of days. So ultimately, I decided I would fly 1,700 miles in a practically untested airplane at the drop of a hat, simply for the chance of having an aerodynamic genius work his magic on my airplane.

* * *

On April 4, 1992, I took off from Nut Tree Airport, where I was then basing the Sabre, and headed east. After overnighting in Gallup, New Mexico, I arrived in Guthrie, Oklahoma, on April 5.

Leo Loudenslager met me at the Bakal Aeronautics hangar on the Guthrie field. A tall, serious man with shaggy gray hair, he moved around the hangar with tight efficiency. The hangar—huge, white, and spotless—was used for building composite aircraft parts and drones, and Leo had recently helped them design an all-composite wing called the Edge for Unlimited competition aerobatics. Leslie Bakal, one of the owners, was driven and talkative, and Mark, her husband, was a quiet, deep thinker. I couldn't help but enjoy Leslie's focused attitude and Mark's laid-back, wry humor, despite my anxiety.

Another pilot had his plane—a four-cylinder monoplane called a Lazer with an Edge wing—in their shop, and he worked on it alongside some of the mechanics from Bakal. The pilot introduced himself as Joe Haywood. He was a friendly, slightly rounded man who liked cracking jokes. He owned his own business, and spent most of his free time out at the airport.

Leo focused intently on my description of the problems with the Sabre, circling the plane as I talked. After I removed all the Styrofoam from my cockpit and gave him a quick briefing, he climbed in the plane and took off.

It's strange seeing someone else in your single-seat airplane disappear into the distance. When he landed, he gave me a quick precis of the aerodynamics of the plane in a brisk, no-nonsense manner. I took notes as quickly as I could. Mark Bakal came out onto the tarmac and listened along to Leo's report.

"The rudder is too big, as is the elevator. That's what's giving you the problems with the heavy control forces." He rattled off a set of formulas for the optimal area for the vertical stabilizer, horizontal stabilizer, and control surfaces.

"Is it possible to cut down the existing rudder?" I asked.

Leo squinted at the Sabre and slid a hand over the vertical tail. "I'd build a completely new set of control surfaces. You'll need someone who can do precision welding and can also do fabric work to cover the tubing when it's done."

I felt sick. It was only seven weeks before I was due in Ohio for the team practice session at Rickenbacker Field. I'd been hoping Leo would recommend a couple quick fixes, and then I could get down to some hard practicing. His suggestions sounded like they would take a long time.

"You can try some bigger spades on the ailerons and build some for the rudder too." Spades are aerodynamic counterbalances that are usually mounted aft of the aileron hinge and provide a boosting effect, kind of like power steering for control surfaces. They make the aileron forces lighter.

"Rudder spades?" I'd never heard of them being used anywhere other than ailerons.

Leo frowned at my airplane. "You're not going to like this, but if you really want my advice, I'd ditch the entire wing. That's an old-style wooden wing, solid but an obsolete airfoil."

I choked. "You want me to swap out all the tail surfaces and the wing as well? What'll be left of the airplane, the serial number?" I could see dollar signs in the air, as well as my chance to compete in the Worlds floating away.

"Do you want a plane that can compete at the highest levels or not?"

"But there's hardly any time left! I still have to practice and learn to fly the airplane. Plus, I don't have the money to make major changes. I spent every penny I had on getting the airplane as far as it is now."

Leo shrugged. "Well, if you were to decide to do it, you just happen to be at the best place to get work done on aerobatic aircraft." He pointed at Mark Bakal, standing off to one side quietly listening. "No one can build a better aircraft than this guy. If you mounted an Edge wing on your plane, it would solve many of your problems right there."

The suggestions were coming too fast for me to take in.

"Tell you what," Leo said. "You asked me for my recommendation, and I'll give it to you. It's up to you whether to take it. I recommend you try a few minor changes that Mark can probably knock out over the next couple of days. See if that helps. If it doesn't, maybe see if you can fly an Edge somewhere, see if you like it. Then I'd recommend doing the complete retrofit with an Edge wing."

Joe Haywood, who had wandered up to our conversation, said, "Why don't you fly my airplane and see if you like the Edge. Do that before you make any decisions."

"You'd let me fly your plane?" The guy had only just met me thirty-five minutes earlier, and he was offering to let me fly his $100,000-plus custom aerobatic machine.

He grinned. "You're not gonna break it, right?"

I laughed nervously.

Less than half an hour later, we loaded my Styrofoam cushions into Joe's Lazer and he briefed me on the cockpit and airplane. I sat in the plane as Joe went over a last set of instructions on the landing speed and the plane's idiosyncrasies.

It's not too unusual for Unlimited aerobatic pilots to fly each other's airplanes. It's usually assumed that by the time we get this good, we're not going to do something stupid and crash. But there were so many things that could go wrong.

My arms and legs were shaking at the thought of taking off in this unknown plane. I could barely reach the rudder pedals. The Styrofoam cushions helped somewhat, but they still didn't give me that last inch without straining. I couldn't help hearing Louie Robinson's voice: "You need that last half inch for spin recovery."

I decided I wasn't going to try spins, just some turns, rolls, and maybe a snap or two.

The plane felt unstable on takeoff, wiggling as I sped down the runway. Once in the air, the airplane flew lightly. I couldn't believe the aileron response—so precise and nimble and worlds better than the heavy, somewhat ponderous feel of my plane's ailerons.

I was already grinning, even before reaching altitude. Out over the bisected green fields, I looped and rolled and snapped and pivoted. When I landed, I announced, "Let's do it."

But it wasn't that easy. First, it would take the Bakals a few weeks to build a brand-new wing. We didn't have enough time for that. So where could I get a used one? Mark Bakal knew of a used Edge for sale on the East Coast. That was probably the best bet.

But the bigger problems were financial. I was tapped out after buying the Sabre. I couldn't afford this retrofit project.

But then the Bakals made me an offer hard to refuse. "We'd really like to see an Edge fly in the World Contest," Leslie told me. "How about if we sponsor you with all our labor? All you have to do is pay for the used wing, and any parts."

"Wow," I said. "That's an amazing offer." I was still worried about the cost of even the used wing. On the other hand, I was desperate. There was no way the Sabre could fly Unlimited as is. It needed a major retrofit. And here Mark Bakal was offering it to me at a substantial discount. I couldn't *not* take his offer. I struggled to think of where I was going to come up with the extra money.

But I knew I was going to do it. It was just one more impossible thing.

And then, there was the time factor. "Is it even possible to do all this work in the next few weeks?" I asked Mark. "I've only got seven weeks before team practice. Could you do it in four weeks?"

Mark scratched his head very slowly, and gave the Sabre another long once-over. "How about five?"

That would only leave me two weeks before the team practice. No way would that be enough time. Two weeks to train to Unlimited-level competency in a plane I'd barely flown? And that wasn't even considering how much time it would take to test-fly a brand-new airplane.

I also had to trust that Mark could actually deliver in that short time frame. In fact, I was hanging everything upon believing him. We'd only spent a few hours getting to know each other, but strangely, I already felt like we were old friends, Mark and Leslie and me.

I decided to trust.

I spent the rest of the day getting a tour of the Bakal hangar and learning more than I ever knew was possible to know about composite aircraft. They had a large government contract to build military drones and a giant oven where they cooked the composite materials into aircraft parts. I marveled at the high tech, amazing precision work, all the equipment, and how they produced such incredible craftsmanship in such a small space.

I also spent hours talking about how nerve-racking it is to start a new business with Leslie, the business owner.

By the end of the day, they told me to cancel my hotel reservation and stay in their beautiful Midwestern-style house on a quiet tree-lined street. I spent the next few days hanging out with them 24/7. In the evenings, we talked in the kitchen as Leslie cooked dinner, with me helping however I could. "When we were first getting the loan from the bank for this business," Leslie said, "they wanted us to use our house to secure the loan. But I refused. I didn't want to mortgage my children's future. The bank didn't like that, but eventually they gave me the loan."

"Banks make a lot of money off loans," I said. "But you can sometimes get them to compromise."

"Yes, they act like they're doing us a favor, but really, we're the customer."

We understood each other, two women business owners trying to make it in the field of aviation.

They gave me a large, quiet room finished with hardwood floors and ringed by dormer windows. Ruffled flounces encircled the double bed piled with quilted pillows. Out the window, huge maple and oak trees crowded the yard. I hadn't stayed in someone else's house for a long time—not since I was a child visiting relatives. As an adult, whenever I traveled, I picked the cheapest motel and stayed there.

It was different being welcomed into someone's home. The Bakals had opened their hearts to me. Yes, they hoped that I would showcase their wing at the World Championships, but there was no guarantee I could even fly it. They offered me kindness of a sort I hadn't imagined would ever be possible outside my own family.

We set up the final plans. Mark and Leslie would drive to the East Coast with a trailer so they could pick up the wing and drive it back to Guthrie within the next week. I was stunned at how much they were willing to do for me. All of this was free of charge.

All that was left for me was to go home and keep up my aerobatic tolerance by flying in the Pitts. At home, Ben had become a staunch supporter, following my progress eagerly and cheering me on after every competition. Although he still refused to attend local events, citing a disdain for hangar food, I was touched when I found out he planned to come to the World Contest. What's more, he'd gotten his parents involved and excited. To my delight, his father and mother both said they'd come to France to support me, joining my own parents, who were also planning on making the trip. My parents were absurdly proud that their daughter was now going to represent their adopted country in an international competition. It gave me tremendous solace to know they all stood behind me, and that no matter what happened, my efforts to compete at the world level had become a family affair. I felt surrounded by love, and it floored me.

I caught a commercial flight home and booked my return flight for five weeks later. Would it work? Even Mark Bakal admitted it was an ambitious schedule. If anything went wrong, he wouldn't hit the deadline. And that would mean missing the World Contest.

* * *

My logbook showed that in the days between April 9 and May 5, I flew nearly every day, often teaching students in several different airplanes and practicing Unlimited sequences in the Pitts S-1T. I'd sold it to a friend in two stages so I could still practice in it while I was waiting for the Sabre to be ready. In May I completed the sale to raise the money I needed.

It made me sad to sell my little Pitts, the plane I had flown from Intermediate through Unlimited, eventually winning a spot on the US Team. I'd flown it over 620 hours—more time than I'd logged in any other airplane. (By then, I had accumulated over 3,000 hours, about half as a flight instructor and over 1,700 in tailwheel airplanes.)

It was quite a journey since the summer of 1985, when I'd taken my first nervous ride in a small plane. And now I was embarking on the most notable journey of my life. I'd gone from being a nobody, scared of flying, scared of *everything*, to a small business owner, a test pilot, an aerobatic instructor, and now, at last, I'd reached the pinnacle of aerobatic competition flying: membership on the US Aerobatic Team. In less than a couple of months, I'd be representing my country in France. Maybe.

My logbook also showed multiple flights with photographers from various newspapers, video flights with TV stations, and all sorts of encounters that really didn't belong in the logbook of a "nobody."

Still, it could all come crashing down. If Mark Bakal didn't deliver on the airplane as promised, if a tornado tore through the Bakal hangar in Oklahoma, if the plane didn't fly well and I couldn't make it snap, if for some reason I couldn't fly—if, if, if. I put all of that out of my mind and concentrated on keeping my g-tolerance up and going through my sequences mentally.

In early May, the call I'd been waiting for arrived. Mark said the plane would be finished on time, two weeks before team practice, just as promised. On May 6, 1992, I took a commercial flight out to Oklahoma. Mark picked me up at the airport, and we talked all the way back in the car.

The airplane was ready. There had been a couple of problems, but he'd solved them, and everything looked good. I was so excited I could hardly stand it. I couldn't wait to fly in the morning. We pulled into Mark's garage as the sun was setting over Guthrie. The lights in the windows of their two-story house were warm and inviting, and I could already smell Leslie's cooking. She came to the door and gave me a hug.

I sat on a high-backed spindle chair at their polished wood dining table under a stained-glass light fixture. We ate tuna casserole with peas as Mark and Leslie regaled me with all the stories of the journey east, how they had loaded the wing on the trailer and driven it back in the rain, all the difficulties getting the airplane together, but now it was finally done on schedule.

I had trouble sleeping that night near the dormer window where the oaks and maples rustled their leaves under the streetlight. The lamp threw a stippled pattern on the wallpaper across the room.

It was my turn now to show I was worthy of their support. What if I let them down? What if I couldn't fly the airplane? What if I didn't perform as well as I hoped?

"Nothing is certain in this world," they'd said at dinner. "Just do your best. We have your back." That kind of support was something I'd always longed for. I was so used to my parents being my only cheerleaders and most people outside my family assuming I'd never accomplish anything.

In the morning Mark and I drove out to the Guthrie Airport to begin the test-flying regimen. Hey, by now I was an old hand as a test pilot. Mark described the flight-test regime he wanted me to go through, and I nodded. It was the same as the routine I'd followed when I first flew the Sabre. I'd start out performing the test sequence at a slow speed, and then gradually increase to redline and beyond. Checking for aileron snatch. Checking for flutter.

The first day would be spent entirely on test-flying. I had to make sure the basic flight and spin characteristics were good before I started doing any aerobatics. Mark eyed me closely to make sure I understood. "Don't just jump in and start snapping it before completing the test sequence." He sounded like a man familiar with aerobatic pilots.

I grinned. "Don't worry," I said. "I'm cautious."

If he knew how cautious I really was, he'd demand his money back. He probably had no idea how long I was going to delay before actually taking off in the new airplane. I preflighted the plane, discussed all the changes again with Mark and his engineer, checked the control surfaces on the ground, opened the inspection plate in the tail to make sure no tools or screws or other loose items had fallen inside the fuselage. All looked good. I did another check.

Finally, there was no more dawdling. I had to do the flight. I climbed in, started up the engine, taxied around the airport several times, did two full run-ups, and finally taxied onto the runway for departure.

As soon as I began the climb out, I could tell something was very different. The plane felt light and sweet. It handled like the Pitts, itching to fly. It wanted me to let loose. It was all I could do to complete the first set of test maneuvers, come down and land, have Mark check out the airplane one more time, put more gas in it, and take off again.

I dove in increments to redline, checking for flutter and snatch. No problems. No problems at all. I pulled up, pointed the plane at the sun, and rolled.

Wow! Four hundred and twenty degrees per second. The world went around in a blur and then righted. I found myself laughing. I hadn't believed that any plane could feel sweeter than my Pitts. But this new plane was even lighter, even more responsive. It was perfectly balanced and neutrally stable. If I pitched up and let go of the stick, the nose stayed there. Exactly what one would want in an aerobatic airplane.

Finally, I let the new Sabre loose. It was everything I hoped it would be. Light on the controls, beautiful snap rolls, incredible roll rate. In fact, the rate was so fast and the controls so sensitive that I was overshooting each roll. Would I be able to train myself to fly this airplane to the exacting standards of world competition in only two weeks? And after that, there were only two more weeks before I had to be in Dover, Delaware, for the departure of the C-5 cargo plane on June 19.

There simply wasn't enough time. It was impossible. But wait, hadn't I heard that many times before? It was getting kind of old. It was impossible for a first-generation child of immigrants to overcome abuse and discrimi-nation, a speech defect, crippling shyness, and a lack of finances, to get to where I was and make the US Team—or so I had once thought.

I'd just have to use every minute I could, so I vowed to get up as early as I could each morning and ride out with Mark before eight when he drove to the hangar. Still, things didn't go exactly as planned. There were mechanical problems, and the changeable Oklahoma weather impacted many flights. More than once, a thunderstorm grounded me, and for two interminable days, it rained steadily from morning until night. I got in some decent practice anyway, even if my flying was serviceable though not exciting. I nervously counted the days until I had to fly to Rickenbacker.

When I met the new US Aerobatic Team coach, would I be good enough?

Chapter 18

On May 21, I departed Guthrie after two weeks of practice and a total of eighteen flight hours in my newly modified airplane. It didn't feel like enough, but it was all I had. It was also my parents' anniversary, and since I wasn't too far from West Lafayette, Indiana, I'd planned to take time out to wish them a happy day and show off my airplane.

As I flew cross-country over the flat green and yellow fields, my heart sang at the sweet feel of my airplane. It was a joy to fly, faster and smoother than with the old wing. Plus, I'd said goodbye to the bullet auxiliary tank. The Edge wing had two seven-and-a-half-gallon internal auxiliary fuel tanks. I couldn't fly aerobatics with any gas in those tanks, but having them in the plane made flying cross-country much easier. I now could carry thirty-nine gallons total: nineteen in the main tank, fifteen in the two wing tanks, and five in a tank behind my seat that could be used either for smoke oil or fuel. Since flight at typical cruise airspeed burned fifteen gallons an hour, I could fly for two straight hours and still have nine gallons of fuel in reserve. The plane cruised at two hundred miles an hour, so I could fly four hundred miles per leg. Sweet!

From Guthrie, I flew to Sullivan, Missouri, then Taylorville, Illinois. Next stop: my old hometown. I flew at seventy-five hundred feet, using only maps and my erratic compass. The Sabre had no navigational aids and the bare minimum instrumentation required for an experimental aircraft. Crossing the Indiana border gave me a strange twinge. I'd only returned to my home state for a couple of short visits to see my parents since I'd left at age sixteen to go to college. And I'd certainly never flown my *own airplane* back to Indiana. It felt like a milestone. I was an independent woman now, a success. I was flying under my own power.

As I flew northeast over Indiana, it surprised me how much of the state was covered by fields of corn laid out in neat, square sections, even though I should have known. The southern part of the state's terrain rolled slightly, but as I approached the latitude of Indianapolis, the land flattened out and became featureless. Except for the occasional red barn, nothing but cornfields studded the landscape stretching to the hazy horizon.

As I approached what had to be West Lafayette according to my chart, I was taken aback by how tiny the town was. It had a population of twenty thousand people. Purdue University hosted forty thousand students. When I had grown up in this small town, it was the whole world to me. My life was delineated and circumscribed by the borders of the town, by the walls of the school yard, by the bullies who attacked me, and the teachers who dismissed me. Had the town really been that small, that insignificant all this time? Dwarfed by cornfields?

I circled to the south and called the tower for clearance to land. The landing was uneventful on the long, wide runway paved with smooth white concrete. This field looked like any other corporate airport. It was a beautiful, warm spring day, one of the best times of year in Indiana. I fueled the plane and rolled it into a tie-down spot. I tied the stick back with the seat belt, closed the canopy, and walked into the terminal.

Through the window, I saw my parents making their way across the parking lot, holding hands. My father once claimed to be five feet six inches tall, but last time I saw him, our eyes were on the same level. Perhaps his spine had compressed with age. He leaned back slightly as he walked, and a gray beret covered his thinning hair. My mom always made sure he didn't forget to wear it.

My mother only reached five feet in her modest heels. Her coarse salt-and-pepper hair was cropped short at the sides and back, framing the face she once described as "broad and flat with the family nostrils." It had been over three years since I'd seen them last.

"We want to see your plane," my mother said after we'd hugged and kissed. In addition to being an academic counselor at Purdue, she was now an amateur photographer who'd recently started winning awards for her work, and she'd brought her camera. We strolled onto the field, and she took pictures of me with the red, white, and blue Sabre.

My father scanned the cockpit. "You went to all that trouble and spent so much money on a plane that doesn't even have a passenger seat?"

"I could rent an airplane and take you both up for a ride," I offered.

My father snorted. "Us fly? Are you crazy?"

But my mother appeared thoughtful. Although she was once insistent that I give up my dangerous hobby, her critiques had become less frequent since I'd become a member of the United States Aerobatic Team. She and my father had begun to demonstrate their pride in unexpected ways. My mother designed a set of buttons featuring her photography of the Sabre for me to hand out as souvenirs at the World Contest, and my father asked if his department at Purdue could invite me to give a talk on the physics of aerobatics.

It felt wonderful to finally bask in their approval for my flying. We returned to their car, and I climbed awkwardly into the tiny back seat. As we drove into town, my mother piped up and said, "I'd be interested in some aerial photography."

"I'll see if I can check out a plane," I told her. "What about you, Dad? Want to come up with us?"

He answered, "Somebody in the family has to survive."

We arrived at the 1950s ranch house on 1 Lavender Road that had been my childhood home. I helped my mother fill the bird feeders, and then we sat down at the kitchen table to talk. I'd eaten so many meals at this round white table. Sitting here felt like putting on an old pair of jeans I hadn't worn in years, at first unfamiliar, then the memories came rushing back and fit so well. I had so many conversations with my mother in the kitchen while my father worked upstairs in his study.

"Tell me everything about your latest successes in aviation," my mom said. She sounded excited. "And for our flight, what should I wear?" Her deep brown cheeks took on a slightly rosy tinge. "I have to decide which camera to bring!"

When we took flight later that afternoon, I tried to assuage my mother's nervousness by explaining everything carefully, keeping my banks gentle, and giving her plenty of opportunities to take photos of all her favorite spots. Gazing out over my old hometown, I realized it really *was* beautiful. The town was forested and lush, and the Wabash River curved through it, gleaming in the afternoon sun. I remembered the joyful moments I'd had here, exploring the wooded ravines, picking fresh corn and blackberries, riding my bike alone through the wide streets. Why had I only remembered the negative parts? As my mother exclaimed over her new perspective of her hometown, I realized she wasn't the only one.

When I took off for Ohio the next day, my spirit had been refreshed. I'd counted birds in our backyard and had slept in my childhood bed. I was ready for team practice.

*   *   *

Later that day, I landed at Rickenbacker Field. On the tarmac, a uniformed soldier waving a pair of lighted orange batons directed me to one of the biggest hangars I'd ever seen. I taxied over a vast expanse of patched concrete and shut down the Sabre in front of the giant, nearly empty hangar. The soldier zoomed away on his cart, and I was left alone in the hazy sunlight. I popped the canopy open and climbed out into the humid Ohio afternoon.

I pushed the plane closer to the colossal hangar doors, and an unpleasant smell wafted toward me. The hangar floor was thickly coated with bird guano. I glanced up at the rafters and saw scraggly nests and rows and rows of pigeons and other species of birds. This would be my plane's base for the next two weeks. I found a corner streaked with fewer droppings, unrolled the wing and canopy covers, and hoped for the best.

Rickenbacker Air National Guard Base was located in central Ohio, not too far from Columbus. It was recently transferred from active-duty

Air Force control in the early 1980s and was scheduled for closure in the following year or two. It was presently a mixed-use airport, hosting military units including the National Guard, Navy Reserve, and Marine Corps Reserve as well as civilian flight operations. It covered acres and acres of land sprinkled with many empty ex-military buildings. There was plenty of space, and more importantly, lots of relatively unused airspace and not much aviation traffic.

I heard the sound of approaching propellers, and ran outside to see a couple of gleaming monoplanes taxiing in. I was about to meet my new team members. Would they like me? Would my flying be good enough?

They greeted me politely and rolled their airplanes into the hangar. I was one of two newcomers to the women's team; the others were veterans, some having flown for the team for over a decade. They joked and laughed with each other while I stood on the edge of the group, smiling nervously. A van arrived to transport us all to our lodging on the base. I loaded my duffel bags in the back and sat quietly in one of the rear seats.

We drove for miles, crossing the base on long, empty roads, occasionally passing apparently uninhabited buildings. At last we pulled up in front of a pink stucco World War II–era building labeled Base Officers' Quarters—our home for the next two weeks. Inside, the furnishings were neat and utilitarian, each pair of rooms sharing a bathroom between them. I quickly unpacked and hurried to our first briefing.

Ex–Air Force colonel Matt Corcoran was this year's official US Team coach. The briefing was scheduled to begin at 4 p.m., or 1600 hours, and he began speaking exactly as the second hand touched the twelve. He'd prepared a packet of information for all of us, and our time was scheduled to the minute. A couple of the senior team members rolled their eyes, and I even heard groans. The previous coach, apparently, did not require such military precision.

Two team members sauntered in ten minutes late, and Matt interrupted the briefing to tell a story: when he was in the Air Force, if the briefing was scheduled to start at 1600 hours, at 1555 the room was empty, and at 1600 precisely, the room was full. No one said anything.

The pilots had expected to fly two thirty-minute flights per day, as was typical in the past. But Matt told us everyone would get three fifteen-minute slots per day for coaching. You'd enter the box at your assigned time and depart it fifteen minutes later, to the minute. It was a much shorter time period than I'd ever practiced, and I wondered silently whether it would be sufficient. Although there was some argument from the senior team members, Matt prevailed in the end.

We were to meet with our assigned coach, either Matt or one of his two assistants, for half an hour every morning to discuss the day's plans. After each flight, we'd land, fuel our planes, and go to the video room to view our fifteen-minute tape. At the end of the day, we'd meet again with one of the coaches to discuss progress, weak areas, and strategies. I couldn't help feeling something like euphoria at the thought of all this concentrated attention from some of the best trainers in the world. It was the kind of coaching that many of the top pilots paid thousands of dollars for—and that I'd never been able to afford.

Every day, the flying would start at 8 a.m. and continue until sunset. At first, Matt wanted to start at 7 a.m. "Sleep? Who needs sleep? I'll sleep when I'm dead," he said.

However, faced with nearly united opposition from both pilots and support crew, he backed down. Although I wouldn't have minded spending nearly every single minute on flying, I was secretly relieved along with everyone else.

The efficiency and expertise was at a higher level than I'd ever encountered. It was exciting. From early in the morning until we went to bed at night, it was all about flying—in the air, on the ground, reviewing our videos, talking over meals—all the time. At first, I was still bobbling my snaps and overrotating my rolls with my new wing, but I sharpened up quickly under concentrated training. The military precision worked.

No time was wasted. On bad-weather days, we gathered in the briefing room to discuss strategy and procedures. Everybody kept a notebook in addition to their flight log to jot down problems with their flying, tips for improving various maneuvers, and general suggestions. The international rules differed from the US rules, so we had to train to fly to these standards in preparation for the upcoming competition in France. Additionally,

Matt gave us a set of specific procedures that we were to follow from engine start to shut down. It surprised me how every movement of ours was planned in advance. But there was logic behind everything he said. For example, he cautioned us not to rely on terrain features as references, a common practice at US contests.

"Rely on box markers alone," he said. "In the 1984 World Contest in Moscow, in the former Soviet Union, the box was laid out on the tundra, and there were very few landmarks. Pilots from all over the world arrived for practice and got one flight in the box, and they all tried to orient themselves by a road here, a hill there. But on the first day of the contest, they found their Russian hosts had shifted all the box markers by forty degrees. As a result, everyone who flew based on landmarks had memorized the wrong sight picture. People were over-rolling, under-rolling, and just getting confused." He paused to gaze at each of us, one by one. "The Russians won that contest. Fly only based on the box markers."

"At the international level, it's all about winning," said Dale Brandt, a five-time team veteran. "They'll look for every loophole in the rules, so you have to be prepared for anything."

Off the record, over beers in the base mess, Matt told us that European judges placed an emphasis on style, not just precision. He reminded us to keep our figures tight in the box and retain cadence and rhythm. He repeated that we were there as a team, not a collection of ten individuals. A crucial part of our job as team members was to support the other pilots.

"Oh, and one final warning," Matt cautioned us in a briefing. "Don't fly over the nuclear power plants. It's against the law in France, and they take it seriously."

* * *

One day, I got to see a copy of the press releases that had been prepared. The articles all stated that the women's team was strong this year because of the three veterans, Jennifer White, Marge Denny, and Karen McKinley. Jennifer, a six-time team member, had brought home multiple medals for the US since her first competition in Austria in 1982. She now managed an aircraft museum in Florida. Marge (the one who'd called me "granola") had been on the team since 1984 and had a similar record of achievement, and her flight school, M&D Aviation, was nationally known. In 1986, Karen made the team for the first time, and had been the top-placing woman pilot in the 1990 World Contest. They were illustrious colleagues. I noticed that no mention was made in the press releases of me or the other newcomer to the women's team, Lily Anderson, a stockbroker from Chicago. Lily and I spent many hours comparing experiences and working with each other to improve our flying. When the press came with cameras rolling to interview the three veterans, Lily and I sat off to one side.

At least I didn't embarrass myself at practice, I consoled myself. Maybe nobody expected much of me, but I was a credible performer, and no one said anything about not taking me to Europe. Everyone agreed that my new airplane was very visible in the box and had the potential to score well because the judges could see it easily.

"Big improvement in visibility over your Pitts," Matt had said. He'd been at Nationals the previous September and had apparently been watching me closely. "Unfortunately, that five-degree over-and-back on rolls also shows very well. If you overrotate, just hold it," he instructed. "Sneak it out in the pull. Remember, the World judges tend to be biased against newcomers, so if your scores are low, don't take it personally."

I nodded and kept my face neutral. I'd certainly overcome bias in my life. The most important thing was not to dwell on it—it would only make me miserable. I'd just do my best. Accept it and move on.

"Don't worry," he said, breaking into a smile. "Sometimes the newcomers surprise us all. After all, Melanie Thompson was a first-timer at the last contest, and she came home with a silver medal. It's too bad she's not here this year, but you show the same kind of promise."

I'd become a world-class competitive athlete working at the peak of her abilities. The days were invigorating, and I slept soundly every night. My body hummed with energy—every muscle, every cell, tuned to its prime. The bruises on my thighs became nearly permanent, the yellow smears of older bruises fading under the angry red marks of the newer. Behind my eyes and within my head an unfamiliar sensation emerged, as though the blood vessels inside my brain had grown stronger, tougher. I developed a tolerance to motion sickness of any kind. I rode the tilt-a-whirl and roller coaster at the local carnival one evening without a hint of dizziness. I'd become the woman with the cast-iron stomach. I could read in the car—an unexpected bonus.

I was pushing nine negative and pulling twelve positive g's every day, shifting within seconds from weighing nine hundred pounds hanging in the straps to bracing myself under half a ton of my own body weight. It was more than I'd ever experienced before, but I never came close to blacking out.

When the two-week practice was over on June 5, 1992, Matt pronounced me in impressive shape, especially considering I had so little time in my newly modified airplane. He advised me not to go home to California, but to practice between now and June 19, when I was due in Dover, Delaware, for the C-5 to fly us all to Europe.

"You're flying against the best pilots in the world. You need to give yourself every advantage."

I nodded and said nothing. But inside I wanted to protest, *I've already taken practically the entire summer off from work, and I've used up almost all of my funds. How am I going to be able to afford another two weeks?* But I also knew I'd find a way. I had to.

I spent the following two weeks flying from contest to contest around the Midwest, visiting various airports, practicing with local pilots and other team members at each field. I also spent most of those days staying in people's houses and making many friends.

Another team pilot told me he never liked staying in other people's houses, that he always preferred to have his own space in a hotel. Looking back on the experience, I wouldn't have changed a thing, even if I'd had the money to stay in hotels. Although it could be awkward being a guest in someone's home, something happened to me during those weeks that I'd never encountered before.

As an itinerant, I lived through some of the old-time hospitality that I'd read about in books. In the past, if a traveler knocked at your door, it was expected that you would open your hearth and home, share your food, and give them shelter. I thought that kind of hospitality no longer existed. But I was wrong.

It might have been that people were supportive of me because they wanted to help a US Team pilot. But it also might have been that there were just many more kind people in the world than I had ever imagined. It takes significant effort to host a stranger in your house, even for a few days. I needed to be driven to the airport every day. People made me special meals, although I asked them not to.

It seemed like a small miracle to me—not only that people helped me out, but more importantly, that they cared about me and wanted me to do well. I felt loved in a way that I had rarely experienced. The aviation community had become my family. I realized it was normal for people to reach out to one another and offer each other care. The part of me that had always been suspicious of others began to loosen and warm, and I began to trust on a regular basis.

And trust, it turned out, would matter more than I ever expected.

Chapter 19

I knew it was going to be bad news even before the flight briefer opened his mouth. An ill-defined cloud layer had settled over the Ohio airport, and the trees at the end of the runway stretched misty and gray into a low-contrast sky. I was due in Dover, Delaware, in only a few days to catch the C-5 to the World Aerobatic Championships in France. If I couldn't make my next planned stop in Salem, Illinois, I might not make it on time.

The briefer scratched an ear and shoved his faded red baseball cap further up his forehead. "IFR conditions all the way to Salem." He pivoted to the second terminal behind the counter and began typing.

IFR (Instrument Flight Rules) meant the weather was bad, and there was no way my tiny, one-seat experimental airplane that lacked instruments could carry me to my next destination. Not only would it be dangerous, it would also be illegal. My airplane wasn't certified by the FAA to fly in those conditions.

"If you don't get to Dover by the nineteenth, they'll leave you behind," coach Matt had warned the team members. "That C-5 will take off when it's scheduled and not a minute later."

"Any chance of conditions improving by this afternoon?" I asked the briefer as I lowered my gaze to my flight pad and gripped my pen more tightly, as though I could somehow squeeze better weather into existence.

He typed at his terminal, and the white *O* on his baseball cap wobbled back and forth. "There's a warm front coming in. Conditions are gonna get worse, and the front is forecast to stall over the area for the next week."

My fingers slipped on my pen. One week would be too late. I glanced out the wide plate glass window at my red-and-blue airplane perched on the tarmac, sporting its sleek new white wings.

The old insecurities rose up within me again. What was I even thinking? Flying a plane that had been cobbled together from a half-finished, experimental project in order to compete at the world level?

Now it seemed I wasn't going to make it, defeated by a little bad weather before the contest had even begun.

The other team pilots were taking off on instrument flight plans. They had installed the latest avionics in their top-of-the-line planes, and some had even hired staff to drive across the country, following them to airports to maintain and take care of their airplanes.

Me? I was on my own. No staff, no instruments. I stared glumly out at the low clouds. And now—it seemed—no flight. I leaned on the counter and tried to imagine what it would feel like when the rest of the team flew in France and I had to stay home.

A voice from behind startled me. "Hey, you on your way to Salem?"

I turned around to find Paul Newberry, one of the more senior members of the team, smiling at me. A quiet, heavyset man with an air of calm certainty, he piloted his plane with a hand as steady as a rock. In Vietnam he'd flown helicopters.

"Doesn't look like I'm getting out of here with this weather."

He raised his eyebrows. "That front's going to stall."

I shrugged. "No instruments."

His smile was open and welcoming. "How about you fly formation on me?"

I stared at him. Flying in formation—staying on Paul's wing and using his instruments to navigate—was the only possible way I could get out of here in these weather conditions. But I'd had exactly one brief lesson in formation flying, and it was a finicky and demanding skill. It wasn't something you just did casually, without extensive training. The risks could be life-threatening. But still, something inside me leaped with hope.

"Are you sure?" I asked, scarcely believing my luck. "I don't have much formation experience." Here it was again: That amazing level of acceptance and trust I kept encountering from acquaintances and even strangers in the aviation community. Over the last five years, I'd been learning to count on other pilots. But this was something more—a life-and-death gesture of kindness I wasn't sure how to accept.

The corners of Paul's eyes crinkled. "Sure. You're a fellow team member, aren't you?"

But I might put him at risk, or at least slow him down. He was offering to do me such a big favor. Why? Why would he be kind to me?

I remembered a day in sixth grade when I learned what I thought was an important lesson about kindness. I stood on the pavement in front of the elementary school, waiting for my mom to pick me up. Don was running around with his friends. I hadn't yet experienced the full force of his malice toward me when he skidded to a stop in front of me that day. "Hey, Rod-REE-kezz. Want some gum?" He held out a yellow pack of Juicy Fruit, one stick poking out enticingly.

I hesitated. Don had never been nice to me before. But my mom had said that people were good underneath. Maybe it was a peace offering. Maybe I should be more trusting.

"Thanks," I whispered, and reached for the stick of gum.

Snap! A metal tab sprung up and slammed my finger. I jumped back in pain. Don and his friends shrieked with laughter. "What an idiot, Rod-REE-kezz, falling for that old trick." Don waved the device triumphantly and ran off to find another gullible fool.

Unlike the boys from my childhood, Paul was a nice guy, wasn't he?

"Thanks!" I said finally and smiled. "I can finish my preflight in ten minutes." Would I actually make it to Dover to catch the C-5 after all? Maybe I would.

We taxied out together, the damp air blowing through my open canopy and chilling the chin strap of my cloth helmet. I mentally reviewed everything I knew about formation flying. As the wing pilot, I'd have to match my airplane precisely to Paul's throughout the flight, relying completely on him for direction. Midair collisions and fiery crashes flashed through my mind, but I pushed them away. I had to stay utterly focused on the task ahead.

I swung onto the runway, did my checks rapidly, and positioned myself on Paul's wing. Through my windshield, I fixed my gaze on his flight helmet, lining it up with a spot of blue paint on his fuselage. I had to keep those two references aligned for the remainder of the two-hour flight.

He started his takeoff roll, his Extra accelerating away from me. I advanced my throttle. It was important not to drift out of position, even while still on the ground. My eyes were locked to his aircraft, maintaining the sight lines. Oops, I was overcorrecting, closing in on him too fast. I eased the throttle back. My tail lifted as I reached flying speed. Paul rotated for takeoff, and I matched him. We took off together, a single organism in two bodies.

I always feel an incredible thrill when my wheels are no longer in contact with the ground. I was free, free of the heaviness of my everyday life, transformed into a being for whom miracles were possible. My heart lifted even as we soared into the murky skies. But then something felt wrong.

My six-cylinder Lycoming engine was growling unusually softly, and we were climbing much more slowly than normal. All my muscles tensed. Was there a mechanical problem? If my engine failed, I'd have to find a field to land in. But I didn't dare look away from Paul's wingtip to check for obstacles on the ground. My breathing shallowed.

Then it came to me. Paul must be making a reduced-power takeoff. If he used full throttle, there was a risk I wouldn't be able to match his climb, and any small error would mean that I'd have no chance to ever catch up. I sighed in relief.

Paul radioed to switch to our in-flight frequency, leaving the tower behind. I'd punched in the frequency in advance, so I could just hit one button and wouldn't have to take my eyes off the lead airplane. *Click.* "Sabre Four Four One One Foxtrot, reporting in." I made a tiny power correction and nudged a couple of inches closer to Paul's dark-blue wing hovering in the gloom. Okay, I could do this. I took a deep breath, then another. Then another.

There was no response on the radio. I double-checked. Nothing but static over the roar of my engine. I tried calling Paul again. Nothing. We had somehow lost radio communication. What if he needed to do something unexpected? How would I know what to do?

The smell of alfalfa rose from the gray-green fields below, fields I couldn't see except out of the corner of my eye. I stayed absolutely focused on Paul's wing. We were cruising at only a few hundred feet above the ground, almost brushing the ragged edges of the cloud layer. I wasn't even sure where we were. My map was strapped to my leg, but at this altitude, I couldn't read it without losing control of the airplane. My hand clenched on the stick as I realized I'd become lost, flying at a dangerously low altitude, pinned under an implacable cloud deck.

Scanning my flight path earlier that morning, I'd noted tall towers dotting my chart, and here I was speeding over the ground well below their heights. If I lost my formation position on Paul, I might smash into one of those towers. That is, if I didn't crash into a hillside, or run out of gas first, flying in desperate circles above unknown terrain.

All the colors dimmed and muted as earth, trees, and fences flashed by below. It was impossible to detect any landmarks. I was alone. Although I was inches from Paul's wingtip and my engine blared, the silence on the radio overwhelmed it all. Cut off from human contact, I was encapsulated in a bubble of mist, my senses muffled. I could barely see. I could hear nothing.

There is a strange fatalism that overtakes you in a life-threatening situation. Your mind narrows, and you hang on to the only thing that matters. For me now, my life dangled by the thread of my ability to make tiny corrections with the throttle, to nudge the stick ever so delicately, to lock myself onto those imaginary rails in the air that promised me safety.

I might have prayed. Somewhere deep inside me, a voice was chanting a mantra, a wish, again and again: *please, please, please* … Above it all the roaring silence, and the unutterable, intense need, the absolutely essential requirement to stay in position, to clamp my body and mind in place and focus them on one single action, one single lifeline.

For the next two hours, I had to fly formation as though my life depended on it. Because it did. The only thing I could do was what I had always done: keep going.

Paul's plane drifted a fraction of an inch away. I brushed the throttle lightly, ever so tenderly, and eased back into the correct spot. Sweat broke out on my forehead and under my palms. I gritted my teeth. I was not going to stray by a millimeter.

The smell of wet grass from the fields below overlay the slightly acrid odor of burnt metal and gasoline fumes. It tickled my nostrils, but I refused to sneeze. I sweated inside my five layers of clothing, every muscle in my body rigid as I balanced just on the edge of shivering.

Paul banked his Extra, turning very slightly to the left. I inched the throttle forward just a hair and matched my wings parallel to his. When he leveled off again, my engine noise quieted. I noticed I had brought the throttle back almost to the stop. He must be reducing power for a descent. But why? Then I glanced to my left and saw the familiar lines of our departure airfield below us.

Paul was returning to the airport. Relief poured through me as though I'd been released from a giant vise grip. We'd be on the ground in minutes instead of hours. I wouldn't have to fly all the way to Salem after all. I took a deep breath and let it out raggedly. For whatever reason, Paul had decided to abort the flight. I wasn't going to die today.

We flew the pattern, turned onto final approach, and touched down on the wide runway side by side. It wasn't until we had taxied all the way back to the fuel island, shut down our engines, and popped open our canopies that I was able to talk to Paul again.

"Why?" I asked him, still trembling. "Why did you turn back?" Now he'd be stuck behind the bad weather along with me. It could even cost him his spot in the C-5.

He raised his eyebrows. "We were out of radio contact, and that's a huge risk. The lead pilot always looks after his wingman."

It finally came home to me: Taking off on Paul's wing had been my deepest act of trust yet. I'd put my life in his hands. Despite my recent experience, I'd never fully trusted anyone outside my family. People left you behind, ignored you, and played tricks on you. But now this seemingly ordinary, slightly paunchy man with a soft voice had watched out for me.

"Of course, I came back," he said in that voice that was like a rock in the fog and mist, utterly certain of the world and what was right in it. Of course I could rely on him.

For the first time, I realized I could put my entire self—my fragile and tentative life—in someone else's hands, and they might hold it gently and return it to me. And even more important, this was the way it was supposed to be. People were meant to share and hold one another, to lift a hand in support. I'd rarely known that growing up.

But now I saw beneath the surface of things to a web of interconnection, a silent, secret structure underlying everything. Could the world really be so different than I'd assumed? All my instincts—to cringe away in fear, to always anticipate a blow—were they wrong after all?

By the time Paul and I had refueled our airplanes and taken off again, the ceiling had lifted, against all expectations. Slender ribbons of fog thinned in the river valleys. My wings cleaved through the clear air, and my plane held me securely three thousand feet in the air, my engine thrumming as we sped over the wide, green, undulating hills.

Chapter 20

Landing at Dover Air Force Base requires special permission. We were only given a small window of time in the afternoon of June 19 to enter their airspace and land at the field. Paul, Lily, Jennifer, and several other team pilots gathered at Summit Airport in Delaware to fly in formation into the base. I needed to file a special flight plan, get advance permission specific to my N-number, and send a copy of my passport and other personal information to verify my identity. (And this was in the days before 9/11.)

At that time, it was still possible to fly over Washington, DC, and flying in formation with other US Aerobatic Team members over the nation's capital was an unexpectedly stirring experience. Our formation was loose enough that I could sneak glances at the glittering city below me and the monuments that evoked power and history. I suddenly felt an emotion that took me a while to identify. It started as a feeling of warmth inside my chest, and then spread through my limbs and up into my head until I felt a pricking behind the backs of my eyes. Could it be … patriotism?

I'd grown up believing that patriotism was a bad word. As a child in the 1960s and '70s, I'd developed scorn for politicians after seeing the corrupt paths our government had taken and witnessing what seemed like meaningless war. Washington, DC, felt pretentious to me then, too consumed with its own importance.

But now, as a national representative, I felt something different: a sense of connection to that larger community and a reverence for the history of our people and the tradition of democracy that had led us this far. I'd been told to "go home" by people who proclaimed they were patriots, people who didn't think there was room for me in this community. Becoming part of something larger was a healing balm on those scars. An upwelling of joy and respect overwhelmed me, and I had to fight back tears as I flew.

We received clearance and landed in sequence—one, two, three, four, five. I touched down on the right side of the runway, slightly behind and to the right of pilot number four.

Dover Air Force Base was imposing. It had a military feel that was more serious than the small, sleepy airports I'd been visiting for the past few months. I became abruptly aware that the formal part of my journey as a representative of my country had begun.

The humid June air shimmered above the expanse of concrete as I taxied behind the other pilots to a vast hangar crowded with H-60 helicopters and a partially disassembled C-5A cargo jet dwarfing the rest of the aircraft there.

We were housed at the Base Officers' Quarters once again, which was a long, pale-yellow stucco building. It was a relief to unload my duffel bag in the spartan room and take a short nap before our next briefing. From now until the end of the World Contest, my time would not be my own.

At the briefing, we were informed that we would travel "space available," meaning we had to wait at the base until our transport was ready. In past years, team members sometimes had to sleep on the hangar floor if there was a flight delay. So we settled in to wait. Paul, Lily, and I talked about flying and exchanged sequences. We all visualized our routines, and took naps. I bought a lot of chocolate from the base vending machines. One day slipped by, then another.

Then at four o'clock one morning we got the wake-up call and were told to pack our things and assemble for a van ride to the hangar within an hour. The US Aerobatic Foundation was paying $150,000 to rent a return leg of a C-5A. These huge cargo planes carried all sorts of large material all over the world on military or humanitarian missions. Often, however, they would fly cargo in one direction and then return to their origin empty. To recoup some of the fuel costs on these empty legs, certain carefully vetted civilian cargoes were permitted. We had won one of these spots. (This practice was discontinued after 9/11, and today the US Team has to disassemble their airplanes and put them on container ships for a six-week, overwater journey to the World Aerobatic Contest.)

Our team put our small airplanes on dollies and rolled them into the belly of the C-5. News and television crews were there to film this. It took several hours of careful work, with all the team pilots, mechanics, and staff working alongside the military handlers and cargo masters, who weighed each of our planes and noted the numbers on clipboards.

By placing them nose to tail, we were able to get all ten of our aircraft to fit inside the cargo hold, which ran the entire length of the C-5. It was a tight fit, and we did have to take the propeller off the nose of one team member's Sukhoi, but we got them all in.

My plane, which was loaded near the beginning of the process, was rolled up the ramp and secured at the far end of the cargo bay by heavy webbing around its wings and landing gear, then ratcheted with huge hooks to giant metal loops in the floor. We all double-checked each other's airplanes to make sure they were secure and would not shift during flight. The planes were stacked within inches of each other, so we didn't want them to move and ding each other.

At last everything was ready, and we climbed the narrow metal staircase from the cargo hold up into the passenger compartment. On the flight were Coach Matt and his two assistants, the videographer, the team manager and his assistant, several team mechanics, a few other team personnel, and the ten team pilots. The seats all faced backward, five across on either side of the aisle, with utilitarian green belts. There were no windows. We all spread out and claimed a row.

We belted in and took off. The cabin was much louder than a passenger jet, and there were no amenities. No in-flight meals or flight attendants coming down the aisle with drinks. We all brought our own food and water, and Matt had also brought a supply of water bottles and snacks.

As the big jet climbed to altitude, one of the team pilots regaled us with stories from his previous career as a military cargo pilot. He was now a commercial airline pilot. "I spent an entire season flying troop transports," he told us. "The worst were the marines." He shook his head. "Of course, if they got too rowdy, we could always turn up the altitude."

"What does that mean?" I asked.

He grinned. "From the cockpit, you control cabin air pressurization. Normally you set it at eight thousand feet above sea level. When the marines started to get too loud, we'd turn it up to twelve or fifteen thousand feet. Then they'd all go to sleep, and we'd bring it back down."

"Ever been tempted to do that on a commercial flight?" someone asked.

"Tempted, yes. Never done it, though—at least not that I'll ever admit to."

Eventually everyone left the conversation and went back to their row to sleep. I went to mine and tried to sleep, but I couldn't. The passenger door near the front of the plane sported the only window anywhere in the cabin: one small, round porthole at about eye level. I peered out, but it was nighttime, and we were flying over a solid cloud deck, so there was nothing to see. I guessed that we were flying fairly far north on a great-circle route between Delaware and Germany, so even if there were no clouds, all I'd see would be icy-cold ocean.

I couldn't help imagining what it would be like if the plane lost power and we had to make an emergency landing in that frigid Arctic sea. Here we were in a bubble of light and activity, suspended above reality, isolated from our true existence as humans on the surface of the planet. We were in a cocoon, warm and safe, hurtling through the thin and frigid air. At thirty-eight thousand feet, there was insufficient oxygen to sustain life. If the metal skin were to peel away, we'd die.

When one of the C-5 pilots exited the cockpit and stopped to chat with me, I pushed away my fears. He was interested in the team, and asked me several questions about aerobatics and the g-forces we experience. "Would you like to sit in the cockpit jump seat during approach and landing?" he asked.

I was delighted. "You bet. I've never seen a jet land from the cockpit." I followed him up the aisle and through the cockpit door, where he belted me into a jump seat. I eagerly looked around me. The cockpit was studded with dials—many familiar, but some not. There were four throttles, one for each of the four engines.

My stomach ached and burned from the sleepless night, and my eyes stung. I felt exhausted, and part of me wanted to get up and return to my comfortable seat where I could lie down, but I didn't. I'd probably never get another chance like this. It was exciting to watch the smooth cockpit coordination of the crew as they prepared for the instrument approach into Ramstein. The pilots used Jeppesen charts just like I did, flimsy sheets of paper they each clipped to a mount on their yokes.

I watched, rapt, as they made calls for the descent, flying precisely down the centerline of the approach. We were in clouds for a very long time, and there was nothing to see out the wide cockpit window.

At last we broke out under a gray overcast at around one thousand feet, and the runway spread before us in the early-morning dimness. When we were still what felt like hundreds of feet up in the air, the captain initiated the round-out for landing, and the nose began to rise. Before I expected it—while our eye level was still more than fifty feet above the ground—the wheels contacted the runway, and we had landed at Ramstein Air Base in Germany. We'd made it.

I thanked the pilots and returned to my seat. The rest of the day passed in a blur. We unloaded the C-5 in reverse and taxied our planes to another large hangar. Some of the team personnel had already arrived, and they brought several vans. They drove us to the Base Officers' Quarters, where we were each assigned a key. I grabbed my stuff and headed up to my room, stopping only to buy a bar of hazelnut chocolate. I fell into an exhausted sleep on the narrow bed.

* * *

Jennifer White, the most experienced of the team pilots, had flown in Europe many times before. She'd been on the team since 1982, and I felt a little intimidated by her. She also owned something that gave her a clear advantage: a GPS with a worldwide database, which was rare in those days. She would lead us as a flight of ten across European airspace and to our practice site on the north coast of France.

Flying over Europe was very different from flying over the United States. In the US, almost all the land is laid out on section lines, with a grid of roads cutting a checkerboard of half-mile squares aligned to the compass points. It was the mark of a country where ownership of land was a relatively recent development, a place where land was parceled out by a central authority. In Europe, land ownership grew organically, and as a result, the fields appear haphazard, a crazy quilt of thin, oblong, or meandering shapes following rivers and ancient boundary markers. The lines went this way and that. I'd never realized how much I counted on those section lines to maintain my sense of direction until I flew over the fields of Europe. I was very glad Jennifer knew the route.

There were other differences. France generated much of its electricity through nuclear energy, and the countryside was studded with nuclear power plants. These were all marked on our aviation charts, and, as Matt had warned us, we had to avoid flying over them or risk the consequences.

The flight from Ramstein to our practice site on the French coast went smoothly in the clear weather. Saint-Valery-en-Caux was a small fishing town whose airfield was notable for its large runway, a now-derelict paved strip that had been built in 1944 by American troops during World War II. We touched down in sequence on that runway, one of the bumpiest I'd ever landed on. I winced at the thought of what it was doing to my wheel fairings—the fiberglass covers that streamlined airflow around my tires— but this was just another unexpected expense of the World Contest.

After taxiing to the central aero club building, I was surprised when we were greeted by a crowd of people who cheered and applauded as we shut down and opened our canopies. Even the mayor of the town came out to greet us. They'd set up a microphone for her to make a speech.

I'd often heard that the French held a disdainful view of Americans, but none of this was evident that day in Saint-Valery. White-haired and impeccably dressed, the mayor stepped up to the microphone and read a speech in heavily accented English. "We are proud to welcome the American delegation to our city. It seems only appropriate that we host American pilots at our airfield, since it was you Americans who built our runway in 1944."

Built nearly fifty years ago, I thought, rubbing my tailbone. I'd taxied around numerous potholes and passed by an unrepaired bomb crater on the way in.

The mayor wound up her speech, growing increasingly emotional. I was standing in the front row and could see her rouged cheeks growing redder as she read, "You Americans are heroes to us, as you were on that day in World War II when you landed here in 1944 and liberated us from the Nazis. I was only a little girl that day, but I still remember how we cheered your arrival." She stopped to dab at her eyes with an embroidered handkerchief. "I remember how all the soldiers seemed larger than life, as you Americans entered our town, bringing freedom at last. It seemed like at last light was dawning after a long darkness. We cheered you then, and today we wish to cheer for you again and thank you for all you have done for our city and for France. Welcome!"

The audience of about a hundred mostly white-haired men erupted in loud cheering. The team members glanced at each other, a little embarrassed, since most of us hadn't even been born during World War II. But we smiled and shook many hands. The city residents who had come to greet us remembered World War II, and they spoke to us effusively. Most of the team couldn't understand French, and as one of the only members of the US delegation who knew the language, I was pressed into service as an informal translator. The message was quite clear even to those who could not understand the words: we were most welcome and would be offered every hospitality.

The French aero club that hosted us at Saint-Valery lived up to that promise over the next two weeks. We were given an entire building on the airfield for our personal use, which gave us a place to practice our sequences, work on our flights, and set up our video equipment for training. There were even quiet rooms where we could sit alone, take naps, take notes on our critiques, or redraw our sequences.

They also provided us with three huge and delicious French meals each day. The food was wonderful, and I ate so much rich food, cream sauces, and heavy desserts that I was sure I'd gain ten pounds that week. But the scale in my hotel bathroom remained constant. Those physically demanding Unlimited aerobatic flights I flew each day must have burned up all the extra calories. I briefly entertained the thought of writing a book called *The High-G Diet: How to Lose Weight While Eating All the Calories You Want*.

It was a wonderful time. We benefitted from the same intense training that we had back in Ohio, but we ate far better, the temperature hovered around seventy-two degrees each day, and the locals were constantly dropping by to give us gifts or offer encouragement. Some even professed loyalty to us over their own French team.

Before the trip, I'd exchanged emails with a French pilot named Pierre Collet, who shared useful information with me on the rec.aviation newsgroup. (In those early days of the internet, only computer geeks used email, and there was a single international group of a few hundred pilots communicating online.) That week, he stopped by my hangar several times to talk as I washed and waxed my plane. I learned a great deal about aviation in France. It was far more expensive than in the US, beginning with the cost of aviation fuel. One liter of French avgas cost more than one gallon of US avgas. Also, at every airport, no matter how small, there was a substantial landing fee every time an aircraft's wheels touched the concrete. My new friend, like me, had to sacrifice to afford the high cost of flying.

Toward the end of the week, Pierre offered to give me a ride over the countryside in a rented Robin DR-400. As we flew low over the magnificent Étretat chalk cliffs, swooping barely above a natural arch framing the blue-green sea, we agreed that the joy of flight was more than worth the cost.

It was an idyllic time for me, but all too soon, practice would be over, and it would be time to fly to the contest venue in Le Havre.

Chapter 21

It was spectacular to be a participant in the World Championships at Le Havre. Wearing our formal uniforms, we lined up for the procession of seventy-four pilots from twenty different countries, ready to march across the field. A band played, and a large crowd had come to the field to cheer us on, including Ben and my parents and in-laws. As "The Star-Spangled Banner" rang out, we marched together as a team behind a huge American flag, passing before a review stand where dignitaries shook our hands. Cameras clicked and flashbulbs flared. PBS's *Nova* filmed the team for the documentary "Daredevils of the Sky." Behind velvet ropes, spectators cheered and shouted. All the pomp and ceremony moved me in a way I hadn't expected.

In the past, overt displays of patriotism made me nervous with their hidden political meanings. But on this day, it was all about the simpler joy of belonging to a group I felt proud of. The best pilots from Russia, Lithuania, France, the US, and about twenty other countries had come together to compete against our peers for the title of World Aerobatic Champion.

I was so proud to be the first Latina on the US Team and to have overcome so many obstacles along the way. And I felt I was truly representing all Americans here in France, especially the underdogs, all the Americans who had come from behind, all the immigrants who'd arrived with their own dreams and had contributed to building a better country. Now it was my turn to contribute.

It was particularly poignant to be part of an international event at that time because only a couple of years prior, history had been made when the Berlin Wall came down. In those heady and exciting years of democracy breaking out all over the world, it seemed as if human society were finally maturing. As a member of an international team, I had a front-row seat. By meeting pilots from many countries, seeing them face-to-face as human beings and not as stereotypes or faceless enemies, I'd become immersed in history as an active participant rather than a mere spectator. Russian and Ukrainian pilots, no longer Soviets, flew as guests at our national championships. One of my most vivid memories was watching the former Eastern Bloc pilots at a Holiday Inn buffet, piling their plates high with fresh fruit, something they clearly weren't accustomed to.

In a group conversation, a US pilot asked a Russian pilot what he thought of the fall of the Iron Curtain. "Communism was a grand seventy-five-year experiment," he pronounced. "We are never going back."

The first to be held since the effects of the fall of the Berlin Wall were realized, the 1992 World Championships marked a number of its own firsts as well. In past contests, the Soviet team had been led by longtime Soviet national champion Jurgis Kairys. He was now, for the first time, on the Lithuanian team. Several other countries that had never competed in the World Championships were now fielding teams, such as Romania. The Russians walked behind a white, blue, and red flag that had been adopted less than a year prior. No more hammer and sickle. The men wore bright-red uniforms and the women long, flowing white dresses. The Cold War was over.

* * *

The pilots' briefing was held early in the morning on Tuesday, July 7, 1992, in one of the huge, white tents. We assembled on folding chairs lined up in neat rows, and the contest officials sat at a long table in front of us. An official placed a large burlap bag on the table. Rather than randomly assigning the order of flight in a back room, it was to be decided here, in full view of everyone, to ensure fairness. The order of flight matters tremendously in a high-stakes competition. Just as in US competitions, the first pilot ends up being the "wind dummy" and must contend with potentially lower scores due to mistakes made while misjudging the wind. In addition, the first few flights at a World Contest have historically received lower scores. No one is quite sure why. Perhaps it takes the judges a while to warm up, or perhaps they are subconsciously saving their top scores for later. In any event, no one wanted to draw numbers one through nine, and I sat there with my pulse racing as I waited for my name to be called.

The official procedure called for the pilots to be summoned, one by one, to the front of the room by name, where each would draw a numbered plastic disk from the bag: one to seventy-four. The drawing order was alphabetical—first by name of country, in English, then by personal name.

The first pilot, Christian Lesage from Belarus, was called and walked up to the front. He stuck his hand in the bag, rummaged around, and then drew out a disk and held it up. "Fifty-four," announced the woman at the microphone.

I looked at the disk raised in the air and couldn't believe what I was seeing. They had embossed digits! There was no doubt in my mind that when Christian put his hand in the bag, he could feel those raised numbers. I leaned over to mention this to Matt, who frowned. The seated teams began to whisper to each other. Were others also noticing the raised numbers? Should I say something?

Because of how the drawing order was determined, the United States would pick after everyone else had selected their numbers. We would be at a disadvantage before the contest had even begun. I nudged Matt again, and he nodded. He stood up and walked to the front of the room to confer with the judges. There was a brief whispered conference, and then the woman at the microphone announced, "The drawing of the lots will continue."

More whispering and dismay arose from the US side. France, Russia, and the United States were the three main contenders for the team championship. Was this a deliberate effort to assure supremacy of the French team, or a simple oversight? I remembered Matt's description of the box shenanigans at the contest held in Russia. The murmurs continued. I remembered that the French team had spent a few weeks practicing in the competition box earlier this summer, something no other team had been allowed to do. I started to simmer with a feeling of injustice. Was there something I could do? Or did I just have to accept my fate?

Finally, it was the Americans' turn to draw our flight order.

"Cecilia Aragon," the announcer called, and I made my way to the front.

I plunged my hand into the bag and felt the eight remaining plastic disks. I could easily read the numbers with my fingers, all only a single digit. I picked number eight, the highest one left. Every US team member ended up scheduled in the first ten flights of the contest. The very last person to pick drew number one, and everyone clapped and cheered as they held up the booby prize.

Would this obvious unfairness be corrected or not?

Our team manager filed a formal protest. By international rules, the jury had two hours to consider it. We waited uneasily. Would we have to go get our airplanes prepped for our early flights?

Fortunately, after a short conference, based on the irrefutable evidence before them, and the fact that the United States had, despite all laws of probability, become the wind-dummy squad, the international jury declared a redraw.

This time, all the disks were placed face down on the table, and we each had to select a number without the option of touching them. The picks appeared random this time. One of the French pilots ended up with the number one disk, and she held it up, smiling ruefully, as everyone else cheered and clapped. When it was my turn, I drew number twelve. A good draw. Relief flooded through me. Twelve was not so early that the judges wouldn't be warmed up, yet not so late that they would be tired or the flying would go into the next day.

I headed off to meet my family and get my airplane ready. Ben, his parents, and my parents were staying in a nearby hotel and helping me with the airplane. We'd all eaten lunch at a local restaurant that had completely revamped their menu for the championship. I'd ordered the *salade voltige*, or "aerobatic salad." Not only was it delicious, but it was on the house when the restaurant owner found out I was one of the competition pilots. I felt so honored.

On the airfield, my mother had been eagerly handing out her homemade Sabre buttons, and they'd become a big hit with the international pilots. It was cool to see so many people wearing my mother's photographic art around the airport. It was my turn to feel proud of her.

Practice flights were scheduled all afternoon. Each of the seventy-four contestants was allowed ten minutes in the box to practice. The box was lined up with the coast and not with the runway, making it challenging to stay oriented. I had a hard time concentrating on my sequence because the French coast was so gorgeous, the blue Atlantic unfurling into the distance, the patchwork of green fields arrayed helter-skelter in the opposite direction. But the box markers were clear, and my flight was clean. I landed, drenched in sweat but exhilarated.

The next day would bring six of the most important minutes of my life, bearing the weight of all my expenses and donations, hours of practice, and the hopes of our supporters back in the US. My performance during those all-important, precious moments would, in part, determine the United States' standing in world competition.

In the 1960s and '70s, the US had dominated world aerobatic competition. But in the 1980s, due in part to diminished financing on our side and the Soviet and French governments' full funding of their pilots, the French and the Russians had won the championship consistently, with the US coming in third. We hadn't won a world contest for a long time. This was our chance to reverse that trend and to win back the World Championship for the United States.

* * *

The next day, shortly before my contest flight was scheduled to begin, a pilot from one of the other teams approached as my husband, parents, and in-laws were helping me take the wing covers off the Sabre. He wore a brown shirt and neatly pressed black slacks rather than an official uniform. He introduced himself as Gheorghe Militaru, one of three pilots from the Romanian team.

"It's exciting time for Romania," he said in fractured English. "This is first year Romania sends delegation to the World Aerobatic Championships." He went on to tell us that after the fall of the Berlin Wall, he took part in demonstrations that led to a national uprising against Communist dictator Nicolae Ceauşescu. The first free elections since World War II were held in his country in 1990. And this year his government had decided to send pilots to the Championships. His pride fairly radiated from him.

He'd been walking around the field, examining many of the other pilots' aircraft, and he was especially interested in my Sabre. "You did not buy it from factory?" His eyebrows lifted.

I explained that it was one-of-a-kind and that I oversaw its construction, telling him a little about the Edge wing and my journey to the World Contest. He listened with rapt attention.

He knocked on the surface of the wing. "Is carbon fiber?" he asked.

I nodded. "Rated to twelve g's."

"And made in family business, like you are here with family." He gestured to my husband and father-in-law and cracked a grin. "Homemade."

I returned his smile. "Yes, homemade."

He understood, I realized with a rush of emotion. Like me, his team also operated on a shoestring. He'd seen an uprising of the common people succeed against the rich and powerful, and now he was going to pour all his energy into his flight, just as I was. Although we barely had a mutual vocabulary, Gheorghe and I had a great deal in common.

My family all helped me finish rolling up the wing covers, and I began a thorough preflight inspection. A light breeze had sprung up as PBS's *Nova* reporter interviewed me before the flight. My father-in-law told them how he had been a Korean War pilot and how pleased he was to support the US Team. My mother-in-law squeezed my hand and told me under her breath, "He's so proud to have another pilot in the family."

Before I climbed into the plane, my mom gave me a big hug and kiss and told me to stay safe.

"Always," I assured her.

My dad told me his buttons were popping, and that my plane looked beautiful. Ben's eyes were glittering. "*You* look beautiful," he said. "Fly as well as you always fly."

It was almost time for me to roll my plane into position. The flight for my homemade airplane and the test of my homespun, grassroots approach to flying would be coming up soon. I took a last swig of water, jogged to the outhouse and back, and strapped in. This was it.

I took off and circled over the blue, blue ocean. It was a gorgeous day, sunny but not too hot. The air was crisp and cool and not at all humid—perfect for aircraft performance, and a joy for its pilot. The Sabre *wanted* to fly. I felt its eagerness in the way it leaped off the ground and banked crisply into turns.

I'd flown the 1992 Known Compulsory many times, as well as visualized it in my mind on the long cross-country flights over empty terrain in the US, while standing in line for a brioche at the bakery in Saint-Valery, before going to sleep in my narrow hotel bed, and first thing in the morning when I woke up. Would I be able to fly it as perfectly as I had in my imagination?

I dove to enter the box, and the Sabre screamed as the airflow past my fuselage built to a crescendo. The box markers gleamed bright and clear in the morning sun. The fields below shone vividly green, and lights like jewels flashed off the windows of the city of Le Havre. To my left, the endless blue Atlantic rolled, its gold-tipped waves shimmering in the brilliant sun.

I pulled up for the first figure, breathing deeply, letting the clean air flow into me and through me, taking in the energy of the earth and the sky and the sea. I nailed the vertical line, paused, hit the points of the roll up, one, two, three. I pushed up and over the top, inscribing a perfect half circle in the sky. On the downline, I held an absolute vertical, straight toward the ground. My wings vibrated in the still air. Then I entered an outside snap roll that threw me hard against the straps with six negative g's of force. I relaxed my entire body and breathed gently so as not to build up too much blood pressure in my brain. The horizon and earth gyrated around me, and I pushed full opposite rudder to stop after exactly 450 degrees of rotation. Perfect.

I held the downline long enough for it to show well to the judges and paid no heed to the way the ground was coming closer and closer as I was pointed straight at it under full throttle.

Fear? What was that? I'd left the fear of dying, the fear of humiliation, the fear of letting down my team behind me now. There was only the joy of the airplane and me linked together as a single being, flying in partnership with air and gravity, pirouetting over the earth.

It seemed that as I flew, time slowed down, and I had all the time in the world to watch my wind drift, to note the locations of the box markers, to adjust my sequence so all the figures were positioned just right. I felt the rhythm beneath me, the rhythm of the tides and the sea and the winds, the rhythm that created me as a full member of the human community, the pull of gravity and physical laws, the striving of life toward the sun. This was the way it was meant to be. At last I felt one with my world, my life the inevitable extension of fundamental principles, my emotions and desires the purest expression of the urgent drive upward.

The last maneuver was a full outside snap on a vertical upline followed by an inverted exit.

It was crisp and beautiful, breaking free from the line the way I'd broken free from my fear. I exited the box inverted, and over my head, through my clear wide canopy, spread the green earth. Below my feet lay the sky, and I knew at last this was my birthright, as it was the birthright of every living being: to be at one with the planet and a part of the spectacular and complex universe.

* * *

I landed to the cheers of my teammates, the pilots from other countries, and my parents, in-laws, Ben, and many friends, all beaming with pride. I knew I'd flown well but wasn't sure how that would translate into a score. But to my delight, at the end of that day, I was ranked first in the world among women. I wondered how this could be true. And yet, it was. For that one day I was number one. The French magazine covering the championship reported that day: "Excellent performance from the United States with the best place of Cecilia Aragon. First among the women pilots for the moment, she's confirming the American strength."

After all the women had flown the Known Compulsory program, I ended up in fourth place overall. When the final accounting was done and my rank was announced, I beamed with joy and ran to find my family to tell them the news. I'd never seen such big grins on my parents' and in-laws' faces. Ben lifted me up in the air and twirled me around. I also turned in the second-strongest flight among my teammates, which was quite a surprise from a rookie from whom no one expected too much.

I left the World Championships ranked one of the top aerobatic pilots in the world. I'd achieved a goal I once thought impossible. Now I was ready to take those lessons to the ground and achieve other dreams.

Epilogue

It took me decades to fully understand the positive impact that flying had made on my emotional life and self-confidence. I had faced death and survived. I now knew deep in my heart that I could carry on in the face of fear, that I could do difficult things, and that my mathematical system of solving life's challenges one operation at a time was a superpower I could use whenever I needed. Flying also fed me that essential nutrient I'd missed during my childhood: validation from a community. The support and friendship of other pilots taught me that I was worthy of inclusion and that I could trust people to be there for me.

When I looked back at all the obstacles I'd faced in my journey to the World Championships, I saw that persistence, creativity, and dogged determination—as well as a little math—could get me through. And so, I began to take joy in being badass. In 2003 I reapplied and found funding to return to the graduate department where a professor had once told me women didn't have the intellectual ability for computer science.

I finished my doctoral dissertation in a year and a half. And yes, I still experienced moments of sheer terror. When I was writing my first solo academic paper, I procrastinated for days because I was afraid my research wasn't good enough. But when I finally talked myself past the fear and did the work, my paper was not only accepted, it was awarded best student paper at the conference.

Eventually I came to understand that those feelings of not being good enough were coming from forces outside of myself. As my flight instructor Louie Robinson had once said when he set up the Pitts cockpit, "You might blame yourself, but it's your environment that's setting you up for failure."

I now wonder how many young women and people of color have been overwhelmed by similar feelings of low self-worth formed in childhood and end up not trusting themselves due to a lack of validation.

And what will it take to give them a way out?

After I landed my dream job as an engineering professor at the University of Washington in 2010, I turned my attention to mentoring students, to helping others achieve the academic goals that had been so challenging for me. I particularly wanted to support underrepresented students, such as women and Latinxs seeking STEM degrees who were struggling from a lack of support.

In 2018 University of California, San Diego, engineering professor Olivia Graeve sent me an article she'd coauthored that showed me just how high the odds had been stacked against me. Her data showed that "while the total number of Latino engineering faculty as of 2016 is close to 600, only 48 of [them] were born in the United States."

I knew that Latinxs were underrepresented in engineering, but seeing the low percentage of Latinxs born in the United States who've became engineering faculty was shocking and made me see my own struggles and accomplishments in a new light. I'd always assumed it would be more difficult for foreign-born immigrants, who had to navigate both cultural and language barriers, to win a position in the highly competitive engineering faculty job market. And yet there were fewer US-born Latinxs in those positions? The data defied all expectations.

As I continued to read Graeve's research, I learned that US-born Latinas had fared even worse than their male counterparts. Out of the more than twenty-six thousand engineering professors in the United States, only *ten individuals* were US-born Latinas. I was one of *three* US-born Latina full professors. Three in the entire country!

I thought of my father, a Chilean immigrant, and how he had been able to accomplish his academic goals with less anxiety than I had. Of course, he'd experienced racism in the US as an adult, but he hadn't internalized it; he remained supremely confident in his own abilities his entire life. But I, a girl who excelled in math *and* a Latina daughter of immigrants, had internalized my teachers' and peers' expectations from childhood. My identity had been shaped by my environment. I'd learned early to doubt my abilities, to stay quiet, and to stay safe. I learned not to reach.

I once told a white acquaintance in Seattle about the time a store clerk in Indiana turned away and refused to serve us when my mother and I approached the counter. The acquaintance crossed her arms and said, "Well, maybe all that bad treatment in childhood is what gave you the strength to be such a success today."

The comment took me aback. Could anyone possibly believe that childhood racism or sexism gave people strength?

My childhood experience with these things didn't make me strong. Instead, I doubted my own abilities for decades. I developed imposter syndrome. Every time I worked on the math and computer science I loved, I struggled with self-doubt. Fear, seared into me at a young age, threatened to overwhelm me as I worked on the very challenges I knew I could surmount.

I almost gave up. And yet, something kept me going. For me, the way out—my strength and my saving grace—was my parents' belief in me. Their faith gave me the inner strength to fly, to finally return for my PhD, and to find my career path. My parents believed in me when no one else did. My mother loved me and taught me to face fear. My father loved me and told me I was smart. No matter what happened, he never stopped believing I was a genius.

"Will you still love me even if I fail my PhD exams?" I tearfully asked my father once.

"If you fail, I'll love you more," he said.

It only takes one person who believes in you. It only takes one voice to give you strength. I was lucky. I had two.

* * *

"When I was in my early twenties," I said into the microphone at a conference in 2016, "no one would have thought I would become a pilot or even do anything risky. I was scared of heights. Timid."

I stood at the podium in a large auditorium, gazing out over an audience of several thousand people—mostly women—at the Grace Hopper Celebration of Women in Computing.

"Once," I continued, my amplified voice echoing off the high walls, "I would've defined myself as unable to speak in public, as a person whose introverted personality required me to take a quiet, background job." The fact was that public speaking still made me nervous. However, that nervousness itself now buoyed me as I addressed the crowd. I asked the audience, "How many of you are—or once were—afraid you weren't good enough to complete your degree in math, computer science, or engineering?"

Almost everyone raised their hands. These were women at all levels in technical fields—and most were still going through the same self-doubt I'd encountered.

A relentless message has been drummed into us: Only the best survive. If you don't make it through your educational program, it's because you're not good enough. It couldn't possibly be because it's a hostile environment, because sexual harassment exists, because racial discrimination exists, or because there are subtle forces arrayed against anyone who's different.

It couldn't possibly be because your environment—or cockpit—wasn't designed for you.

I saw recognition in their eyes. They needed to hear this. "How many of you have felt afraid that you're not good enough at technical work, and that at any moment, someone will find out?" I asked them.

Hands shot up all over the auditorium. "How many of you have felt like you didn't belong?"

People nodded vigorously, and some called out, "Yes!"

"You're not alone!" I said. "And just because you're afraid, just because you feel you're alone and out of place doesn't mean it's a sign you should give up. Facing your fear is difficult, but once you do it, even a little bit each day, it becomes easier the next time."

I went on to talk about mathematical induction, the dominoes falling one by one, and how math—plus a voice or two of support—had brought me full circle to stand in this place. I talked about my long journey starting in childhood and how I had come to fly free.

Acknowledgments

This memoir has been twenty years in the making, and I owe more people gratitude than I can list. To everyone who sustained me on the long and turbulent journey to publication, thanks so much for giving this story wings and setting it loose to fly free.

I am deeply indebted to my inspiring teacher and mentor Theo Nestor, who showed me how to discover the heart of my memoir and then worked with me over multiple drafts to deepen and strengthen it. I owe you more than I can say.

Countless thanks also go to Lane Heymont, agent extraordinaire and sales genius, for believing in me and my story and consistently exceeding my expectations.

I am enormously grateful to Vikki Warner, visionary acquisitions editor at Blackstone Publishing, for having enough faith in this book to bring it to light.

It's been such a pleasure to work with my amazing team at Blackstone. I couldn't have asked for a better flight crew. Thanks to Alenka Linaschke, for creating a stunning cover design; to Holly Rubino, for sharp and detailed improvements to my prose; to Michael Krohn, whose copyediting was not only meticulous but inspiring; and to everyone involved in the magic of production and marketing: Jeff Yamaguchi, Lauren Maturo, Megan Wahrenbrock, Mandy Earles, and Josie Woodbridge.

My dear friend Toni Littlestone read the very first draft of this memoir and provided encouragement and support when wished for and expert critique when needed.

Æleen Frisch wrote with me at the inception of my memoir in 1997 and supported my writing career with kindness, tough love, editing, and one of my longest and closest friendships.

My wonderful writer friend Alice K. Boatwright shared fantastic marketing and editing advice, support, lunches, and long walks with me.

My beloved writing and marketing teacher at Hugo House, Waverly Fitzgerald, read an early draft of this memoir and gave me feedback and advice on marketing and finding an agent.

Special thanks go to the incredible and knowledgeable 15th Avenue Marketing Group—Waverly Fitzgerald, Annie Pearson, Alice K. Boatwright, Jeffrey Briggs, Janis Wildy, Luanne Brown, and Rachel Bukey—for the gift of delightful Friday mornings, for teaching me surprising details about the book business, and for loyally attending my book talks.

I am also grateful to the members of Theo Nestor's yearlong memoir class at the University of Washington, who read and critiqued early chapters of this book and provided reassurance and helpful feedback. Thanks to Ron Schulz, Jennifer Phipps, Sharyne Thornton, Paula Cunningham, Bonnie Dixit, Gail Nunn, Natalie Serianni, Mary Walter-Feltner, Jenna Jue, Andrea Blander, Alyssa Singh, Kaitlyn Kelley, Rebecca Romanelli, Erika Stanley, Diane Perry, and Ruthann Martin—I can't wait to read all of your memoirs. Special thanks go to Bonnie Dixit, who lovingly and thoroughly line-edited a first draft of my book proposal.

I would also like to thank all my NILA friends, colleagues, and teachers, who started me off on this phase of my writing journey and helped prepare me for the writing life:

Rob Land and Renée McCormick, sophisticated and generous critiquers, for the years of friendship and support both tough and inspirational. In particular to Rob, for loving dragons even when they didn't make it into this book.

Carmen Bernier-Grand, for teaching me how to avoid the "sagging middle"; Bonny Becker, for your deep and thoughtful critique and workshopping tips; and Wayne Ude, for your thorough and fascinating classes on narrative craft.

Jillian Fox, Debbie King, and Jamieson Haverkampf, for your critiques and ongoing literary camaraderie.

Many thanks to my MFA cohorts at Hamline University, the Benign Violations and the Headless Gods, for endless good cheer and creative sustenance, and to my mentors at Hamline—Nina LaCour, Laura Ruby, and Anne Ursu—for your gentle yet relentless encouragement to seek out my voice as a writer.

Thanks to Bobbie Peyton and Lily LaMotte, wonderful authors and critiquers; to Kessa Shipley, for reading an early draft of the book and offering support and critique; to Julia Drake and Jodee Blanco, for freeing me to listen to my inner voice; and to Lorrie Penner, who combed through back issues of Sport Aerobatics on short notice to help me fact-check.

Thanks also to the YA Book Group, for ten years of reading and sharing stories close to all our hearts, and to my dear Binders memoir group, for your speedy, voluminous, and supportive feedback on every single one of my questions. May all your publishing dreams come true.

And most of all, my deepest thanks to my family, whose nurture and support has made everything possible:

To my mom, Katinka—photographer, quilter, and author—who taught me to love books by driving me to the library every week during my childhood and who first inspired me to write this memoir by coming to me for advice on her own, Birthdays in the Cemetery.

To my dad, Sergio, physicist and storyteller, who never stopped believing I would do amazing things, despite all my failures and restarts, who told me on the day after I shook President Obama's hand, that he was the lucky one to have met me.

To my husband, Dave, who has fed and sustained me, stayed "beside me for companionship and behind me for support" for over thirty-five years, and accepted my many flaws and unexpected flights.

And to my children, Diana and Ken, who endured my preoccupation with writing and work, and listened over and over again to my life story without complaining (too much).

I love you.

About the Author

Dr. Cecilia Aragon is director of the Human-Centered Data Science Lab, professor in the Department of Human Centered Design & Engineering, founding codirector of the University of Washington's data science master's program, and senior data science fellow at the eScience Institute at the University of Washington (UW) in Seattle.

In 2016 Aragon became the first Latina to attain the rank of full professor in the College of Engineering at UW in its hundred-year history. She earned her PhD in computer science from UC Berkeley in 2004, and her BS in mathematics and literature from the California Institute of Technology in 1982. She also holds a 2019 MFA in creative writing from Hamline University.

Her research focuses on human-centered data science, an emerging field at the intersection of human-computer interaction (HCI), computer-supported cooperative work (CSCW), and the statistical and computational techniques of data science. She has authored or coauthored over 100 peer-reviewed publications and over 130 other publications in the areas of HCI, CSCW, data science, visual analytics, machine learning, and astrophysics. Her book using human-centered data science to study distributed mentoring, youth, and fanfiction—*Writers in the Secret Garden*, coauthored with Katie Davis—was published by the MIT Press in August 2019.

Aragon is the coinventor (with Raimund Seidel) of a data structure, the treap, which has been commended for its elegance and efficiency, and is now widely used in production applications ranging from wireless networking to memory allocation to fast parallel aggregate set operations.

In 2009 President Barack Obama awarded Aragon the Presidential Early Career Award for Scientists and Engineers, the highest honor bestowed by the US government on outstanding scientists and engineers beginning their independent careers, for her work in collaborative data-intensive science.

Cecilia Aragon's research has been recognized with over $27 million in grants from federal agencies, private foundations, and industry, and has garnered six Best Paper awards since 2004. She is a 2017–18 Fulbright fellow. In 2015 she received the HCDE Faculty Innovator in Research Award from the University of Washington. She won the Distinguished Alumni Award in Computer Science from UC Berkeley in 2013, the student-nominated Faculty Innovator in Teaching Award from her department at UW that same year, and was named one of the Top 25 Women of 2009 by *Hispanic Business* magazine.

Her work on the Sunfall data visualization and workflow management system for the Nearby Supernova Factory helped advance the study of supernovae in order to reduce the statistical uncertainties on key cosmological parameters that categorize dark energy, one of the grand challenges in physics today.

Aragon has an interdisciplinary background, including over fifteen years of software development experience in industry and NASA, and a three-year stint as the founder and CEO of a small company.

Aragon is also active in program service and supporting diversity in computing. She is a founding member of Latinas in Computing, was a board member of the Computing Research Association's Committee on the Status of Women in Computing Research, a founding member of Berkeley Lab's Computing Sciences Diversity Working Group and Women in Science Council, chair of the IEEE Computer Society's Computer Entrepreneur and Computer Pioneer Awards committees, and has served as a reviewer and program committee member for numerous computer science conferences.

She has also been a test pilot, aerobatic champion, and medalist at the World Aerobatic Championships, the Olympics of aviation. She holds the record for shortest time from first solo in an airplane to membership on the United States Aerobatic Team (less than six years), and was also the first Latina to win a slot on the team. She has logged over five thousand accident-free hours, flying airshows and competitions throughout the United States and in Europe. An active flight instructor since 1987, Aragon is a pioneer of "unusual attitude recovery training," where flight students are taught how to recover from emergency situations in flight. She was the founder of one of the first aerobatic and tailwheel flight schools in the San Francisco Bay area in 1989.

Aragon and her husband have two children. She enjoys reading, walking, biking, and flying. Her Erdős number is 3.